Praise for Eai
The Astrological Elements вook 2

"These are transcripts from classes at the Center for Psychological Astrology, and carry the vital richness of inspired teaching at work and play. Great insights!"
— S. Roher, Amazon

"Ms. Costello has a love of literature and etymology that makes her lectures an erudite experience. She quotes poets and writers and has a strong appreciation for Western literary tradition, but there is something else at work here - she is familiar with the imaginative realms, with astrology as a language of Soul and Spirit, and her teaching unabashedly conveys this view. Her thoughts will serve to fuel the imagination of any who may feel stuck in too literal a view of how the elements act in a human life."
— Mary Plumb

"Yes, the book is quite thorough in its analysis of the water and fire elements. Yes, there is a lot of information to digest and yes, I learned a lot. But the absolute value of this book for me was the shift in perspective on how I consider the elements."
— Fabienne Lopez

"The value of Ms. Costello's two (Elements) books comes from challenging the current point of view on how to pair the elements. Modern astrology tells us that Earth and Water are compatible elements. The same goes for Air and Fire. By using the traditional rulership system to pair the elements together, Ms. Costello adds another layer of understanding of the four elements. One that points out that Fire, Earth, Air and Water are interconnected and inseparable."
— Fabienne Lopez

EARTH & AIR
The Astrological Elements

Part Two

Also by Darby Costello

The Astrological Moon

Water and Fire:
The Astrological Elements Part One

Pockets Astrology
with Lindsay Radermacher

EARTH & AIR
THE ASTROLOGICAL ELEMENTS

PART TWO

DARBY COSTELLO

Raven Dreams Press
Portland, OR

Published 2018 by Raven Dreams Press
2621 NE 7th Ave #301
Portland, OR 97212
www.ravendreamspress.com

First published 1999 by The Centre for
Psychological Astrology Press.

E-book published by the Centre for
Psychological Astrology Press, 2013.
E-book republished by Raven Dreams Press, 2018.

EARTH AND AIR

ISBN 978-1-7326504-0-4
LCCN 2019930943

British Library Cataloguing-in-Publication
Data. The original catalogue record for this book
is available from the British Library.

TABLE OF CONTENTS

ACKNOWLEDGEMENTS

In working on this seminar I have realised how many ideas from other people have gone into forming my own perspective as an astrologer. A whole generation of astrologers gave their ideas generously to us in our formative years, and they still do. I wish to thank that generation of teachers. And the students I teach, at the CPA, and elsewhere, for the wonderful discussions that inform my work. My gratitude to Stephen for his untiring support and patience, and the fine and discriminating eye he brings to the text. To Jules Cashford for conversations that inspired my imagination and fine-tuned my thinking. And to Liz Greene for creating such a delightful environment in which to work and publish.

PART ONE

EARTH,
the Ground of Life

*This seminar was given on 20 April, 1997 at Regents
College, London as part of the Spring Term of the seminar
programme of the Centre for Psychological Astrology.*

ROOTS

Fifty thousand years ago we roamed the planet, following the herds and fighting constantly for survival. We were totally dependent on the Earth's bounty, and were in constant danger of being destroyed by the harsh conditions on the planet. Somehow we managed to survive. Over time, the climatic conditions in certain regions became more temperate, and even allowed us some rest. In those places, something happened which allowed the development of a part of ourselves which saw ourselves as separate from this Mother Earth who held us to her in such dependence. We began to relate to the Earth more and more as Other. We began to experiment with ways of regulating her bounty to our benefit. We sought to maintain whatever security we found, and improved our situation whenever we could. It must have seemed a good thing to do, considering how intense our struggle was for so many thousands of millennia. Today we are so far from the Earth that we are in danger of destroying ourselves. Our desire to maintain and improve our condition has become an obsession to completely control her every production.

The separation of our consciousness from the Earth has progressed considerably since our first moments of awareness, and the further we get from the beginning, the more we are interested in our past. We are such a young species on the planet, and during the last hundred years our interest in our earlier selves has been stimulated by archaeology and the development of new forms of dating. We are continually discovering a whole world of knowledge about our very ancient ancestors from all over the Earth. Through studying bone, stone and ivory tools and artifacts, through studying drawings on cave walls, we are acquiring new notions about ourselves as a developing species. We have centuries of records under the ground that show us how we lived together above the ground, once the climate became warm enough for us to cultivate the land. We have evidence from everywhere that from the beginning of thought, nature was held to be sacred, female, and mother-source. From Tiera del Fuego to the steppes of Russia, we know she was treated with respect and awe from the very dawn of consciousness.

Today we shall be talking about the element of earth. Before we begin our discussion of astrological earth, I'd like us to wander back in time so we can get a sense of our early history here on Earth. Traces of those long years of struggle survive today in all of us. Then we'll go on to talk about each of the earth signs – Taurus, Virgo, and Capricorn – and how the planets might express themselves through those signs. We'll look at their associated houses – the 2nd, 6th, and 10th – and earth Ascendants. I have a chart to show you which will demonstrate earth in its various manifestations.

A brief history of the world

For a very long time, the earth was first too hot and then too cold for our species to develop beyond simple survival. It seems a miracle that we did survive, considering the weather that swept across the planet. Our earliest ancestors kept on the move, hunting and gathering food where they could. Some of them were making tools, and some of them were even burying their dead with rituals involving red ochre and hematite, half a million years ago. Later records tell us this was considered "blood of mother earth". We don't know when that thought began. Some time around 50,000 BCE, give or take a few thousand years, we began using bone, stone, wood, and ivory tools to fashion artifacts. I once had one of these ancient artifacts on the desk where

I worked in the 1970's, at the Museum of Man and Science in Johannesburg. It was ivory, about six inches long, with twenty-eight notches on it. It was thought to be a woman's stick for noting her menstrual cycle, and it was around 30,000 years old. I mentioned it when we did the seminar on the Moon. I used to hold it, dreaming of the women who had held it before me, wondering who they might have been.

By around 20,000 BCE it was still very cold, something like modern Siberia, but it was warming up. Figurines, mostly female, have been found from that time in our deep history. Sometimes as small as two centimetres high, they were full-breasted, deep-bellied and wide-hipped. Soon after that, we began drawing on the walls of caves. We drew the animals we were hunting: woolly mammoths and the woolly rhinoceros and bear and reindeer. We lived in caves when we could, but mostly we had to keep moving, following the food. Over the next 10,000 years, carvings and cave paintings of animal and human figures began to appear everywhere from Spain to Siberia. There were horses, bison, wild ox, and deer. These figures suggest rituals which attend the hunting and killing of animals, and a recognition of what we would today call a "soul" in the animal which had to be respected in the life-for-life battles. Other cave paintings showed encounters with the elements and with plant life, each with their attending rituals. Between 15,000 and 11,000 BCE, the figurines and the cave art throughout Europe and into Russia were telling us stories which showed that, for us, the Earth and all its produce were alive and ensouled. We would say today that we lived with a "sense of the sacred". We perceive a coherent symbolic imaginal language expressed in this early "art", and we can find its traces throughout later, very sophisticated cultures and religions.

Some time around 5,000 years ago, the weather seemed to stabilise and become fertile in the Mediterranean basin. The battle for survival grew less fierce. Some of our ancestors settled quietly there and began to have enough time to grow crops and start thinking about things. They began to abstract principles from the things they collectively knew about life, and to articulate, in a rather organised way, some of the underlying patterns they recognised in nature. It's a fascinating moment to consider – when our all-consuming instincts for physical survival began to give way to thinking as we know it today.

Audience: We've all been watching the comet, Hale Bopp, and last night some of us were wondering what it would have been like watching it the last time it came by, in around 2,000 BCE.

Darby: Yes! Isn't it an extraordinary sight? I saw it last month in France. It was a very black night, so it shone bright with its glorious tail. There were several of us, and we were telling each other tales of what it must have been like the last time this comet had swung past the Earth. We imagined our ancestors watching it, and wondered what they were discussing as they stood and gazed at it.

Audience: And who will we be next time it comes round, in about 5400 years?

Darby: Who will we be? Well, around its last visit climatic conditions were fairly stable on the Earth. But there were two real disasters – the volcano which erupted in the Mediterranean in 1500 BCE, which nearly wiped out the beautiful Minoan culture, and then the one in 1300 BCE, which pretty well did wipe it out. But on the whole, we became accustomed to relative stability, and slowly began detaching more of our minds from the Earth around us. Because we were not face to face with it every minute of every day, fighting for survival, perhaps we had time to begin to think about it. For a very long time we remembered how powerful it was, and we were careful to treat its every manifestation with respect and reverence. Along the way we developed and devised ways of approaching it in all seasons and moods, in all times and places. We had become accustomed to its rhythms and cycles and its endless variations. As we were absolutely dependent on its bounty, we worked very hard to treat it with appropriate respect. It was our mother; all nourishment came from its body. We could not afford to mismanage our relationship to it or to any of its offspring.

Evidence from Minoan, Sumerian, and Neolithic times shows us that trees and rivers and mountains and valleys and plants and storms and clouds and birds and fish and animals and even insects were everywhere considered worthy of respect. Each thing had its own particularity, its own spirit, and we had rituals for every encounter. There were rituals for making rain, and rituals to the Sun and the Moon, and everywhere, rituals associated with receiving and accepting the bounty of Mother Earth. There were rituals for hunting and for killing animals, and rituals for planting and for sowing seeds, and rituals for taking things out of the ground. Every tree and shrub and bush and stone, every animal, was alive, and each thing had to be engaged in a particular way. Presumably we could feel nature's myriad rhythms and heartbeats in our own heartbeat, as people who live very close to the Earth still do today. These people still carry the memory of hard times in their bodies, and they rarely forget that hard times can come again. This is the melancholy of earth, and the deep practicality.

The Earth deities

So many names come down to us from those faraway times, names associated with the Earth and its offerings. Probably the most evocative of these names is Dionysus. He seems to gather in his web a great many Earth deities – those who had powerful and complex relationships with their mother/lover/sister, and who embodied the stories of nature's dying-resurrected cycles.

Those gods were all associated with trees – many were tree spirits – and all of them died and were resurrected in one way or another.

James Frazer's *The Golden Bough* gives a catalogue of these spirits, deities, and minor gods which is a bit like the *Iliad* and its catalogue of ships. And like the *Iliad, The Golden Bough* is certainly worth reading. It will bring you right into the labyrinthine depths of our early – and therefore now mostly unconscious – relationship to our Earth. It is not a book for the faint-hearted. It is both romantic and brutal, repetitive and endlessly fresh. It takes endurance and the willingness to be bored while it bores into your consciousness the amazing complexity and simplicity of our ongoing struggle with Earth reality. It calls for patience and concentration. It is truly about Earth.

Frazer weaves a tapestry which reveals how we related to the Earth before we had time to begin the process of abstracting universals from particulars. *The Golden Bough* describes the same rituals rising out of tribal life, everywhere and in all times. Throughout early Europe it traces the deep connection between the tree spirits and the spirits who are associated with the corn. These spirits are often depicted as goats or bulls. This connection between tree and corn spirits and goats also appears in Egypt. Osiris was, according to Frazer, first a tree spirit and later Lord of the Corn, with all the attendant rituals of death and rebirth. He is connected with Dionysus in Greece. His wife-sister-consort, Isis, was Lady of the Corn. She is called "creatress of green things," "green goddess, whose green colour is like unto the greenness of the Earth," "Lady of Bread," "Lady of Beer," "Lady of Abundance." The Greeks identified her with Demeter, their grain-goddess; the Romans with Ceres; the Attics with Cybele. These divine figures are associated with deities such as Inanna and Ishtar, the great Babylonian and Semitic goddess of growth and vegetation – and, of course, grain. And they all have their son/lovers who die – as nature dies, as the grain dies – and are born again next year.

Listen to Frazer: "Under the names of Osiris, Tammuz, Adonis, and Attis, the people of Egypt and Western Asia represented the yearly decay and revival of life, especially of vegetable life, which they personified as a god who annually died and rose again from the dead."[1] Attis was consort to Cybele, great fertility goddess of Phrygia – a god of vegetation whose death and resurrection were mourned and celebrated each spring. The worship of Adonis was practised by the Semitic peoples of Babylonia and Syria, and the Greeks borrowed it from them seven centuries before Christ. He was also called Tammuz, who was consort of Ishtar, who was the Semitic great mother-goddess and who embodied nature's seemingly infinite capacity to produce and reproduce. Adonis, the beautiful lover of Aphrodite, was also one of these dying-resurrecting gods of vegetation. And he is the Semitic Adon, which simply means "lord". And, of course, Aphrodite was also Ishtar, who was Astarte, the Evening Star, goddess of ancient Syria – our own Venus.

When I was in France last month, I went to one of the markets in the square of the local village, and saw a table of corn dolls. I bought one. She reminds me of all the cultures who have had, and still have, their grain goddesses and their yearly rituals to the grain deity for a successful harvest. Demeter has her stalk of corn, and we know that as long as corn has been grown, there have been maize-mothers and corn-goddesses. But there have also been wheat-mothers and barley-mothers and, in the East Indies, rice-mothers. The myth of Demeter and Persephone is the one we know best, as it contains the seeds of so much that is still a familiar part of our psyche. And Dionysus is again found here. The great rituals of Eleusis which held sway over the Greek world for a thousand years bound people together in conscious acceptance of the cycle of death and rebirth. But I am ahead of myself here. If you read Frazer, or Joseph Campbell, you will see

---

1   Sir James Frazer, *The Golden Bough*, Macmillan & Co Ltd, London, 1954.

how creative we have been in developing rituals to work with the spirit of the Earth, to produce good crops from the soil. These rituals developed from the earlier rituals which were part of the hunting and gathering of food, and they go back to the very beginning of consciousness. All magic begins here.

Magic and religion

You may find it odd that I want to discuss magic in this seminar on the element of earth. When I was thinking about earth and preparing this day, I found myself remembering the *sangomas* whom I worked with in South Africa, and how much time they spent on preparing substances which they gave to the people who came to them for various ills. The most common questions they were asked had to do with securing love, health, and work. The substances they prepared had to do with providing physical, emotional, and spiritual support in these three realms.

Audience: Oh, I just saw what you are saying – love, health and work: Taurus, Virgo, and Capricorn!

Darby: That's it. I was remembering Ndlaleni, the *sangoma* I was closest to during my years in Africa. She was always collecting and preparing herbs, roots, and bark for her patients. She had been trained, but was continually learning all sorts of new combinations of substances which could help them to overcome whatever problems they had, to maintain or to improve their situation and to bring order into their lives. No one ever went away without some sort of *muti* – healing substance – which she prepared, and which contained something of the spirit of her ancestors, for the spirit of the patient's ancestors. Ancestral spirits came to heal their descendants through nature's substances. The *sangoma* served the spirits through finding and mixing these things. The patient received these substances in rituals and used them in ritual. If all was done properly – if the laws were obeyed – the situation was meant to improve and order would be restored.

While I was thinking about this, I returned to *The Golden Bough*. I had first read it in Africa, when I was working with the *sangomas*. Frazer has an interesting discussion about magic as the root of science. He said that magic and science are both based on "faith in order as the underlying principle of all things". Both magic and science assume that nature has immutable laws. By knowing the laws and following a particular sequence of actions based on this knowledge, you can change specific situations. He thinks magic is false science simply because the "primitive" people who use magic have false perceptions of the laws of nature, and science has true perceptions. We could talk about this for hours, but it would take us too far away from earth.

Audience: It will be interesting to see what we discover with the new sciences of chaos and complexity theory.

Darby: Yes. Our vision of matter is changing again. Very exciting, but it will take centuries, as usual, for us to bring it right into our day-to-day Earth life. Frazer is right, in that there is probably a lot of nonsense in many of the magic rituals performed by early people – but I'll bet there's not an inconsiderable amount of nonsense contained within the rituals and practices of modern science. In any case, each system of magic had its own rules, but all are aiming for the same outcome: the maintenance and improvement of some situation – order instead of chaos. Frazer compares magic and science to religion. It is an interesting discourse and worth reading. For now, let me say that rituals may lead to magic and magic to alchemy. Religion is rooted in there but becomes something else in the end, aiming far beyond improving life, aiming beyond matter.

The *sangomas* I worked with for all those years used ritual and magical practices to maintain, improve, and bring order to the lives of those around them. Every ritual included the use of substances. Whichever substances were chosen – root, herb, bark, stone, shell, feather, organic or inorganic matter – it was very important for the *sangoma* to treat it in just the right way, and to insure that the patient did the same. Rituals done correctly allowed the laws of nature to work on behalf of the patient. And, as every magician in the world knows, the ritual must be followed precisely.

Audience: That's just the same as working with computers. If you make the smallest mistake, a comma instead of a full stop, then you don't get what you want. They also require patience and endurance, and anyone who really works with them is constantly fiddling around trying to improve them so they will serve better. All very earth, don't you think?

Darby: Now, that's very interesting. I've never thought of computers that way. But most people do consider them magical. Remember, effects are called magical when we cannot see the laws operating. There will always be magic because there will always be processes where we cannot see the underlying laws. And we will always experiment to find the laws, and these experiments, if they seem to be effective at all, will become our rituals. People have awe, fear, and fascination with computers because they are still mysterious territory to many – although most of us know they operate with known laws and so are science rather than magic. This notion of maintaining and improving things is at the heart of both magic and science, and the element of earth. And as we know, wanting to improve things can lead to trying to control them. Today we talk a lot about "controlling nature", but originally we simply wanted to survive, to maintain ourselves. Now we seem to want to control everything. Things have got a little out of hand here. When does magic become an evil art? When does our desire to maintain and improve our situation become greed and self-destructive madness?

It is very easy to see the roots of religion in our early struggle with the Earth's unpredictable and hostile environment. But the tree certainly looks different from the roots, and with the development of religion we seem to leave the Earth and reach up into the air. As our consciousness began to separate from the Earth's body, so we saw nature's spirit separate from her body too. Out of the vegetative and, especially, the corn spirits, arose Demeter and her lost, or perhaps wayward, daughter, Kore, who became Persephone, queen of the underworld. Out of the drama of their story rose the Eleusinian mysteries, which took our consciousness into new dimensions. Sky, Earth, and Underworld opened. Out of the mysteries of these realms, Christianity arose, which has taken us even further from the Earth and, in fact, can be held partly responsible for turning us against it.

Psychological and alchemical earth

In his book, *Man and his Symbols*,[2] Jung tells us a Chinese story about a tree and an "earth altar". The "earth altar" is usually an unwrought stone, round or square, at which the people offer sacrifice to the local deity who is felt to own that portion of land. Jung says that this symbolises our need to consciously surrender ourselves to the processes of the unconscious in order to become truly individuated. In following the promptings of our unconscious in a particular way, we can develop an ear for hearing our inner deity. The "earth altar" reminds us that there is a god who speaks to us through our bodies. This god is the local deity who owns this piece of land – our physical bodies. Through developing a habit, or even a ritual, which includes sacrifice to

---

2   C. G. Jung, *Man and His Symbols,* Aldus Books, London, 1964.

this deity, we may learn to hear what is required of us in relation to the material world we inhabit.

Then there is the classic Jungian classification of intuition, sensation, thinking and feeling types. He says, in *Psychological Types,* "Sensation establishes what is actually present, thinking enables us to recognise its meaning, feeling tells us its value, and intuition points to possibilities as to whence it came and whither it is going in a given situation."[3] The one I am interested in here is the sensation function, which "establishes what is actually present". This is connected to the element of earth. We tend to associate the sensation type with the element of earth. Planets in earth signs are said to see what is in front of them as simply that which is there. They do not seek meaning from it, or look for its ultimate purpose in the scheme of things. It is "What is happening here?" rather than "How do I feel about this?" or "What will this lead to?" They look at things as they are, and then they see how to make the best of them. People with earth rising generally look at themselves this way – they ask themselves what their talents are and how they can best work with them.

Alchemy is the great earth science. It is earth science reaching beyond itself, beyond perfection into transformation. You can see how far its child, chemistry, is reaching today. Paracelsus, that great healer and alchemist of the 16th century, had Capricorn rising and Mars in Capricorn in the 1st house. In "Paracelsus as a Spiritual Phenonemon", Jung quotes him as saying, "Nature is so careful and exact in her creations that they cannot be used without great skill; for she does not produce anything that is perfect in itself. Man must bring everything to perfection. This work of bringing things to their perfection is called 'alche-

---

3   C. G. Jung, *Psychological Types,* Vol. 6, *Collected Works,* Routledge & Kegan Paul, London, 1971.

my". And he is an alchemist who carries what nature grows for the use of man to its destined end."[4]

And again, "All things on Earth have been given into the hands of man. And they are given into his hands in order that he may bring them to the highest development, just as the Earth does with all that it brings forth. But this highest should be for man the lowest – a beginning; it is a seed which he is beholden to shape into something greater."[5]

Well, you can see the classic prejudice: man is above nature, and all of nature is ultimately there for our use. But you can also see the earth in his chart coming through, especially his planets in Capricorn. He was a Scorpio with Pluto in Scorpio and Capricorn rising, and with Neptune, Mars, and Uranus in Capricorn. He had Jupiter in Virgo and a Sagittarius Moon. He was a transformer (Sun in Scorpio) in a generation of transformers (Pluto in Scorpio), and he had the work of perfecting nature as his high aspiration. He had the natural powers of a magician with both Scorpio and Capricorn planets. If you want to see magical abilities, start your search with those who have Uranus in earth!

Alchemy requires infinite patience as the work is repeated over and over and over again. The end of the alchemical process is the *coagulatio*. The alchemists write about the process of *solutio* and *coagulatio* as two poles – water and earth. The alchemist goes on and on dissolving and coagulating until eventually the stone is formed. We are speaking here of the philosopher's stone, the goal of the alchemical work. The stone is under the influence of Saturn. It is the goal of the work. Jung saw in alchemy a parallel to the process of individuation. If you subject the raw, base instincts to a certain sort of scrutiny, a precise and careful conscious pressure (a Jungian would say, for example, in the

---

4   C. G. Jung, "Paracelsus as a Spiritual Phenonemon", *Alchemical Studies*, Vol. 13, *Collected Works*, Routledge & Kegan Paul, London, 1967.

5   *Op. cit.* (Note 4).

alembic of analysis), and if you are patient and do it properly, then the work will produce the gold of true wisdom. If you slip up and lose heart half way through, it leads to foolishness or worse, madness. However, the prize, the philosopher's stone, is considered worth all the effort. The wisdom gained through this sort of long, hard work is wisdom of the highest order. It is not wisdom separated from life, but wisdom based on the experience of the best and the worst of life, from the sublime to the ridiculous and back again. With Jung's Moon in Taurus conjunct Neptune and Pluto, he was a natural for this work.

In speaking of matter, Jung said, "We describe its physical properties, we conduct laboratory experiments to demonstrate some of its aspects. The word matter remains a dry, inhuman and purely intellectual concept without any psychic significance for us. How different was the former image of matter, the great mother that could encompass and express the profound emotional meaning of mother earth."[6]

Gaia consciousness

In 1969, a book called *The Silent Spring* came out. It was written by Rachel Carson, and warned us of the dangers of our increasing ignorance – our ignoring – of the laws of nature. It warned of the dangers of the increasing use of pesticides on our crops. It told the big chemical company magicians that they were going too far in their tampering with nature, and that there would be a huge price to pay in the future. She was hounded and threatened for stating her views, but her book became a bestseller. Many people paid attention to what she said. Don't you think it was interesting that she wrote this book when Uranus and Pluto were conjunct in Virgo, sextile Neptune in Scorpio? And now, as Pluto is going into Sagittarius and Uranus and Neptune in Aquarius

---

6   *Op. cit.* (Note 4).

– all these squares to those Virgo and Scorpio positions – we are starting to collectively notice the disturbing effects of all the tampering that has been going on in the name of improvement.

And then, in 1979, came a book called *Gaia, A New Look at Life on Earth,* by James Lovelock. By now, many people were aware that something was wrong with our relationship to the Earth and its produce. His book brought this awareness into sharper focus. It called for a reanimation of our relationship with the Earth. He brought the name Gaia out from the past, reminding us that this was once the name of the goddess of Earth. He developed the Gaia Hypothesis, in which he described our planet as a living, self-regulating system. "Gaia consciousness" is the recognition that Earth *and* her creatures are an organism in itself. We human creatures are one species amongst many which form the body of this living planet. Since its publication, many have come to fear that this living organism might die before its natural time through our ignorance, negligence, greed, and stupidity. Or the Earth might "shrug off" its destroyer and continue on without us. Whether this is true or not, we do not know, but it has become a very powerful story in the collective mind.

Audience: Someone pointed out to me recently that, just as some of us in the 20th century West are developing the awareness that Earth is a living organism that needs attention and care, so pre-industrial societies all over the planet are being taught an archaic science which tells them that the Earth is a mechanical thing with impersonal laws, not the living, sacred being they always thought it was. Isn't that bizarre? The so-called Third World is being taught the science of fifty years ago, while our science has leapt into a new dimension and is reporting back from the future that everything is teeming with life, that everything is in relation to everything else, near and far, and that our Aristotelian notion of a mechanistic universe has been proved redundant.

Darby: Yes, I've been told that, too, from someone who visited schools in Indonesia recently. Here in the West, more of us are sensitive to environmental issue since those books were published. Here the battle rages between those who think our modern life is life-threatening and those who think it life-enhancing. But I think this consciousness is now everywhere. From one pole to another, and at every latitude across the planet, we talk about the dangers of pollution, of chemical farming, cutting down rain forests, experimenting on animals, genetic engineering.

There are people working indefatigably to counterbalance the unrelenting drive towards improvement which was once seen as good magic and is now, in many quarters, seen as bad magic. It is less than thirty years since we first saw our Earth from space. Seeing our planet from afar has given us a new awareness of the earth we tread. Images touch us more deeply than anything; they go straight to our hearts and imaginations. This image of our planet from space is probably the most powerful image of the last thousand years. I wonder how this image is working on us, and how it will transform our consciousness in the future?

Audience: Most of us are so cut off from our own bodies and the Earth that we cannot even imagine resisting the destruction. We are all either exploiting matter or buying into the exploitation.

Darby: And there are people who are trying to find their way back now, and exploring avenues that may give us all solutions to the problems we are creating. We can only begin from where we are. Having separated from our matter, we may now be starting the return journey. Of everything we may ever own – land, houses, cars, books, tables, chairs, watches, computers – there is only one thing we will have for certain for our whole lives. It is our bodies – the only piece of property we will ever truly own. As we develop our awareness of the harm we may individually and collectively do to our planet, so we might also develop the capacity to attend with respect, if not affection, these bodies that carry our consciousness around. Our modern notions which centre around appearance, and even some of our notions of health, are often damaging to our bodies. Wouldn't it be satisfying to figure out how to develop a healthy affection for our bodies? At the moment we veer between dislike and obsession, with ignorance and indifference in between. But here we are, in the 20th century, and the battle for survival goes on, although in most of the Western world it is at a more subtle level. And everyone is still trying to improve conditions, for better or worse. Living on the Earth, it seems we cannot stop mucking about. It is the nature of our nature.

ASTROLOGICAL EARTH

Astrological earth is differentiated in three ways: Taurus, Virgo and Capricorn. Taurus is ruled by Venus, Virgo by Mercury, and Capricorn by Saturn. Venus, Mercury and Saturn: let's look at our now familiar diagram of the signs by elements and by their rulers. Just to remind you, we are using the traditional rulerships first, as they work strongly through the signs on a personal level.

fire	♈	♌	♐
ruler	♂	☉	♃
earth	♉	♍	♑
ruler	♀	☿	♄
air	♊	♎	♒
ruler	☿	♀	♄
water	♋	♏	♓
ruler	☽	♂	♃

We have looked at this in each of the seminars on the elements. Both fire and water are ruled by Mars, through Aries and Scorpio, and Jupiter, through Sagittarius and Pisces. Then there is the Sun at the heart of fire in Leo, and the Moon as the soul of water in Cancer. If we look at air and earth, we have Mercury ruling Gemini and Virgo, Venus ruling Libra and Taurus, and Saturn ruling Capricorn and Aquarius (with Uranus as transpersonal ruler). What can we make of that?

Audience: It makes me want to know what the similarities of earth and air are.

Darby: There is good food for thought here. Venus, Mercury, and Saturn are the rulers of both earth and air. Venus represents the principle of attraction and our notion of beauty. Mercury is the principle of exchange and our method of adaptation. And Saturn is the principle of action and reaction, and our internal reckoner. Goddess of Love, God of the Crossroads, and Lord of Time: these three symbols, with their great webs of mythology behind them, rule the elements of earth and air.

The importance of ritual

We discussed ritual in our early relationship to the Earth. When you are looking at planets in earth, you are looking at planets that respond to rhythms, cycles, and seasons, and so get into habits and rituals. Planets in earth signs describe habit formation and a tendency towards ritual. These rituals form the basis for creative expression. I don't mean they are its cause, but they provide a container for creative expression. Earth signs develop habits of response to situations, often ritualistic, which, seen from afar, look to be monotonous repetition. But when you look closely, you can see that small things change each time, and eventually this swings the cycle into a new rhythm. Ritual is developed both as a response to unstable conditions and to further nature's productivity, even if it's the productivity of the person's own nature. Sometimes these rituals are obsessive and neurotic. Sometimes they are healthy and deeply sane. Earth signs first establish what is in front of them, and then they set to work, each in their own way. They are not about looking at things as they should be, could be, or if only, if only they would be! Earth looks at a field and sees what can be done with it. Each of the earth signs will have different ways of doing this, but each will do it.

Audience: I've also noticed this ritualistic tendency in earth. Planets in Taurus are more instinctual and unconscious in their rituals. Virgo is nervy, of course, and sometimes I can't tell if their rituals are keeping life at bay or keeping it in order.

Darby: There is a very fine line in Virgo. Taurus can look stuck, and then in a moment it all changes and renewal takes place. Habits become rituals become inertia. It waits for crisis to change something.

Audience: Capricorn brings ritual to an art form, and in the end it thinks the rituals it has created are the law of the land.

Darby: That can definitely happen. And remember, these rituals that rise out of earth are the human response to the variations within the natural rhythms and cycles of life. They are, at least partially, survival strategies. Planets in earth describe where we become familiar with our territory through observing the rhythms and rituals of its nature and inhabitants. They are always working towards securing territory in some way, and they do it according to the sign and its occupying planet. Once there is a measure of safety, then the work to keep it secure begins. Part of this work involves bringing comfort and beauty to the environment. Comfort and beauty are inextricably woven together for the earth signs.

Audience: But earth signs seem so matter-of-fact. Are beauty and comfort so important?

Darby: Yes, they are. The matter-of-factness can be a kind of defence – they have not worked out a way to get the right environment for themselves. It can be a form of patience. Once they find a way to better their situation, they move! And then they become creative. They work to bring as much comfort and beauty into their world as they possibly can.

Fred Gettings, in his *Dictionary of Astrology*, says that earth is "restricted in its ability to express itself, and usually achieves self-expression as a result of a drive towards self-improvement."[7] He notes its inclination to inertia and what he calls "inhibited will force". He says, "An earth type who succeeds in galvanising his will force becomes a most powerful personality, and is often deeply creative." I am interested in the phrase "inhibited will force". The will force of earth does not operate unless it is pushed – and often by discomfort. Earth planets indicate where we will fall into inertia unless cross aspects make us uncomfortable. Earth is self-sufficient and self-contained, not easily pulled out of its rhythms. Planets in earth will develop and maintain habits until the weight of these habits becomes too uncomfortable because they no longer suit the circumstances. It is discomfort which will push earth into action, and this action naturally aims for self-improvement. Of course, your earth planets may be pressured by aspects from other planets into something that looks like more than simple improvement. When fire and earth get together, the simple desire to improve a situation can become a burning vision to transform the world or, at the least, one's own world.

Audience: The element of earth is associated with melancholia in the medieval system.

7   Fred Gettingss, *The Arkana Dictionary of Astrology*, Penguin, London, 1991.

Audience: Fire is choleric; air is sanguine...

Audience: Water is phlegmatic and earth is melancholic. Do you use those classifications?

Darby: Not overtly, but I am aware of them in the background. For example, if you start with the notion that the earth is brown, then you can see all the other colours that might be earth. If you start with earth as melancholy, then you can find all sorts of other hues which might deepen or reduce the basic temperament. Fiery people are moved by images which spring into being – hence the choleric, immediate responsiveness of fire. Water is drawn down by its memories and so may become phlegmatic. And earth...

Audience: Earth is deeply forgiving.

Darby: Now, that is interesting. The notion of earth bearing with things is very strong. People with a lot of earth planets do seem to bear a lot. Juliet [Sharman-Burke] and I were speaking on the phone last week, and she said, "I think earth is really patient." The word "patience" means *to bear*. It comes from the Latin *patior,* which means "to support" or "suffer", "undergo". But it's also associated with firmness, unyeildingness, and hardness.

Audience: It sounds like a description of those people we call "the salt of the earth."

Audience: Do you know *The Devil's Dictionary* by Ambrose Bierce?[8] He defines patience as "a minor form of despair disguised as virtue."

---

8   Ambrose Bierce, *The Devil's Dictionary,* Oxford University Press, Oxford, 1997.

Darby: Fred Gettings says earth is "esoterically an 'incarnating' principle, which seeks to either draw or invite the immaterial into physical form: any incarnating spirit feels the weight of such form, with the result that the element is also associated with inertia, with physical and mental passivity." Ambrose has a neater turn of phrase!

Of course, planets in other elements will interfere with the pure impulse of the earth planets – vision, ideas, and feeling will be imposed on the earth planets. Earth is something that other elements act upon, or try to. Uncultivated land is something we itch to interfere with. Planets in other elements crossing or opposing planets in Taurus interfere with their rhythm, and yet force them into activity, which usually ends up improving some situation in a creative way. Perhaps it is the discomfort that gets them moving. Planets in Virgo describe areas of great sensitivity, and so planets coming at them from awkward angles make the Virgo planets nervous. They agitate and throw the Virgo function off its counting and listing of things. Yet they also drive the planets in Virgo into creating better and better systems, and this is the development of culture. Planets hitting any Capricorn planets get into a battle immediately. There ensues a battle of will from two dimensions of the person's nature. "I will! You won't! My way! No way!" Often a great deal is accomplished – empires come out of the battles – but oh, what a struggle!

Earth knowing is sensible knowing. It knows through its senses, and it uses its senses to know. Earth is slower to accept things than fire, air, or water, but it does not let things go without a struggle, unless they are toxic. Then it expels them if it can, sometimes violently sometimes gracefully. Earth keeps that which is useful, and tries to get rid of that which isn't. Earth is sensible.

Earth is about manifestation. Ideas, visions, feeling all manifest themselves through the physical plane. Earth is slow, but incredibly malleable. Someone has a vision and a plain becomes a city. The Earth is patient, has forbearance, is often passive. Fire and earth produce metals and diamonds and trains and planes – and volcanoes. Water and earth produce bricks and every sort of dwelling – and quicksand. Air and earth move everything around all the time – and produce sand storms. Earth can be very resistant and can seem revengeful: not many deserts have been turned into cities yet. If any of you have tried to make anything – a pot, a sweater, a house, a boat, a good meal – you know how careful and patient you must be if anything worthwhile is to take shape. It can seem indolent, inert, and lacking in spirit, especially when you want something from it that is not appropriate to its time or condition. When you misuse earth – your own body, or your possessions, or nature itself – you discover how resistant matter can be. And yet earth is "patient" and submissive, and seems to tolerate long periods of misuse. Earth seems to really put up with things.

Audience: I was thinking about the Earth, and wondering how it is going to expel all the toxins we have put into it. We'll need some pretty heavy magic there.

Earth stelliums

Audience: I have a question. In the fire seminar[9] you said that people who have lots of fire can have a difficult time. I have six planets in earth, and I don't find it difficult to live on the earth. I feel in contact with earth energy. Is it generally easier to have lots of planets in earth than in fire?

Darby: That's interesting. If you had six planets in fire, then the other four would be divided between earth, water and air. These planets must bring the fire down into manifestation in one way

---

9   See *Water and Fire,* Darby Costello, Raven Dreams Press, 2018.

or another, or the fiery person stays locked in their imagination and out of contact with other people. With so many planets in fire, there is more chance of introversion. Now, with six planets in earth, the other four are divided amongst fire, water and air. All your earth is drawn up into expression through those elements. When you are not expressing yourself through them, you may sink into your earth and become enslaved to the daily grind. To avoid that, you have to keep alive to the other elements and their action.

Audience: It's odd, but I know several people with lots of earth and little or no air, and they are all real thinkers – heavy thinkers, you might say! I am always surprised how deep our conversations go, but come to think of it, I am using words like "heavy" and "deep" here, without thinking about it. I am assuming that thought is the realm of air, and very earthy people would not think so much!

Darby: I don't know about Eastern philosophers, but many Western philosophers often have four or five planets in earth. You would think that the more earth there is, the less ability to abstract or imagine. But remember, the more planets you have in one element, the more the other planets will have to do to be heard. An earth planet tends to look at reality "as it is", so it is a good element for a philosopher. Even Jean-Jacques Rousseau had four planets in earth – but I have to admit that three of them were Uranus, Neptune, and Pluto! He was certainly an idealist and, true to form, he had four air planets. Bertrand Russell had Moon in Libra and five planets in Taurus. The American philosopher William James had six planets in Capricorn, and Neptune in Aquarius.

When your outer planets are in earth – such as the group with Pluto and Uranus in Virgo – you already have a head start with planets in earth. Those of you born in 1961 have Jupiter and Saturn in Capricorn, too. You only need one personal planet in earth and you are an earthling and perhaps a natural philosopher! In my generation, with the outer planets all in fire and air, you have to have a lot of personal planets in earth to be really earthy. We are natural idealists.

Audience: So do we find more mystics with lots of planets in earth?

Audience: The Buddha was said to be a Taurus.

Audience: That's the kind of mysticism which requires you to be in the here and now.

Darby: I think it would be going too far to say that. But I am glad we have got away from the conventional notion that earth people are the ones who won't accept what they cannot see with their eyes. Earth looks hard at reality: the shadow of earth is denial. The mystics look at things as they are in the deepest possible way.

No earth

Darby: When someone has no planets in an element, then those people tend to get excited about that element. No earth indicates an obsession or rejection of the material realm. No air – a love or mistrust of reason. No water – a fascination or repulsion with the emotional realm. No fire – moths to the flames of other people's inspiration, but they can also be exhausted by it. If there is only one planet in an earth sign, then that planet carries a lot of responsibility for working with things "as they are". The whole material realm gets channeled through that one planet, bringing a huge sense of responsibility with it.

A person with no earth will get extremely excited about a practical problem or a material object. It's not the really earthy people who go all gooey over landscapes, nor is it earthy people who scream and shout and kick their car when it doesn't work. Well, not unless there is fire interfering! Having no planets in earth signs is usually more of a problem for other people than for the one with no earth. They do seem to float around a bit. Those who love them will worry, "Why can't she save money?" "Why doesn't he take better care of himself?"

Audience: I have a friend with no planets in earth. He has stayed in the same job, which he hates, for twenty years, and the same flat, which he dislikes, for ten years. His friends are always saying, "Why don't you move?" And he says, "Oh, well." He's got this obsession about planting trees on a common a train-trip away from his home. He goes up regularly on the train with rare seeds, and plants these trees. If you ask him about any tree, he will give you the Latin name and its whole story. But that may be because he is a Gemini.

Darby: People with no planets in earth signs are not good at working to improve their own situation, but your friend is certainly improving the general situation by planting those trees. A missing element does often seem to operate in a sort of impersonal way, through the person rather than for the person. This is why we say that a missing element can operate like Jung's "inferior function".

Shadow and denial

The psychological notion of the shadow comes from the very physical reality of the shadow cast by the Sun on an object on the Earth. There are day shadows and night shadows. The fuller the Moon, the deeper the shadows it casts – moonlight and moon-shadow. Now, there's a world of poetry and speculation!

Audience: The shadow of the Earth falls on the Moon, and we have an eclipse. On Earth, you can only see shadows when there is light, with the exception of those times when the light is directly overhead.

Darby: Can we make any bridges between what you are telling us and the psychological notion of shadow? What do you think might be the shadow of earth?

Audience: The brighter the light, the deeper the shadow. The lower the light to the ground, the longer the shadow. The dimmer the light, the less the shadow.

Darby: Interesting.

Audience: It must have something to do with not accepting the natural processes, the natural rhythms. If you don't accept natural processes, you cannot work with them, and you do violence to the Earth.

Audience: Isn't greed one of the shadow sides of earth?

Darby: I think it is one of the principal things that arises in the shadow of earth. Nature maintains systems of delicate balance. Everything has its cycles of birth, death, and rebirth, and everything is connected with everything else on Earth. If one species takes over a territory completely, it ends up destroying its sources of nourishment and, therefore, itself as well. Greed often leads to destruction and devastation, as any of you know who have become greedy about anything for a period of time. I suppose you could say, if you want to destroy yourself, get greedy.

Audience: What about addiction?

Darby: Besides being a response to deep pain, addiction can become unconscious greed, if we believe that we each have responsibility for our lives. But we need to walk carefully here, and look at our own sometimes disguised greed before we judge others' manifestations of it. Do you know Robert Bly, the poet? He wrote about denial in a book of prose and poetry called *The Rag and Bone Shop of the Heart*.[10] He addresses it to America, but it could as easily be addressed to England. I quote him here because I think denial of reality "as it is" is the real shadow of astrological earth. He says: "Denial can be considered as an extension – in all levels of society – of the naive person's inability to face the harsh facts of life. The health of any nation's soul depends on the capacity of adults to face the harsh facts of the time. But the covering up of painful emotions inside us and the blocking out of fearful images coming from outside have become in our country the national and private style." He goes on to say: "Denial begins with the refusal to admit that we die." "Breaking through the wall of denial helps us get rid of self-pity, and replaces self-pity with awe at the complicated misery of all living things."

Now, I wonder how many of you in this room immediately experienced a resistance to this phrase, "the complicated misery of all living things"? Do you accept that notion, or do you think that if people ate better, thought better, got better analysis, lied less, created more practised kindness more often, meditated more, there would be less "complicated misery"? Do you think you would be happier if you were better loved, smarter, wiser, thinner, richer, living in a better house, living with someone or living alone, had a child or a friend or a better mother or father? It's not easy to accept reality "as it is."

The Japanese say, "eat bitter." Robert Bly says, "Eating bitter means to turn and face life." He talks about life in all its ugly,

---

10   Robert Bly, *The Rag and Bone Shop of the Heart,* Harper Collins, London, 1993.

painful manifestations – the cruelty and stupidity, the neglect, and the sheer animalness of each of us with our unglamorous animal bodies which have their own needs. "If we have turned our backs on life, don't be surprised if we kill the poor, the homeless, ourselves, and the Earth. Getting rid of denial, then, means getting used to the flavour of 'bitter', getting used to having that flavour of bitter truth in the mouth."

Audience: Is he speaking from earth planets?

Darby: It sounds like it, doesn't it? The further we get from the Earth, the more we deny its reality – that everything eats everything else to survive, and the strong destroy the weak, and all individual things weaken in the end and die, and new life comes out of old.

Audience: Are you saying that people with lots of earth are more prone to this denial?

Darby: I am saying that denial of natural processes is the shadow of earth, and this denial can activate fear, which often leads to greed. When you see manifestations of denial of the way things are "in all their complicated misery", then you often see depression masked by greed as a response to it. How many of us are going flat out, all the time, to get as much as we can of everything? Is this zest for life, or is it greed? Earth bears with things, and through bearing with things it works with them, keeps things going, improves things where it can, brings things to their peak, then watches them die. Everything else is distortion.

Audience: Isn't there a shadow element in earth's tendency to see everything in such a matter-of-fact way that there is no magic at all?

Darby: I don't think so. Earthy people know about magic. If they appear "flat" and skeptical sometimes, it is probably because they are skeptical about what is arising in a particular situation or conversation. Fiery or airy or watery people can hold out against what they experience. Earthy people can't. They are too deeply based in reality. So they will instinctively reject false magic, but equally, they will recognise true magic. They recognise when something is real, when something works, whether they understand the laws behind the manifestation or not. The shadow is something to be recognised and acknowledged. In many situations, the ability to deny the horrors of life can also be a strength. But it is never a real or lasting strength if the denial is unconscious, because that leads to greed, which leads to destruction. But perhaps even that is part of nature's story in the end.

I have copied here a poem called "Faith" from *The Rag and Bone Shop of the Heart.* It is by Czeslaw Milosz.

> Look, see the long shadow cast by the tree;
> And flowers and people throw shadows on the earth:
> What has no shadow has no strength to live.

TAURUS

This is the first of the earth signs, and it is fixed earth. In the northern hemisphere, where astrology began, it coincides with deep springtime, when everything is humming and buzzing with fertile richness. Taurus is ruled by Venus. It is the sign most naturally associated with the beauty of untrammeled nature. It is also about the basic necessities of life. I remember this from my first class with Isobel Hickey in Boston, in the late 1960's. She said, "Taurus is about food, sex, and shelter." And I thought, "This astrology is going to be easy to learn." The seductive power of Taurus, even in that!

The Earth waits for spring. The rain comes, the heat comes, and the Earth wakes up and begins her extraordinary season of fruiting and flowering. Everything happens in its appropriate sequence – it happens the same way every time, and yet each new fruit, flower, lamb, flea, is different to any other. Taurus is the Earth which waits for the spark which will begin the process of manifesting life. Taurus is the Earth from which every basic necessity arises, but in its own season and time. There is a great deal of waiting in Taurus' energy.

Audience: And there is a melancholy in Taurus, because the waiting may not bear fruit.

Audience: And the fruit may not be eaten. Human beauty, especially youthful beauty, is almost unbearable at times.

Darby: Why unbearable?

Audience: The shadow of death. The transient nature of beauty, of life.

Darby: And yet, contained in the Taurean field is the awareness of constant return. Taurus bears with things, because embedded in its nature is the sense of renewal, the constant flow between death and life that is part of nature. The waiting, the flowering, and then the return to waiting. Death's seed in the fullness of beauty. Life's seed even in death. And even the uneaten fruit, part of the cycle, fertilising the next generation. Venus is ruler of Taurus, Lady of the House. She infuses her subjects with a grace and charm that comes from the promise of new life. Planets in Taurus offer a promise of fruitfulness. Their seductive power lies in the promise of something better.

Audience: Even Hitler, a Taurean, sold himself by appearing to offer something better.

Darby: True. And always, having been seduced, we are then called to the work of tending and maintaining that which has come from our willingness to be seduced. Venus charms us into getting to work through Taurus. Sex leads to creation and a lifetime of work. Taurus is a lot about sex, in the sense of both a deep appreciation of bodily pleasures and a natural instinct for procreation and generation. Think how important procreation was to our species in all those long years of struggling to survive – thousands and thousands of years fighting the elements. And the moment of rest and comfort, even a moment, must have given birth to something in our notion of beauty. All of our early magical rituals were for securing the things of Taurus' realm – food (survival), sex (survival of the species), and shelter (to nurture new life).

Audience: There is a conflict today. Modern magic is generally worrisome to Taurean people. It feels like perversion. It is since the Pluto in Leo generation was born that we have had such a conflict – love of youthful beauty and hatred of the "black magic" that can preserve it. That is one of the Leo-Taurus conflicts – obsession with "the child" and the aversion to the unnatural.

Darby: You are right. Planets in Taurus are resistant to the artificial. Artificial fertilisers, plastic surgery, GM foods, and happy pills are distortions, from the Taurean perspective. It is conservative by nature and tends towards the traditional in most ways, preferring time's seasoning. When those with planets in Taurus go for the artificial, it is either greed, or the impulse is coming from somewhere else. Some idea or emotion or vision is interfering with Taurus' natural inclination. Once the Taurean part of ourselves discovers the inherent rhythm in something, it works with that rhythm and will not want to change it – well, not much. Planets that form awkward angles to planets in Taurus seem to push and pull them out of their natural rhythm. They interfere with the slow development of what those planets describe. If the pushing goes on and on, then they blow like a volcano.

Audience: I just thought about the power of a bull. If you quietly lead them around, they will go softly, but if you are harsh or quick, they resist and become dangerous.

Darby: Absolutely. Watch your planets in Taurus and the planets that aspect them, to see where you are naturally slow and patient and what constellates "being pushed" for you. Those of you with planets in Leo squaring your Taurus planets: notice how "righteous indignation" gets mixed up with anger when you feel as though you have been pushed too far. With planets in Aquarius afflicting Taurus planets, you will see how "idealism" interferes: "It *should* have happened this way, in this time." "I *should* be allowed to do it my way, because it's the right way." With Scorpio planets opposing Taurus planets, you will see long periods of quiet and then huge battles of wills – one side demanding and the other side silent and resistant. With all these conflicts, compromises have to be made for peace and security to be reinstated. The Taurean planets are thrown out of the garden of Eden by the "afflicting" planets, but new and, often enough, improved conditions emerge out of the discordant energies.

Venus will always stand behind any planet in her sign. It is always important to find her in the chart when we are trying to understand planets in Taurus. Then we will have a starting point for understanding what sort of blooms those planets are cultivating – whether they are relatively quick-blooming, or take a long, long time to arrive and last a long time.

There is a deep resistance in Taurus. This resistance to force is not just physical. It also operates mentally and emotionally. If you bring a new idea, notion, plan to the part of the chart where Taurus lives, expect resistance, unless your idea is brought with charm and grace. If there is the slightest whiff of complicated motives, of hidden agendas, or of coercion in the area represented by Taurus or where Taurus planets reside, they will dig their heels in and not be moved. Venus rules here, and Mars is in detriment in Taurus. Force is destructive in Taurus' domain.

Audience: You have to get Taurean planets to *own* anything new that comes in – an idea, a plan, a possibility.

Darby: That's a good way of putting it. But no matter how charming or seductive you are, if the idea does not make sense to them, there will be little movement toward it. Sense and beauty are one here.

Audience: So they'll stay in relationship if you can convince them that you are the best thing ever, and as long as you keep putting on the charm.

Darby: Hm, do I smell a bad experience with Taurus? Giving and receiving pleasure is the currency here. After all, Venus is about seduction and charm and beauty and grace and mutual attraction. So it would be churlish to suppose that her sign should not need to give and get what is her great power and strength. We are rightly suspicious of charm, because it usually leads us into something that demands a great deal of us, one way or another. Through psychology we have seen past the surface of charming and seductive people into the dark and controlling nature that is often under the surface. The secret of true charm is that you cannot really charm anyone else unless you are charmed yourself by a notion or a plan, an object or a place. The very nature of true charm is that it has a natural grace and beauty to it, whether it be an idea, a chair, or a meal. Taurus teaches us simplicity, and simplicity *is* charm. Most of us are charmed by nature, aren't we? We rarely admit, any more, the dark and controlling aspects under the charm of nature, because nature seems endangered now. But under all the beauty of nature there is a relentless force which is about survival and evolution.

The dark side of all that fertility and grace and beauty of rhythm and love of form is cold and relentless. We often portray it as awkward and misshapen. Think of the Earth-gnomes and goblins and demons that reside in nature. Think of the wicked nature-spirits who steal gold and silver and babies and the breath out of bodies. They have to be propitiated and attended and paid, like Mafia, if they are not to come out in the night and steal the very heart out of our bodies. They are greedy and cruel, manipulating and ruthless. They are, in some part, our way of understanding something frightening about nature – that it is only on our side if we are useful to it and further its ends. It cares little for the survival of one or another individual.

Audience: Is this the shadow of Taurus you are describing?

Darby: Yes – and its power. When it takes over and reveals itself without its grace and beauty, it becomes...Well, think of your worst nightmare Taurus person.

Audience: My ex-husband.

Audience: Hitler.

Darby: And there we are, in nightmare alley. Which is not where Taurus would ever *choose* to be, for any reason.

Planets in Taurus

When the **Sun is in Taurus**, people are born to be the caretakers of natural rhythms, in one way or another. And so they will develop at their own pace, no matter how much you push them toward yours. A Taurean child needs to know that things can take time – that all the rushing and buzzing that other people do is fine and dandy, but the flowers and fruit that are growing here, in this ground, will develop in their own time and in their own way. Taurus Sun will resist being forced to grow in a way that feels unnatural, and so it gets a reputation for being stubborn. This Sun carries an image in its heart which is attuned to furthering or creating an environment in which people and animals can find peace and security. It works to make a space in which its own values can take root and grow. No matter how warlike it may appear to be, its highest values circle around ownership of territory where peace and tranquillity can lead to security and prosperity of one sort or another. Anything that is sensed as opposition to this urge is to be resisted.

Audience: You were speaking of the pathological side of earth. My uncle had Sun in Taurus, and he was so much a part of the rhythms of nature when he was young. He worked and built up a farm, but he became very, very greedy, and he couldn't let go of any of his possessions. And that pulled him under.

Darby: That sounds like earth and water together: quicksand.

Audience: My son is a farmer in New Zealand, and is Taurus with Moon in Aquarius. He is caught between the desire for money, which he will get by growing "unnatural" crops, and the desire to live simply, growing only "natural" crops.

Darby: Being a farmer today must be more demanding than ever before, not only physically but morally. With Uranus in Aquarius now and Neptune coming up, the choices will get even stranger.

Audience: I think **Moon in Taurus** is even more possessive than Sun in Taurus, but it doesn't know it. They get very attached to what is familiar, and are totally charming until you try to get away. My mother and grandmother have it, but I have Moon in Aries. I've been running away from comfort for as long as I can remember, but I have to fight to do it.

Darby: Moon in Taurus is not conscious of the possessive moves they make on those who inhabit their feeling world. Its seduction is to offer comfort and to help you to get more comfortable in one way or another. When crossed by aspects which indicate a need and love of freedom or solitude, they get into turmoil. They can have the same arguments over and over and over with those who are part of their intimate circle. But Moon in Taurus can generate a magic circle of warmth and security, and it really gives an instinct for how to make the most of any environment. But one must never take that quiet warmth for granted. They can become unrelentingly vengeful when they feel betrayed. It may seem a peaceful placement for the Moon. It rarely is. Volcanoes be in that earth!

With **Mercury in Taurus**, then knowledge will be sought which can bring peace or security to the Sun. As Mercury is never more than 28° from the Sun, only Ariens, Taureans, and Geminis ever get the benefit of this information-gatherer alighting on the use of beauty and peace. No matter where Venus is, this Mercury is almost always slow and retentive. Taurus will naturally find it easier to bear the slowness of Mercury in its own sign. It will take in the information the Taurus needs at the pace it can accept and retain. It will not gather information that is not necessary or useful for the Taurus Sun. However, Mercury in Taurus can be frustrating for Aries or Gemini, and each of those signs can be impatient with the slowness of their own minds.

Audience: Or maybe it is more a matter of other people learning to appreciate their minds. Both my father and I are Aries, but I have Mercury in Aries and he has Mercury in Taurus. When I was young, it used to drive me crazy that he would repeat everything he said twice. Whenever he told you something, he would say it, and then say it again. As a teenager, I could barely tolerate being in the same room with him. When I finally started studying astrology and saw that he had Mercury in Taurus, everything changed. I went home and told him, and he said, "Good, well, good, I'm glad that helps you. I'm certainly glad."

Darby: I have two friends who are Aries with Mercury in Taurus, and they repeat everything, too. I wonder if that is usually the case? If they say something once and it sounds good, they have to say it again, partly for the pleasure of saying it and partly to feel the weight of it. And that's another thing about Mercury in Taurus. Unless it can take pleasure in learning, it cannot learn. Unless it can take pleasure in information, it cannot or will not – and I'm not even sure it should – take in the information. If Mercury is "afflicted", then it must be creative in finding ways to absorb the information it needs, because the "afflicting" planet will get in the way of its pleasure. And so it must "trick" itself into finding a pleasurable way to take in the information. Venus will tell you something more about the sort of pleasure that will turn this Mercury on. It will tell you what will motivate this Mercury to improve itself so that the Sun might be better served. But remember, you cannot push Taurus. You cannot force it to grow faster. You can only provide conditions in which its nature will flourish. A child with Mercury in Taurus, who is not learning to read, seems lazy, isn't interested. But provide that child with beautiful books, books that appeal to his or her sense of colour and shape, books with wonderful pictures, and that garden might begin to grow.

Venus in Taurus is a happy position, and I think this is true no matter what the aspect. Venus is so strong in Taurus that no harsh aspect seems to be able to stop her taking pleasure in the good things of life. It is like Venus herself, who is never, ever a victim. A person with Venus in Taurus may go through fire after fire and still come out with something velvet or mossy to sit on. Somewhere it always knows where to find a bit of wealth, a bit of comfort.

Audience: What about when it's square Pluto, as several of my recent clients have? Each had a different story, but each story was painful when it came to love.

Darby: That is often the case, isn't it, with Venus square Pluto in Leo? The Pluto in Leo generation is about self-transformation, self-consciousness, bringing light out of the darkness, making the unconscious conscious. When it is squaring Venus in Taurus, it makes the waiting and the apparent passivity seem wrong, and the waiting and passivity get forced into trying to become conscious.

Audience: Venus in Taurus square Pluto recoils at first from that Plutonian impulse.

Audience: But it will also attract passionate people.

Darby: When it is square Pluto, it can attract sexual energy before it is sexually awake. Venus in Taurus is naturally slow to awaken sexually, but Pluto can force it to consciousness, like chemical fertilisers force plants to grow faster. Venus in Taurus then retreats, and won't easily come out again when there is sexual energy around. The slow gestation was disturbed, and so it becomes suspicious.

Audience: What do you mean?

Audience: Well, it is not the natural expression of a planet in Taurus to be quickly roused to passion. It wants to stay where it is, wherever that is. When it is being provoked by something as heavy as a Pluto square, its first inclination is to retreat deeper into its "sleep." I have Venus in Taurus square Pluto, and I experience it like that. Of course, it isn't allowed to retreat completely, and so the tension builds until it breaks, and then there is a new consciousness. But it's a heavy process.

Audience: Venus wants to attract in Taurus.

Audience: It does. But it doesn't know that, and when Pluto in Leo calls for transformation, it does it through physical experiences.

Audience: I agree. I also have Venus in Taurus square Pluto. Once conscious, it is very sure about what it is doing, as well. It wants to stay in control, but it has to find something incredibly passionate out there to feed off. It will eat it. But it will put it in its mouth to taste – it doesn't particularly want it in its belly. It just takes it that far into sensual pleasure. So you can imagine that on a psychological level, it's the same thing. It only goes so far.

Darby: I've noticed that need to stay in control with Venus in Taurus square Pluto people, and I've wondered if it stemmed from the fear that loss of control will take too much away – it will be all-consuming.

Audience: That's it. So one finds a way to have sensual pleasure without being consumed by it. The need to sink into the earthy unconsciousness of the senses is challenged by the need to stay aware of danger. So we look for "earthly delights" that will allow us both.

Darby: And that way Venus can have her pleasure, even in the dangerous zone of Plutonic intensity.

Audience: I have **Mars in Taurus** square Pluto, and I feel as though I am sitting on a volcano most of the time. When it explodes, it is inevitably very destructive.

Darby: Mars is traditionally in detriment in Taurus, being in the sign opposite to its natural domain, Scorpio. This tells us that Mars is not at its ease in Venus' world. Remember the trouble that Hephaistos made for Ares and Aphrodite when they leapt into bed with each other as soon as they had the chance. Think of the almost comic discomfort that men experience in traditional female places. When Mars in Taurus is activated, it seems like "a bull in a china shop". People with Mars in Taurus are not comfortable conquering new territory, defending or protecting their own territory, moving fast, or competing for prizes. They can react to love as if it is a threat, and to aggression as if it is love. You must remember to look at where Venus is in the chart, to see what will set off this Mars most naturally. Venus will be the value which will activate Mars' "defend, protect, conquer", impulse. And because Mars is in Taurus' earth, it will work all its life to improve its ability to protect its own territory and to find a comfortable way to do it. It will not give up on this, and slowly but surely, it will gain the ground it wants.

Audience: I have Mars in Taurus in the 8th and Venus in Leo on the MC, and it is true that I am very steady in improving my financial situation as I go through life. I started out in a poor family, but now I am getting quite prosperous. Now, the other part is interesting, because I am an actor, and I am improving my financial situation through my work, mostly on TV. But I don't understand what you are saying about looking at Venus to see what is setting Mars off.

Darby: Well, your Venus in Leo in the 10th house is the value behind the work that Mars does. Although it may seem as though you are working for Mars – financial security – the inner motive is perhaps the need for love and recognition from "the world" and, under that, from your mother, who perhaps took first place in getting the attention when you were young. It may be this that is behind the seemingly simple financial drive.

Audience: Well, I'll have to think about that – I also have Mercury in Taurus! – but it is interesting. Sometimes I take work that isn't financially good, but I cannot resist it because I know it will be good for my reputation. To convince myself, I tell myself, "It will lead to financially lucrative work later on." My mother was a great woman, who gave her all to keep us afloat, and I'd love to show her that I can take care of her now.

Darby: I think that is also your Cancer Sun speaking, and your Moon in Virgo, but it is worth thinking about the dynamic between Venus and Mars – especially as they are square each other. If you understand that Venus has a strong say in what drives Mars in Taurus, then you are less likely to get disturbed by thinking you are going after one thing while you are really seeking another. You have picked up your father's way of moving from Mars, and yet underneath, your mother's values and the things that she appreciates are a strong factor in drawing you towards certain kinds of experience. This is true for everyone with Mars in Taurus, but it is more obvious when Venus is square to Mars.

But let us think about **Jupiter in Taurus**. What a delicious placement this seems to be. They believe the material world will be safe for them. Whether they are rich or poor, they have an instinctive trust that they will always have enough to live on and that their bodies will not let them down. There is no sense of "sin" in their love of indulging themselves and others in luxury, however limited their resources. Of course, they can take their "abundance" completely for granted, and if they lose their humility, their sense of wealth becomes tinged with something sour. Remember, again, to always look to where Venus is. Then you will see what sort of beauty they are seeking to experience the fullness of this position. Two people I know with Venus in Libra and Jupiter in Taurus express and nourish themselves and others through beautiful objects. Picasso had that combination. But he also had Saturn and Neptune and Pluto in Taurus with Sun in Scorpio, so his hunt for beauty went down more complicated routes. I have known know several people with Venus in Pisces and Jupiter in Taurus, and they all have experienced being "magically" saved from financial disaster at one time or another.

Audience: I have Jupiter in Taurus and Saturn in Libra. My experience is that I can take a certain material abundance for granted in my life, but not people! I have to learn that over and over, it seems. It is as if life gives to me, and I have to give to others and not expect the same back.

Darby: That's interesting. Your nature draws abundance to you through your Venus-ruled Jupiter, but in relationships you have to pass Saturn's rigorous accounting. You may expect the same from people as you do from nature, but it doesn't work that way with Saturn in Venus' other sign. I wish we had more time to explore that combination in various houses.

Audience: Do people with **Saturn in Taurus** dislike nature?

Darby: That's a thought! I don't know anyone with that position who dislikes nature. The people I come across with Saturn in Taurus feel a profound responsibility for the things around them, in very particular ways. They learn that from having seen things taken for granted in their life, and perhaps having taken things for granted themselves. Unlike Jupiter in Taurus, their natural talents do not flower by themselves. They have to work hard to grow their inner garden. Saturn in Taurus puts a high value on talent, and that blocks or at least slows down the development of their own unique gifts. They have to unearth their natural gifts and keep a steady eye on them while they develop. They can lose their focus if they love someone whose talent or beauty they love. That's the Venus connection. When they love, they can lose their own ground for a while. I'm not saying this is wrong, but it does generate frustration, and they can displace this frustration by working hard in other people's gardens. But at some point, when they turn to cultivate their own again, this develops a depth and concentration that others can learn from.

Audience: I want to ask you about **Chiron in Taurus**. I have two clients with it. They are in their sixties, and I have no idea how to interpret it. They come to me for business advice, and I'd like to have some clue about it.

Darby: I have noticed that people with Chiron in Taurus don't have comfortable relationships with their bodies. Their bodies are not sensual objects in themselves. They do not take delight in the body's movement, its appetites, and its natural functions. Now, that is true for a lot of people, of course, but for those with Chiron in Taurus it is the grit in the oyster. There is a gap between their bodily reactions and their pleasure. Whenever I look at the Chiron placement in a chart, I think of that voice in some of London's underground stations: "Mind the gap!" For those of you who do not travel the underground, this voice calls out when the train comes into stations where there is a significant gap between the carriage and the platform. So one must "mind the gap" or fall into it. With Chiron, the sign tells you where the gap is, and the house will tell you where the gap will appear in your life. In the case of Taurus, look for Venus behind the scenes. She will be wildly compensating for the gap, over-stating her particular values.

Having said all that, Sean Connery – a Virgo Sun and Moon – has Chiron in Taurus. It is trine his Moon in Virgo, and it is in the 4th, if the time I have is accurate.[11] His Venus is in Libra, in the 8th, square Pluto, opposite Uranus, and quincunx Chiron. There

---

11   Data for Sean Connery: 25 August 1930, 6.05 pm, Edinburgh, from Tae-ger, *Internationales Horoskope Lexikon*. This data is classed as Group 1*, deemed to be reliable.

is a very harsh and painful story under all that. He has certainly found a way to excite the sensual imagination of the public as an actor. But isn't it interesting how violent most of his films are? Perhaps this keeps his own volcanoes quiet.

When Uranus is conjunct Saturn in Taurus, which it was in 1940, there is an odd twist to it. I had two clients recently say, "I can't understand my Saturn conjunct Uranus in Taurus. No matter what anyone tells me, it doesn't make sense to me." Well, I suppose it wouldn't "make sense" in any conventional sense – that is the nature of this particular conjunction. I have been close to two women with this conjunction in Taurus square Venus in Aquarius. Also, the writer Erica Jong, who wrote, amongst other things, *Fear of Flying*, had this configuration, with Venus on the MC. This group of people seems to be struggling to work out new values, breaking away from the traditions of their roots. Both the women I knew were magicians of a sort. One of them was Ndlaleni, the *sangoma* I told you about earlier in the day. The other was a healer, an extraordinarily gifted Alexander teacher. Both were isolated, unable to feel comfortable in their given communities. Both were attracted to people and communities which were extremely unusual. But even there, they had outsider positions.

No matter what the aspects to Venus, the Saturn-Uranus conjunction in Taurus will alienate you from comfort, drive you to find an art form which is beyond the normal, insist that you cross the boundaries between cultures, age, and time, initiate you into the secret mysteries of nature, and isolate you from you own kind. It will also open lines of affection between you and individuals you could not have imaged before you met them. But having met them, you cannot go back to your own traditional ways of relating. You now expect to find a unique gift in everyone, and that can feel like a gift itself, or it can feel like a burden.

Unless life expectancy increases a great deal, none of us have or will experience **Neptune or Pluto in Taurus**. But we are still strongly affected by the generation with Pluto in Taurus, and some of them had both Pluto and Neptune there. These were people born between 1874 and 1884, give or take a few months. Albert Einstein had both of them in Taurus, though not conjunct. Picasso had them together, and with Jupiter and Saturn, too. They were all opposing his Sun-Mercury in Scorpio. Pierre Teilhard de Chardin, whom some of you might know, had all of those, plus more in Taurus. I will speak about him later. Spinoza was a Sagittarius with Jupiter conjunct Pluto in Taurus, opposing his Mercury in Scorpio. Jung had his Moon in Taurus conjunct Pluto, and we all know the wealth that came from that particular mine.

Planets in the 2ⁿᵈ house

Darby: Now, what about 2ⁿᵈ house planets? What's the difference between having planets in Taurus and planets in the 2ⁿᵈ?

Audience: Planets in Taurus come from one's own nature, and planets in the 2ⁿᵈ are about one's relation to one's material environment. One is inner and one is outer.

Audience: With planets in Taurus, you are born stubborn. With planets in the 2ⁿᵈ house, you learn to be stubborn!

Audience: With planets in the 2ⁿᵈ house, you develop a fixed or stable attitude through experience.

Audience: Sun in Taurus has a fixed attitude to life. There is something stubborn in the character, something solid and secure. But someone with **Sun in the 2ⁿᵈ** house will give priority to things remaining the same – to money, to possessions. It will work to keep the things it has. Sun in Taurus is the way it is, and that is that.

Darby: Yes, planets in Taurus attend the things that belong to their territory by simply keeping an eye on them. They develop a rhythm of response and just keep doing it that way, because it works well enough. With planets in the 2nd house, you are drawn to the development of your resources in different ways at different stages of your life. You work to improve your material life and to secure your relationship with what belongs to you.

The 2nd house is the place where you can recognise your basic attitude to your primary resource, your body. This matter, your body, is the only piece of property you will ever really own. How you treat it says something about your attitude to matter. It is the resource which contains all the other resources, and so it is worth understanding your underlying attitude to it. Without it, you aren't going to do very much here. Well-aspected planets in the 2nd house will show an easier relationship with your body than planets that are tensely configured, of course. This has nothing to do with whether you are short or tall or fat or thin or ugly or beautiful according to the standards of your culture. The seeds of your natural talents and gifts lie here. We all are born with something of value that can be developed, either to make our own living or to serve those who support us. Your 2nd house contains that which, when brought out and appreciated, becomes the field you tend.

Audience: I have **Saturn in the 2nd**, and I really feel I must earn my own living, even though my husband is perfectly willing to provide for me.

Darby: Having Saturn in the 2nd house doesn't mean you lack money. It means you lack self-value, unless you are working your own patch. Self-worth and resource management are connected here. Saturn here says that your early conditioning did not teach you sensible rules of resource management. You have to learn through your own hard-won experience. You can feel poor, even if you are rich by other people's standards. As you work to get your material world in order, so you are working for self-worth, but there must be balance here, as always with Saturn. Spend too much time on the material world and you freeze up in other areas. Spend too little time and you can easily fall into resentment, envy, and other such character distortions.

If you have "good" planets in the 2ⁿᵈ house – Sun, Venus, or Jupiter, particularly when they are well aspected – this naturally inclines you to developing your gifts and talents. You develop your natural resources in ways that bring food to your table. You may not feel secure in other parts of yourself, with people or with your mental capacities, but as soon as you put energy into developing your resources, it begins to happen. When transiting planets "interfere" with your 2ⁿᵈ house planets, you may find you have to examine your values around material things and, depending on the aspecting planets, adjust your inner and outer relationship to what you value. Transiting planets remind you never to take "things" for granted.

"Hard" planets in the second – Saturn or Mars, and perhaps Neptune – demand different kinds of attention, but they *must* be attended. By that I mean you must work to bring consciousness to how you care for your body and your body of talents. Ignorance brings trouble. Afflictions to planets in the 2ⁿᵈ, or "hard" planets in the 2ⁿᵈ or aspecting the ruler of the 2ⁿᵈ, simply demand consciousness. Pay attention to the rituals people develop to keep their fields producing, their resources flowing. They will have the flavour of the ruler of the 2ⁿᵈ. Tenanting planets might be said to be the sort of magician who lives in your field.

Audience: I have **Jupiter in the 2ⁿᵈ**, and I have had periods in my life when I had no money. But I always know it will return. No matter how it looks to others, I am always sure that something will turn up.

Audience: I have a fairly well-aspected **Neptune in the 2nd** in Libra, and I feel the same way. But I do get anxious, sometimes, because people tend to tell me I should pay more attention and be more practical. I just glance at my finances now and again, and stay out of debt, and try not to get greedy for things. Mostly, I keep myself "in the flow." Do you think that is right?

Darby: Yes, I do. And perhaps it's important not to air your anxiety too much. Remember, Neptune's realm is a realm of mystery. You may be over-stirring the atmosphere around Neptune by talking about your 2nd house affairs and activating anxiety in others. With Neptune in the 2nd, one's relationship to one's material condition and one's body is strange to most people. No amount of "making secure" can secure material things with Neptune in the 2nd. You simply have to develop a non-material attitude to the material world, for it to work for you. But Neptune in any of the earth houses indicates material anxiety and demands an imaginative approach. For those with Neptune in the 2nd, the longing for beautiful objects or material security is truly a spiritual longing. *Things* carry soul, for those with this position. Those who can recognise this longing for beauty and security as a longing for the soul within matter find their material and spiritual life interwoven in such a way that conventional material security is no longer relevant.

Audience: I have **Moon in the 2nd**, and I can recognise that in myself, although it is more personal. My sister say she can tell how I am feeling in general by my need for or lack of need for material things.

Audience: I have Moon in Capricorn in the 2nd, square Neptune in Libra. I see that I can sometimes blur the edges around what I need for my own personal security and what I long for spiritually. I go from feeling that I have everything I could ever need to feeling as though I am the world in need.

Darby: That can sound like Pluto in the 2ⁿᵈ. But what's the difference?

Audience: I have a client with Venus in Taurus in the 11ᵗʰ square Pluto in the 2ⁿᵈ house, and she is a prostitute. I had been reading a cookbook interpretation by Louis Acker, and it said, "possibly prostitution". I told my client, and she said, "Been there, done that." That must be one way Venus goes to the underworld. You once said that you knew several women with that aspect who were celibate, either by choice or not.

Darby: Yes. One woman told me that she had decided on celibacy in her late thirties because, although she had enjoyed sex, she had never enjoyed the relationships where sex was involved, and so she had given them up for a peaceful life. She was in her mid-fifties at the time, and I don't know if she ever changed her mind.

If you have outer planets in the 2ⁿᵈ house, your magician is truly beyond your control. I have a very old friend with **Uranus in the 2ⁿᵈ** in Gemini and Taurus on the cusp, with Venus conjunct Jupiter in Sagittarius in the 7ᵗʰ. He is a painter, and people are drawn to him. He makes money doing murals and pictures and ceilings and ostrich eggs, and all sorts of things. Money comes from all sorts of meetings. He is not rich, but he never lacks much either. With his Venus-Jupiter, he trusts completely – lucky him! He was very poor in childhood, and developed strange ideas about how money would come in a sort of magical way. He was right. If you try for material stability with Uranus in the 2ⁿᵈ, you get crazy. In a way, outer planets in the 2ⁿᵈ house are always "afflictions", in that you can't control them in any way. You have to let the planet work in its own way. And so, with outer planets here, you will either suffer natural disasters or become an alchemist of one sort or another.

Pluto in the 2ⁿᵈ will attract or describe conditions where your relationship to your natural resources, money, and your body can go through such extremes. These extremes change your values completely. You discover extraordinary treasure in your garden, but it is never completely yours. Your talents wait in the dark, and then come out when the time for them comes round.

Taurus rising

Taurus rising meets the world with charm and grace, according to which sign Venus is in and what its aspects are. No matter how relaxed it may appear on the surface, material comfort is an underlying concern. One is naturally seeking to improve one's situation in very practical ways. In an otherwise fiery or airy nature, it may seem incongruent. Wherever Venus resides in this chart tells you where this person's real security lies, and aspects from other planets describe the sort of conditions constellated by the hunt for security.

Taurus rising is not concerned with amassing wealth. It is concerned with securing comfort. Comfort may mean wealth to some, but to others it will mean discomfort, because wealth demands so much attention. If you have Taurus rising, then simplicity is the goal, both of personality development and life-style. If there are many planets in Scorpio, then one is working through very complicated situations again and again in the search for simplicity. When Venus is in fire, then one imagines all sorts of things or people who will bring comfort and joy. In air, Venus sends her message through ideas, and so all sorts of schemes arise in the search for peace and quiet. When Venus is in water, then emotional comfort is as much a goal as material ease – the two are inseparable. Taurus rising usually appears to be straight and uncomplicated in its approach to others. But remember, Scorpio is on the 7th house cusp, and so the atmosphere of peace and tranquillity is not all that it seems.

VIRGO

Virgo is the second of the earth signs, and it is ruled by Mercury. It is interesting that no planet is said to be in either exaltation or fall in this sign. If we believe that the transpersonal planets have rulership over signs, then Neptune, ruling Pisces, is in detriment in Virgo. Of course, this covers a whole generation of people, most recently those born between 1928 and 1942. We shall speak about Neptune in Virgo later.

Virgo is about intricacy. It is the intricacy and subtlety of nature. It is the subtle interweave of each species with the other, and of each species with its local and particular environment. It is the intricacy of the flora and fauna of each environment and the insects and fish and animals that are part of that environment. It is the infinite usefulness of nature with its remedies, its poisons, and its antidotes. It is the infinite permutations of nature with its intricate order of eat-and-be-eaten and use-and-be-used. It is the tiny detail of the smallest flower under the moss under the tree under the fern, which none of us ever sees – exquisite in its delicate shape, and perfectly woven into the chain of being in that particular wood, as is the tallest redwood in California. It is the very delicate and yet incredibly hardy interconnection of all natural life.

Planets in Virgo are nervous and shy of exposure. They stand behind their work, not in front of it. They are attuned to the delicacy of the balancing act that goes into keeping anything going. Virgo stands between Leo and Libra, and out of the spontaneous outpouring of Leo profusion comes the pruning and refining that will lead to the well-proportioned and graceful expression of art or culture in Libra. Virgo earth, is about maintenance, improvement, and control of the environment from behind the scenes; attention to the tiniest detail, so that what shows to the outside world will seem effortless and beautiful. Virgo attends the spaces between the words on the page and is sensitive to the intervals between the notes. With Mercury as its ruler, it is attuned to the moments between the main events.

Planets in Virgo have the task of noticing that which can stop systems working properly. And so they are sensitive to all sorts of pollution. They smell garbage building up quicker than other signs. I don't mean Virgos dislike conventional "bad" smells – they can usually handle the farmyard better than most. But they have a sensitive nose for stuff that needs to be brought out in the open and cleared up. They are psychically attuned to where the garbage is building up. This is their gift, but like all such gifts, it can get out of hand. Planets in Virgo go about noticing the rubbish, and they can get lost in this noticing unless other influences, other planets, open up their perceptions. Anything that interferes with their work makes them very nervous, yet their work has to be interrupted. Otherwise their world becomes too small and too full of fixing, tidying, and taking out the garbage.

Virgo has to do with cultivation in all its senses. Demeter, goddess of the grain, who rules over all planting and sowing, is a powerful figure in Virgo's field. The Greek story of the loss of her daughter to the god of the underworld, and her subsequent search and eventual return, is a very sophisticated story. At one level, it tells of our intimate and intricate relationship to the seasons and to grain from the beginning of our agricultural evolution. The initiation rites at Eleusis, and their survival for over 2000 years, tell us something about the power of this Goddess of the Grain. Can you imagine the power of the moment in which we discovered we could cultivate crops, rather than simply hunt and find food? In remembering the myth of Demeter and Persephone, I also think of the Virgoan tendency for periodic crisis, whether it be physical or psychical. These crises break the rhythms and rituals of the ever-self-ordering Virgoan world. They break up and break down the inner and outer habits and routines, and when whatever was lost has been found, the world settles again, the world is seen afresh again. New rituals evolve out of new perceptions.

We can also associate Baubo with Virgo. She was the bawdy, ancient crone who so amused Demeter with her vulgar entertainment when she was weeping by the well in Eleusis, searching for her lost daughter. Virgo is said to be prissy and prudish. This may be true on the surface, but not at all true underneath. Their attention to detail extends to noticing bodily processes with a Mercurial, and often funny, eye. There is a bawdiness to this sign that only those who get very close discover. And you do not get close unless you understand how difficult it is at times to tend all the intricate details of the various processes Virgo attends. So many things call out to planets in Virgo for attention, and the tension of attention to everything that needs attending makes people with these planets very edgy indeed.

Audience: What about service?

Darby: The service is the work of keeping things going and smelling out the rubbish and getting rid of it; registering the pollution and telling someone about it; noticing the broken plough and getting it fixed; simply keeping things going. Virgo is also the cup of tea you bring your aunt when she has come home from town tired and irritable. It is the polish you put on the underside of the table, so that the wood can be fed from both sides, whether it is seen or not. It is the accounts you keep so that the incomings and outgoings tally, so that the harvest can feed the community. It is the endless tasks that have to do with maintaining the rhythms and cycles of daily life.

I mentioned the edgy, nervous quality of planets in Virgo. But there are times when simply performing ritual tasks – sweeping, dusting, ironing, polishing, cleaning tools – can be incredibly restorative when there is too much emotion around. But on the other hand, being so serviceable can lead to all sorts of problems for those with Virgo placements and for those they serve. Service which is done simply and quietly is usually not recognised by others. They can feel taken for granted, and those around them can become slothful, unconsciously relying on them to clean up the mess. It is our Virgo function which keeps us aware of the sacred character of true work. It is our Virgo function which keeps us tending the garden of our life, pulling weeds, tidying up the edges, keeping the corners clean. Ignoring that aspect of life often leads to a debilitating one-sidedness in the personality, and you find people who cannot take care of themselves and have to completely rely on others.

Audience: But too much focus on that sort of service is also unhealthy. You hear about people who are obsessively tidy and orderly, and cannot leave the house without putting away every shoe and shirt and cereal packet. I know someone like that, and she dominates her entire family from that almost invisible but powerful place of "service".

Darby: And then there are those who are the opposite. I know several Virgos who are so sloppy and chaotic that they couldn't function unless they had people tidying up after them all the time. But this disorder comes from other placements. The Virgo planets show where one is trying to create order, improve life, develop self-suficiency. It can be quite an inner battle.

Audience: I have noticed something that surprised me about Virgo. I have come to think that they are very social. Have you found that, or is it just me thinking that?

Darby: I haven't noticed that. I wonder. Virgo is about finding its true service, and more often than not, that means service to people. It is ruled by Mercury, and Mercury is also about culture and communication, so perhaps there is a social element from that.

Audience: Virgo goes away and works at what it has been given to do. It will craft and polish and then give it back, but the idea of social dialogue – well, it is not that sort of sign.

Darby: This is interesting. Most of us probably do think of Virgo as a somewhat unsociable sign, more focused on keeping the world in order. But if you think of it, it is a sign that speaks of cultivation. It is drawn to culture. If Taurus is the rock shard that becomes an axe-head, then Virgo is the reed that becomes a basket. It goes one step farther into intricacy and complexity, seeking use in everything. The Egyptian god Thoth always comes into my mind when I am working with Virgo planets. It was he who brought agriculture and art and science – human culture – to the kingdom while his lord Osiris was away. Presumably he had time to work on all the improvements he had been contemplating while he was busy serving his lord. Culture is an expression of, and for, a people.

If Virgo needs people, it is very different from its previous sign Leo. Leo is about heart development. It is very different to the next sign, Libra, which is developing the capacity to balance the ideal with the real in human interaction. Virgo looks for what it can do, and it then does it, somehow or other. It looks around to assess what it can usefully contribute to in any given situation, and then it sets about doing it, to the best of its ability. In general, people with strong Virgo emphasis do not find people their rest and recuperation. "Pottering around" is rest and recuperation. People are work. Life is work and work is life for those with strong Virgo planets. Virgo is associated with healing, more in the sense of attending and tending than the active and radical energy of Scorpio healing. It is also about fixing things, and often about fixing people. Methods, techniques, rituals, substances: Virgo tinkers with things, looking for new ways in which things might work better. The Virgo field is nature's workshop and, if left to its own devices, planets in Virgo would fix and cultivate and improve everything they touched on their path.

Planets afflicting Virgo planets over-ritualise and over-order things, tidying up all the loose ends they can find. They need things to function properly around them, and they can become frenzied when they are not able to do this. They can get really upset, wild, when things don't go according to schedule. It's a very edgy placement for planets, but magic comes out of those placements, order out of chaos, cultivated land out of jungle. Of course, we can see, in the shadows, all the obsessive and ty-rannical cultivations that sap the very life from people and en-vironments, because Virgo cannot handle the messy, untidy, chaotic side of itself and others. In its need to bring forth fruit out of its cultivation, it can section off itself and others. It can reject that which is "not useful" in a way that cuts itself off from its own heart. Its capacity for fine discrimination can become an incapacity to accept the irrational and untidy undergrowth in every situation. In seeing the flaw in the carpet so well, it can develop the habit of seeing only the flaws. Virgo's love of a good harvest and fear of a bad harvest can turn its cultivation skills into destruction. In weeding too well, it can take out the hidden fruit. When Virgo denies the chaotic and irrational it lives in the shadow of its own light. The shadow of Virgo is disorder: chaotic emotions, imagination, or cupboards. And it is in these shad-ows that all Virgo demons are found – demons who, when faced, bring strength, but when projected or denied, bring physical and emotional breakdowns.

Planets in Virgo

Sun in Virgo's life will be dedicated to one kind of service, and once Virgo has found its appropriate field, it can then begin to enjoy its work. The sign Mercury inhabits will tell what is the Sun in Virgo's best tool. Will it be vision and passion, with Mercury in Leo? Will it be an eye for art or justice, with Mercury in Libra? Or will it simply be the scapel of a finely tuned, careful, and curious intellect with Mercury also in Virgo? The house in which Mercury resides will tell you where this Virgo will gain its information for the cultivation of the field in which the Sun resides. Aspects to Mercury will specify how information is gained, and aspects to the Sun will give us information about how much and what kind of work one must do to be satisfied with the results of one's cultivation.

Audience: That sounds very neat – very Virgo-like!

Darby: Yes, I noticed that as I was going along. There is something in the nature of the earth element that seeks to make order out of chaos. It must come from all those centuries of seemingly chaotic conditions on the earth. Once we found a tiny patch of safety, we really worked to find ways to secure it. Once it was secure for a period of time, we began to cultivate that which made us feel secure. This is the Virgo phase. As soon as we are in the realm of Virgo, we seek to find the inherent order, and then to organise it so that we will get the best yield. With the Sun in Virgo, this work engages the heart. When a Virgo finds the field in which he or she can do this, it is very satisfying. Everything else is practise. Because it is a mutable sign, it cannot only rest in one section of the field forever – it has to develop different parts of itself. Once a section of the garden is giving quite a good yield, then the Virgo Sun looks around for something else that can be organised and crafted into use.

Audience: But I have noticed that they also keep busy in order to avoid feelings.

Darby: You are talking about the opposition to Pisces? Yes, that is true. Being useful and busy is the heart's delight for Virgo Sun, but nothing in this human dimension is unmixed. The opposition to Pisces tells us that Virgoans fare best when they can acknowledge the defensive part of Virgo, which keeps any feelings of helplessness at bay. They serve even better when they experience and acknowledge the ordinary human experience of feeling useless at times. When these feelings are allowed to rise to the surface, they evaporate naturally. Kept underground, they waterlog the works and generate neurosis and hysteria.

Now let's look at Mercury, as Virgo's ruler. **Mercury in Virgo** will only serve Leos, Virgos or Librans, as it is never more than 28° from the Sun. Here, in its place of rulership, Mercury in Virgo works with exquisite care and attention to detail. The house and aspects will tell you where it naturally goes for its information. Its natural inclination is to bring that information to the Sun this way, like a perfect secretary might bring information to his or her employer. The danger built into this Mercury is the danger of literalisation. How can you not believe that what you are seeing is literally the truth, if you have a Mercury that is so clear and detailed? Aspects to Mercury will decide whether this literalness is challenged by other dimensions of knowing.

When this Mercury serves the Sun in Leo, an uncomfortable amount of detail can accumulate in the information gathered. Leo can find itself up to its mane in detail and critical analysis in its desire to become central and inspiring to others. A Leo perfectionist is not a happy Leo. But it can also be a very useful Mercury to the Leo who needs a good library of information to bring his or her creative gifts into the light.

Audience: My brother is a Leo with Mercury in Virgo in the 11th house. He knows absolutely everything about everybody in our town. He has been like that since our childhood. I have never known anyone with so much knowledge about other people.

Darby: And then there is Virgo Sun with Mercury in Virgo. This Sun takes the information it receives and easily puts it to use. It may sometimes seem pedantic, but that is because it takes real delight in the details that its Mercury takes in, and we naturally want to share what interests us, as human beings. This combination works to harvest more productively as it goes along, and its rituals and hyperawareness to changes others don't see are part of the cultivation of the territory it serves.

On the other hand, the Libran Sun is drawn by its spirit to situations where balance must be restored. With the information-gathering Mercury in Virgo, it may seem to get caught in the intricacies of tiny imbalances and be accused of missing the larger issues to be addressed. At its best, it has the ability to restore harmony by changing one small detail that others would not have seen. At its worst, it fixates on details that obscure the real imbalance or injustice, and it cannot explain why.

Those with Mercury in Virgo can sometimes seem like magicians or alchemists. This Mercury serves its Sun as if it were assistant to someone powerful and useful. In that position it comes up with small but significant observations and improvements. In its curiosity and tendency to potter around while tidying up, it finds ways to improve the running of the kingdom of its Lord – a very smart, very canny Mercury.

Audience: That's interesting, because I have noticed that **Venus in Virgo** tends to fall in love with very smart, very canny people.

Darby: That's neat. Perhaps it does. Yet it is very earthy. However, anything in Virgo will be highly strung, and Venus here plays the high strings with great delicacy. It gets thrown out of comfort very easily.

Audience: You mean we are prissy.

Darby: I mean that when you are in the right mood, when your nerves are at ease, you can play the game of love with so much delicacy and wit that the earth spirits dance for joy.

Audience: You sound like you speak from experience.

Darby: It takes *all* kinds of experiences to learn astrology, as I am sure most of you are discovering. Are we getting distracted here? Perhaps that is one of the difficulties of Venus in Virgo. Unless the mind and body are playing together, love is an edgy affair. Venus in Virgo is very earthy, underneath its polite demeanour. Pleasure is taken in the tiniest detail. Beauty is found in the shape of a toe, in the turn of a metaphor. Venus in Virgo will get turned on by someone reading a list of groceries, as long as it is read with a particular care and attention. Afflictions to Venus in Virgo twist it out of shape and make it finicky, critical, and cross.

Audience: And a square to Saturn in Gemini makes it even finickier, more critical, and crosser.

Darby: So you have to work harder to find your pleasure zone – I mean one that is clear and free of guilt – and that takes some work. Work one field, then another, until you find one in which you discover the cultivation that brings enjoyment. Once found, it can become more than simply a pleasure zone. It can become your craft, your art. Things must always be developing with this Venus – cultivation in service to culture.

Audience: Yes. My present field is photography. I got there *via* a strange route – not a very admirable route – but now it is really my pleasure and my art. But I'm still finicky and critical and cross a lot. You spoke about the instinct for improvement. When I discover a new technique that works better than the one I've been using, it feels like magic. On a personal level, I even work with techniques that will make me less critical, or perhaps more discriminating in my criticism. I think I'm addicted to techniques. Do you think there is a support group for this addiction?

Darby: If there isn't, you could start one. Of course, you'd all end up exchanging techniques all the time, and so further addict yourselves. But you could experiment with the fine line between techniques and rituals – how art becomes religious expression and religious expression becomes art. You could even end up writing a useful and beautiful manual on it!

Audience: My son has **Moon in Virgo**, and he is so critical of me I feel as though I gave birth to my own worst critic. He has been like that since he was three. Now he's fifteen, and it's at its worst. I know he loves me, and he does all sorts of kind things for me, but I am a huge embarrassment to him.

Darby: Moon in Virgo has the instinct to improve whatever or whomever it feels for. It has an instinct for what is wrong with any system, what is stopping effective action. It is not a restful Moon, easily disturbed physically when it cannot order its world mentally. There is constant adjustment between mind and body. Mercury's position tells where and how this person gets the information with which the Virgo Moon will tend its environment. Its placement also tells us something about the rituals which are most restorative to this delicate lunar position. Mercury's position in relation to the Moon in Virgo tells how easy or difficult it is to access this information. Sometimes you have to go through loops to get the information that will be helpful – there are all sorts of disturbances.

Audience: Most people with Moon in Virgo have a very kind streak, too. You could thank your son every time he criticises you and buy lots of books on self-improvement. He'll either start feeling guilty for being so critical, or you'll improve in his eyes.

Darby: You say that because you have an earth Moon, too. Earth Moons give advice, because they want to improve things. Virgo Moon is in life service to the temporarily impaired or broken things and people of the world. It depends on other things as to what takes their attention – things or people, plants or cats. A friend with Virgo Moon told me that when he walks into someone's house, machines that have been on the brink of breaking finally fall apart with a sigh of relief, because they know their fixer has come. I have another friend with this Moon who cannot open a tin, but she can certainly fix any loss of confidence, trust, or hope with just a few words, especially those whose work she believes in. Unless there are softening influences, this Moon is impatient with those whose problems are truly unfixable, but it never stops trying. One born with this Moon was born to a mother who needed some fixing, and Mother Earth keeps it on duty through its life, attending her material and those who serve her.

Audience: I have **Mars in Virgo** conjunct Mercury, and my garden is the place where I work off the frustration I have with people.

Darby: What frustration?

Audience: The frustration that they are so slow.

Darby: Mars in the realm of the faithful councillor – a warrior in a cultivated and ordered kingdom. What can this warrior fight? And what will it fight for as servant to the king? Do you know that in medieval astrology, we find that "Mars joys in the 6th house"? If you have Mars in Virgo, your fire is lit by the chance to render service in some appropriate way – not just any service, but service that might involve risk and something to be really fixed. The service will come through the house Mars tenants, but without this chance to serve, enthusiasm and vitality are lost. Mars in Virgo will not get excited about something unless there is the thought of something useful coming out of what it is doing. Mind and body unite in service. The possibility of achieving excellence lies in the area where one is giving one's mind and body to a task that brings culture to others. Mars is enthusiastic in the cultivation of talents and resources in others which will enhance their ability to achieve something.

Audience: My mother has Sun, Mercury, and Pluto in Cancer, with Mars in Virgo in the 9th house. She looked forward to us all growing up and moving away so that she could "have some peace and quiet". It was less than a year after the last of us left the house that she left the country and went to New Zealand to set up a school for people involved with her spiritual group. She is working incredibly hard, and when I visited her last Christmas, she was like a young girl again, so full of enthusiasm and excitement. It was as if she had found a new family and a new world of service which suited her even better than her original one. But we do worry – she has burned herself out before, with her passion for service.

Darby: And you fear she might do that again. This is always a problem with Sun-Pluto – do we advise people *not* to get obsessed because it may harm them? But I do like the 9th house touch. Had it been in the 10th, she would probably have joined the civil service.

Audience: I have Mars in Virgo in the 10th, conjunct Neptune. I retired from broadcasting years ago, but I still find myself assisting one or another of my younger ex-colleagues all the time on researching their programs. It took a while for them to start asking me – I didn't think I wanted to – but when they slowly started coming for advice, I couldn't resist. I even like the fact that I don't get paid for it, although my children don't like that. I get all the pleasure of the work without feeling I have to bow to necessity in the way I did when I was on salary.

Darby: It's the Neptune in Virgo connection that's speaking there, but we'll talk about that in a moment. What about **Jupiter in Virgo**?

Audience: It's in detriment. That must say that Jupiter struggles here even more than it would in Capricorn, which surprises me.

Darby: It may not be a question of more or less. It may be something more delicate than that. Remember the interesting thing about mutable signs – Mercury rules two of them and Jupiter rules two of them, and they are thought to be awkward in each other's territory. Mercury in Pisces or Sagittarius can become overwhelmed by the profusion of data being carried on currents of water or fire. Jupiter in Virgo can behave like a newly hired foreign correspondent when the most trivial piece of information comes through the door. Jupiter in Virgo sees the world in every grain of sand, which is gift and grace, but oh, there are so many grains of sand that it is hard to coordinate them into a workable system. So it is a very restless Jupiter.

As Mercury rules Virgo, you must always look to its position to see what kind of library or market place is being raided for information about the meaning of life. Look at its position to see what sort of information is being gathered, and where. I have a client with Jupiter in Virgo in the 5th. He has a delicate but wonderful relationship with his daughter, whom he works to keep safe with every waking breath. He has Mercury in Cancer in the 3rd. You can imagine how long it took him to find the best, the safest car for her. He could not consider her going away to university until he realised her relationship with her mother was harming her, and then he sent her away.

I have another client with Jupiter in Virgo in the 12th and Mercury conjunct Venus in Ares in the 7th. He spent years and thousands of dollars on psychotherapy for his wife so that his life could be more peaceful. In the end she left him, and he is presently struggling with his business partner, who is now the reason he searches for peace alone in the mountains. The times when Jupiter in Virgo is enjoying itself truly are the times in which it is cultivating its field and improving its world, however small or large that world may be. Some do this to great effect. Both Paracelsus and Samuel Hahnemann had Jupiter in Virgo. Both plumbed the depths of nature in search of healing substances. Both came up with rituals associated with healing that are still practised today.

Audience: I have **Saturn in Virgo**, and I can't find any peace unless I actually work for it. I meditate twice a day, and when I don't, I really get edgy and critical and scratchy in my mind and my body.

Darby: Saturn in Virgo demands that one be discriminating about one's discrimination. Perhaps the periods of meditation allow you to sift out the things that you should be critical of from the things that are a waste of time and energy. Saturn here demands a balance in discrimination. One works to improve one's mental and physical faculties so that what you produce is useful to yourself and to others. It demands the development of concentration and attention to detail – but you have to learn what details are important to whatever it is you are trying to produce. One is critical of authority, and that begins in childhood. Children with Saturn in Virgo are attuned to the places in the father's makeup where he is not "sensible" in his discriminative faculties. They are very sensitive to his criticism, and develop a keen critical eye in defence, which they fall back on when threatened. They develop a fine discrimination in one field or another, and for the rest must pay attention that their critical judgements don't isolate them too much from the fertile chaos of emotional life. Saturn in Virgo can easily get into "knowing better", and the Mercury position will tell you how and where they most naturally express that.

Outer planets in Virgo

When I think of **Chiron in Virgo**, I think of the British Rail announcement: "Mind the gap!" I mentioned it when we were speaking about Chiron in Taurus, but I think it is even more appropriate with Chiron in Virgo. Mind the gap between mind and body, between efficiency in one area and coordination of the whole. With Chiron in Virgo, there is a gap between the body-self and the intellect-self, and perhaps between the idea of service and the actual service. The information which comes through the body does not connect directly with the information that comes through the mind, according to the house Chiron is inhabiting. One has to make a leap. Courage is required. Brave deeds are needed to overcome feelings of helplessness in whatever area its house position indicates. You have to build a bridge between your mind and body, and that usually means developing a ritual so that your mind and body can work together. But the rituals break down and you have to make new ones. It never stops, but then, that is the nature of Chiron. Healing is an ongoing process here, not an event.

Audience: I have Chiron in Pisces opposite Uranus and Pluto in Virgo. I recognise what you are saying about boundaries.

Darby: Ah, yes, the Uranus-Pluto in Virgo generation. So many of you have Chiron opposite the conjunction, and all those born between mid-1964 and mid-1965 have Saturn conjunct Chiron, too.

Let me say something about **Uranus in Virgo** first. Earlier, I mentioned that Uranus in earth has a special instinct for magic, if other things so incline in the chart. And remember, magic is that which works according to laws we have not uncovered. If Uranus in Virgo is significant in a chart, then this person will have an instinct for arriving at rituals that take things apart and break things up, rituals that relate to nature in an almost experimental way. Einstein had it in the 3rd house, Picasso in the 2nd. Doesn't *that* make sense? – I mean because of what Picasso did with traditional shape and form. Of course, Uranus can always be a somewhat silent note in a chart. You belong to the group that is experimenting in a particular way, but you may not experiment notably yourself. However, you are experimenting with nature somehow, even if it is in tiny corners. It's part of who you are, as a tribe, and everyone takes part in one or another way.

Pluto in Virgo has a deeper task. In your lifetime, you will be deeply effected by the changes in your physical environment – workplace, food sources, genetic engineering of plants and people. Some of you will see these issues as improvements, others as the destruction of nature. These issues will push your collective buttons, according to Pluto's position. And you have to respond, as you are part of the unearthing of information which is transforming our relation to the earth, one way or another.

Now, for those of you who have **Uranus and Pluto in Virgo**, the work, health, and nature transformations are more intense. If the conjunction is significantly placed in your chart, you are part of the front line – you are actively experimenting with notions and rituals which offer improvements and promises to fix things.

Whether you do or not is another thing. With experimentation, we can never know until we see the results. With Chiron opposing the conjunction from Pisces, there is a struggle between the sense of being nothing and having something *important* to do. I am moving fast here, trying to say a lot in a few sentences. I hope you will use these sketchy notions as ground for experimenting with your own elaborations. When Saturn is conjunct Chiron in Pisces and they are both opposite the Uranus-Pluto conjunction, then, one way or another, it is a big issue. Authority figures, and your need to find a place of authority in yourself, are the work. Otherwise, you cannot help but feel victimised by others who are manipulating or destroying the environment, the workplace, the community. But because this is the most mutable of signs, you have to let the authority rise and fall. You cannot hold onto it. You cannot demand that another be authoritative in all things; you cannot ask yourself to carry authority consistently. Robert, you once said the most interesting thing about this configuration. Do you remember? I was starting to get clients from this age group and I had no idea how it felt to have this aspect, so I phoned you for a clue to begin with.

Robert: Yes, I said it felt like you wanted to be part of the revolution – wherever you saw it – but you were afraid to stick your head above the parapet for fear of getting shot down before you had done anything useful. And when you did speak out, or step out and take risks, you never felt as if it was useful at all. You couldn't *feel* the positive feedback, if there was any. You had to dig deeper into anything you could imagine for the confidence to face the challenge.

Darby: Thanks, Robert. You have to go beyond your own conditioning, and search for solutions outside the normal range. A cultural transition is happening here, and you navigate between two worlds, having to bring about change without the normal ego satisfaction or recognition. But that does not make it less effective, and your place of reward is secret, hidden from view, spiritual, poetic.

Neptune in Virgo characterises a generation which has experienced chaos in all sorts of subtle ways, and dreams of a life of cultivation and order. They are collectively disturbed by excess, and long for lives which run smoothly and simply. As the Neptune in Sagittarius group dreams of adventure, this group dreams of smaller, more discrete pleasures. It depends on how strong this Neptune is in the chart, of course, but in general, they ask for less than the generation which came before them – Neptune in Leo – and the one which comes after – Neptune in Libra. When I was speaking about Mars in Virgo just now, one of you mentioned Mars conjunct Neptune in Virgo. A friend once told me that he feels ill when he is not working, and I started asking all my clients about this. Not everyone felt like him, but all said they needed to be busy to be healthy. The general feeling was that doing something useful kept anxiety at bay. Virgo is an awkward place for Neptune. The longing for a life where one is given time to cultivate one's talents and serve that which their Mercury calls them to, is an undercurrent that runs through the areas of life which are touched by this placement.

Ndlaleni, the *sangoma* I mentioned earlier, had Neptune in Virgo conjuncting her Moon and opposing her Mercury in Pisces. This showed her to be very sensitive to others, and she was fortunate to be called to the art of healing others through magical and material means. Even she was ill quite often, but she had the rituals and routines to deal with her sensitive body-psyche. Of course, I have known very tough people from this generation, too. But all have some particular sensitivity of mind and body that requires them to pay attention to their physical responses in some way. Sometimes it is disguised as oversensitivity to smells or sounds or particular foods or drinks. Whatever it is, it keeps them working towards making their daily environment better. A

kind of nagging guilt or distress of some kind keeps them working for simplicity and the cultivation of wholesome habits. And
they are given the gift of "seeing the world in a grain of sand /
Heaven in a wild flower" in sudden moments of grace.

Planets in the 6th house

When I think about the 6th house, I usually think of Charlie
Chaplin. He had Sun in Aries in the 6th. The Sun's ruler, Mars,
was conjunct Venus in Taurus in the 7th, trine to Jupiter in the 2nd
in Capricorn. I think of the way he developed his "Little Tramp"
character, and the constant work he did to perfect his charac-
terisation. What impeccable co-ordination between mind and
body went into that little person! Over the years I have known
many people with **Sun in the 6th**, and they all work very hard to
get it right, whatever *it* is. Periodically they go through patches
of resentment, as their work is never appreciated as fully as they
would wish. The Sun here shines on the work, and few people
can see how much effort goes into it. Yet that does not stop them
in their quest for perfection. There is always ritual attached to
their work – they seem to have to do the same things over and
over, and attend each detail so the whole will serve its purpose.

Planets in the 6th are landed in a field, and that field must
be cultivated. Nothing must be wasted. Waste is a most annoying distraction which worries those who have planets here. What
do you do with that which is left over, once a creative process is
complete? Planets in the 6th are called to clear up, to deal with
that which is left over. With planets in the 6th, you cannot ignore
your body. It will voice any disturbances in your mind. Satisfaction must be in the work itself. Planets here experiment constantly with method.

Audience: I always thought that planets in the 6th drove people
to neatness, to being tidy. That is certainly not true of my chil-

dren, who all have planets in the 6th. I do, too, and I am a nurse, and I'm not very tidy either.

Darby: I used to think planets in the 6th would tend to order, too. I have a friend who has Saturn there, and he is orderly – in patches, anyway. Unless other things really contradict, it seems to bring great focus to particular areas, but it does not incline to see the whole pattern. And so whatever is being attended now is the whole world. The rest is the chaos out of which this-in-front-of-me is the particular.

Audience: I'm a Virgo Sun in the 8th with Capricorn rising. I have been successful in business for a long time, but I have been trying to transform myself into a writer for several years now. I have **Saturn in the 6th** house in Gemini, square Neptune conjunct Mercury in the 9th. If I don't write every day, I start getting ill. But I travel a lot, and that throws my rhythm out. It takes days for me to get back into it when I return from a trip. It is a constant source of distress to me. When I am writing, I am completely satisfied, and when I am not, I feel hopeless. My success in business counts for nothing compared to this.

Darby: The fact that you also have Capricorn rising strengthens this pattern. I know you started writing late, and there is that Capricorn rising struggle to achieve self-respect from one's work. I do think you will get there in the end. We have spoken about this many times, haven't we? I have learned a lot from you as we have explored it. Mercury-Neptune has to pull you out to strange exotic places, and Saturn then drags you back to "the work" as conceived by your personality. Everything with Saturn takes longer than we would wish. Squares don't stop one achieving. They demand that you include more experience than you thought necessary. Neptune washes away the rituals and habits that Saturn builds, and so you have to build them again. And

Saturn in the 6th will demand constant attention to the work, but Neptune won't allow it. Yet the pattern is there and you have to keep working with it as it is. Your writing gets more subtle, more magical as you progress.

Audience: I have **Moon in the 6th** in Taurus, and it is as if the tide washes in. I clear up my desk and kitchen and attic, and for a short time I feel at peace. Then the tide washes out, and I notice that everything is in chaos again. I can only keep order for short periods of time.

Darby: In the 6th house we are brought to cultivation. Our natures, according to the planets involved, are cultivated, and we develop the power to cultivate something. Cultivation has to do with getting to know the field that you are given and then working with it so that it will produce that which is needed. You have to serve the field, and then it will serve you and produce something worthwhile. So if you look at the 6th house as the field you were given to cultivate, and the planets as the method that is natural to you, then you have some sort of handle on it.

Audience: It has to do with health, too.

Darby: Yes. If the 2nd house is the value you put on your body and the gifts that are natural to it, then the 6th is the way you cultivate those gifts. It tells you the sort of mental and physical routines and rituals that go along with cultivating the gifts of your own nature. Perhaps we could say that your health or lack of it is the weather of this particular land. Some countries have cold and rainy weather most of the time, and others are bathed in sunlight. The 2nd house will tell you about your body as your land, and the 6th will say how you cope with its weather patterns. Do you remember Proust's chart, from the Water seminar?[12] He had Virgo on the 6th house cusp, and Mercury between Jupiter and the Sun in Cancer in the 4th. His delicacy as a child got him powerful attention from both his parents. As an adult, it gave him opportunity to stay at home and write his extraordinary work. He had Mars in Libra in the 6th and Venus, ruler of Libra, in the 5th. His health demanded constant attention and he turned it into an art form in more ways than one. **Mars in the 6th** thrives on hard work. His art thrived on his illness.

I think the 6th is a very complex and subtle house, and it requires a lot of attention to get anywhere near its workings. Thomas Merton wrote *Seven Story Mountain* and became famous overnight, though he was a monk in a silent order of contemplation. He was all fire and air and a bit of transpersonal water. He had several planets in the 6th. Most of the others were in the 5th and 11th. He had Virgo rising and Mercury conjunct Jupiter in the 6th, plus Chiron in Pisces. His health was a major problem in the monastery, but he used it, and the sometimes almost unbearable discipline and rituals of his order, to develop patience and humility. And he kept his sense of humour. If you have planets in the 6th house, that's very important, because they will demand much of you. Often it will seem as though you are getting no reward. The 6th house is where our reward is simply the work. But once a year the harvest comes, and then there is a feast. When the season comes round and you are in harvesting time, it is your planets in the 6th that describe your capacity for joyous engagement in life. The whole cycle of work seems worth it. But then you are brought back to the field, because work is an ongoing process. Here you are best served by developing rituals which foster patience in the process.

---

12   Marcel Proust, 10 July 1871, 11.30 pm LMT, Paris. See *Water and Fire*, Darby Costello, Raven Dreams Press, 2018.

Traditionally, the 6th house says something important about your servants. In South Africa I spent more time looking at the 6th house than I do here. Health issues are not my speciality. Personal relations are, however, and so I was always checking on my clients' relationship to their servants. Personal planet in the 6th describe what sort of servants you attract and how you experience them, sometimes in great detail. The sign on the cusp points you to the planet that gives your general attitude to servants and where they most effect your life. But you are your own servant, too, and the 6th house tells you how and where you serve the whole of your life best. The cusp ruler points to the area of life which galvanises you to develop rituals which will serve your development and maintain and improve your life. Planets in the 6th describe who is running the show from behind the scenes. The 6th house is your workshop, your kitchen, your hearth. It's worth getting to know its nature well. It is where, through repetition and experimentation, your nature produces all the fruits of the talents embedded in your nature. It is a house of work, but magic also comes out of the work you do here.

Virgo rising

Virgo rising is generally said to have a self-contained and diffident air, though this is not always the case. One must look to Mercury to see who is ruling this generally hard-working person. No matter what else is going on in the chart, the development of this personality has to do with self-cultivation. The question for Virgo rising is always: What am I serving? Virgo rising is usually somewhat self-contained and works on its personality development all the time. It is never quite sure of itself, and is very aware of what it must improve in itself. Mercury, by position and aspect, will tell you where and how the improvements are carried out.

The oddest example of Virgo rising I can think of is Henry VIII. We have to assume that his time is correct, as it was recorded by people who took his birth seriously. If it was closer to the Leo cusp, we might think it was a sloppy time-keeper, but there it is in the middle of Virgo. He was a most extraordinary and unusual man, and what we all know about him is that he had eight wives, a huge appetite, and gout in his late years. He may also have been syphilitic. We do not think of him in terms of the service he rendered his people. He was not shy, modest, and dedicated to self-improvement. His Mercury was in Leo in the 11th house, on the cusp of the 12th, and it was opposite Saturn in the 5th, on the cusp of the 6th – very complicated.

Henry was king at a time when the notion of the king as servant of God for the people and servant of the people for God was still alive in the collective mind. All the trouble with his wives stemmed from the fact that none of them could give him male heirs, although, with his Moon in Aries in the 8th house, his demanding sexual nature might have had a say in his decisions too. However, we do know that he really believed that unless he had a son who could follow him, all the prosperity of England, built up by his father and him, would be destroyed in a generation. With Saturn in Aquarius in the 5th, he had the fixed idea that his lack of a male heir would take away prosperity and freedom from his people – Mercury in Leo in the 11th. So he sought to improve his position and serve his people by cutting off the heads of two wives and divorcing two.

Audience: A natural choice, I suppose – very practical at the time, with Virgo rising and that 8th house Moon.

Darby: Yes – but not your average Virgo rising profile, however. It is a very surprising Ascendant. Occasionally you meet the meek, neat little Virgo rising person, dedicated to serving others. But that is because there is a neat and quiet Mercury expression there in the background. Mercury defines the field where Virgo serves, and Mercury's sign defines the style.

CAPRICORN

Capricorn is about the development of order out of chaos into organised systems. It is about the natural hierarchy and order of nature, and how each animal and plant has its place and its function in any well-established environment. It is about the natural hierarchy and order of nature in human communities, too, and how each person and animal has its place and function. Every community, whether it be fish or birds or microbes or people or elephants or forests or fields or lakes or oceans or planets, has a natural order to which it tends. And each community includes members of other communities, so there are overlapping systems everywhere. But here we get into Aquarius.

Once something has become a recognised system, it achieves some sort of stability. When this happens, it can go on for a period of time according to the laws of its being. The laws of its being arise in the formation of its structure; in some way they define its nature. The laws of its being are its structure, whether we are talking about a bird, a land or sea species, a human being, a tribe of people, a company, or an institution. Every separate thing has a beginning, a middle and an end – a life span. This may go on for a day, a week, a month, a year, a century, a millennium, or more. Systems can achieve relative stability for as long as they can "keep moving with the times", as they say.

Many species of birds and animals have learned to live in cities, as their natural habitats have been become overrun with people and their effects. Any system, be it human or animal or vegetable, will colonise as much territory as it can, in its urge to survive. The longer it survives, the more masterly it becomes.

And yet there seems built within every system the seeds of destruction. Mastery has its time. Every system will be overcome by something with a greater mastery. In the end, it is always Death who is the great master. And yet death is part of the system too, for in death the laws are broken apart, and new structures emerge which develop into new systems. Everything rises to its highest peak and then sinks back into the mud, so that new things can arise. And the whole mystery goes on and on.

Capricorn is about the establishment of the well-organised system, and in human terms, that means community. It recognises, at one level or another, the unrelenting drive of any system towards stability, and it finds a way into that system to a place where it can be useful. This ultimate earth sign has the other two earth signs implied within it. There is the slow unfolding of Taurus, and the culture and cultivation of Virgo. There is the recognition and appreciation of natural laws in Taurus, and the need to be harvesting the goods with Virgo. In Capricorn we learn the laws through experience and begin the work to harvest something useful. But here there is something more. Capricorn recognises systems. It does its work and notices the community in which it operates. It recognises that certain products are more highly valued than others. They appear to have greater value because they are considered more important to the survival and prosperity of a community.

This sign has a sense of the structure inherent in systems, and it works to find a place in the structure which will maximise its survival chances. In doing that, it works toward mastery. It finds a place where its talents and gifts can be made useful, even essential. It works for the community because the survival of the community maximises its own survival and the survival of its kin and kind. It needs recognition because those who are recognised as essentially useful have a greater chance of survival. This need for social recognition is a driving force for anyone with planets in Capricorn. It is a carrot dangled before the Capricorn's inner eye. It is survival-based, and that it why it is such a powerful drive. It comes from the earth nature. Planets in Capricorn are sensitive to the laws of nature in a particular way. They are servants of those laws, and once they discover the place where they can best serve the laws of nature, they do everything they can to fulfil their role as maintainers of the laws, for better or worse.

Audience: You are speaking as if Capricorn upholds the conventions in any situation. If that were so, then you would never find Capricorn astrologers or criminals or outlaws.

Darby: I like the groups you have put together there – astrologers and criminals and outlaws. But I see what you mean. If a person with strong Capricorn emphasis finds his or her place in the world of what we call "the establishment", they will uphold the conventions and appear ultimately conventional. In fact, they will aim for the place on the mountain where others look to measure their own standards. Whether they get there or not depends on other things. However, if the Capricorn person cannot find a place where they can feel useful and well connected within the establishment, they will search until they find a community where they can find a place within which they can work. So you have Capricorns with strong Aquarius or a strong Uranus, and they feel like outsiders to the community they grew up in. But then they come into contact with astrology at some point, and as this is a time in history when an astrological community is establishing itself, the Capricorn person is drawn to that community. And if they can find a place where they might grow themselves into usefulness, they will stay. If they have planets in Aquarius or Gemini, then chances are they will bridge communities – they will seek in some way to bring their new community to the "established" community.

Capricorn is about the power and grandeur of nature, too, and the terrible price we pay when we do not obey the laws of nature, whether we know them or not. It is about the way in which each tiniest microbe has its natural enemies and its natural food, and how, when the chain is broken anywhere, there is chaos and destruction for a time. Then order is restored and a new, "improved" chain is created. Capricorn contains the knowledge of the unrelenting growth of any species which has lost its natural enemies and which then destroys everything around. It is the awareness of the natural protection in the law of nature that keeps each species of plant and animal in its place, for the good of the whole. And so, if it falls prey to its own dark side by denying or ignoring its presence, it pays a heavy price.

Capricorn, above all signs, is the sign of the Magus, the Initiate. It contains the *possibility* of the deepest self-discipline and patience, in service to the highest laws. And, of course, it contains its opposite. But Capricorns know the price of things, and so most of them keep to the level they can handle, even though that means frustration. One who didn't was Mercury conjunct Jupiter in Capricorn and Capricorn Sun – Richard Nixon. He made his way very slowly, but then a "stroke of luck" threw him up the mountain, and there he held on while losing his way. He forgot or denied the laws of nature, his own Capricorn nature, and he fell from the mountain in disgrace. He lost the notion of service in perfect obedience to the law – I mean the law according to his Saturn. He had Saturn in Taurus in the 9th and Venus in Pisces in the 6th. What a huge temptation he must have had to turn from simplicity and service. Perhaps his Mercury-Jupiter conjunction told him he was invulnerable.

Audience: And then there is Stalin.

Darby: Yes, there is Stalin, with his six planets in earth, Sun in Capricorn trine a Neptune-Mars conjunction in Taurus trine Moon-Uranus in Virgo, and Jupiter in Pisces. His Saturn was in Aries, squaring his Sun, and Scorpio was rising. I wish we had time to look at his chart, but I have brought someone else whom I am more interested in, so I would ask you to look at Stalin's chart on your own, considering the things we have been saying today. His chart is much less surprising than Hitler's. You look at Stalin's chart and you are not shocked that he became who he did. But there are a few surprises.[13]

Planets in Capricorn

Those with planets in Capricorn are driven to work for the establishment of well-running communities. Whatever the planet, it describes the urge to facilitate this drive. The urge can be misshapen, of course, and the need to create order can become tyrannous. The work of individuation, for Capricorn planets, has to do with recognising this passion for control and the way it can justify its actions in every situation.

People with planets in Capricorn are sensitive to the laws laid down by their fathers. They suffer from bad laws, laws that do not further the community. They hate themselves and others when they perceive lost opportunities, lack of discipline, ineffective or useless rules and laws. They are sensitive to any lack of responsibility in their own fathers, and struggle to take control if they sense that their fathers have abdicated responsibility in any way. They fight any authority, either in themselves or in others, if they believe it is not working for the greater good. They sabotage themselves when they are not sure of their own motives. In those who are unconscious of their own processes, this comes out as blame. Those with Capricorn planets who can take responsibility for their own failure and success at anything are as strong as mountains. The rest struggle with the world and remain victims.

---

13   Josef Stalin, 2 January 1880, 8.15 am, Gori, Tiflis, Soviet Union. Taeger places this data in Group 4, which means it is to be used with caution.

Audience: That's a very harsh judgement.

Darby: I know. Well, sacrificial victims have a role to play in all communities too! Of course, no one with anything in Capricorn would ever wish to be identified with the victim, but this is often the early history of those with strong Capricorn placements. Their road to mastery begins when they perceive their own weakness. At some point they begin to fight this sense of weakness – they are overcoming weakness because they must survive. Later, on their road to a place on the top of the mountain, their motives often change. Their drive to achievement is no longer about survival alone, but about survival and prosperity for their chosen community. Sometimes their "chosen community" is not the one closest to them – it may even be an abstract notion of community. When their community is not their local environment, there is often great loneliness. But the loneliness is second to their need to achieve something, and the work drives them on.

Mars is exalted in Capricorn, and we can see something of the sign's power in this placement. It develops its strength by pushing against the greatest obstacle it can overcome. It has an animal sensible intelligence, and it discovers very early when to fight and when to play dead. As it goes on, it chooses obstacles that are not completely beyond its strength, but ones that are almost just beyond. Venus in Capricorn develops its love nature through recognising quality and appreciating the best over the mediocre. Mercury in Capricorn takes in information in order to cultivate the gifts and talents of the Sun. The Moon in Capricorn finds order and rhythm in its daily life, through which it can nurture itself and others, and the Sun thrives in an atmosphere where there is something to achieve and something to gain by achieving it.

Audience: You can't stop there. You have to say more about each one.

Darby: Is this a have to, a want to, or a should?

Audience: It's a should, since I am a Capricorn and I know what should happen here.

Darby: How could I refuse such authority?

Capricorn Sun carries in its heart the image of a world in which it can find its place, its function, its use. Even a very young Capricorn Sun is uncomfortable in situations where it does not know its role. Capricorn Sun begins experiencing a sense of responsibility at a very young age. But it takes a long time to find the place where its seriousness and intent of purpose can express itself. This Sun usually has to go through a lot of living before it comes into its own power, before the cultivation of its talents can bear fruit that is recognised and respected. Obstacles are its master, repetition its path. No matter what else is happening in the chart of a Capricorn Sun, this slow development through trials and tribulations and obstacles is the only satisfying path. This is the way of the alchemical change that everyone with Capricorn planets seeks. It is never a smooth journey to the place on the mountain where mastery is the entrance fee, but when one arrives, the world is set in order.

In the northern hemisphere, where these symbols were forged, Capricorn is the Sun shining in deep winter. It is light pale and cool, and yet sometimes dazzling. This Sun is ruled by Saturn. How can this be? And yet we have the myth of the Golden Age and its association with Saturn – the just god and the good king, the time of prosperity. When any system is working well, the system prospers. The prosperity of a Capricorn Sun will depend on natal Saturn, which dictates the pace, the road, the laws that must be learned and practised if one is to achieve the aim of the Sun. If Saturn is in Leo, it is one's responsibility to one's creations, children, personality development that brings the sense of success or failure which deepens one's role in the community and earns one the respect, or lack of it, that reflects one's self-worth. A Capricorn with Saturn in Capricorn seeks mastery in whichever house Saturn resides. And mastery is connected with survival, and survival for Capricorn includes the community. So any Capricorn achievement must always be seen in how it effects the community with which it identifies.

Audience: What if a Capricorn has Saturn in Taurus conjunct Uranus, and both are square to Venus in Aquarius?

Darby: Ah, yes, we spoke of that earlier when we were talking about Taurus. Over the years I have known several Capricorns with that combination. I think of you as bridge people. Relationships challenge the development of your natural gifts. They seem to throw you off course. They open up new worlds, and offer you the opportunity to bring a sense of order to chaotic people and disrupt the conventional. You need respect from people, and yet you need people who are not "respectable". You have an odd juxtaposition of gifts with Venus in Aquarius, and they don't easily bring you the recognition you need as a Capricorn. The people you like, the things you love doing, are not usually recognised as "important" by whichever established community stands as the obstacle and the lure of your desire for respect and recognition. And how do you connect the things and people you value in a "proper" work? All that Uranian energy in deep earth Taurus! So there is the "freedom versus commitment" problem, and there is the "Once I get too familiar, I get restless and bored" problem, and the "Now I can do it pretty well, and so?" problem. There are long periods of stability in relationships, and then volcanic activity which changes everything.

Capricorn Sun cannot achieve the mastery it seeks except by doing the same thing for years, constantly improving through repetition and attention. Uranus disrupts that. There's the bridge. They bring "far out" gifts into communities where such gifts would never arrive. I am thinking of two Capricorns with this configuration. The first is a very good astrologer who has never built up her clientele enough to give up her office work. She says relationships have always distracted her. Yet she brings her astrology into everything she does, and so a whole world of people have become comfortable and familiar with it. The other one I am thinking of has strange and wonderful healing gifts. She chooses to live in a small village where people are traditionally conventional. They accept her because she makes wonderful jams for the church raffle, and her garden and cats are so well kept that her exotic healing gifts are less threatening than they would be in someone less conventional. They are even used by many people in the community.

Audience: My mother has Sun and Venus in Capricorn, and she cannot stop telling me how to dress and how to wear my hair and what to say and not say when I am with her friends.

Darby: Where is her Saturn?

Audience: In Libra, in the 11th, and her Moon is in Libra in the 12th.

Darby: Well, there it is. Saturn in Libra is the place where her "orders" are coming from. Everything must be beautifully proportioned, tasteful, socially acceptable. If she can be that – and you are part of her when you are in her social world – then she will have the respect and recognition she needs and, more fundamentally, she will be doing her work, "setting the standard". She has been working at that all her life, and any improvement she can make in you or her home or her mind, she will.

Audience: She certainly will! I have a Capricorn Moon, so I am particularly sensitive to her criticism.

Darby: With Capricorn Moon, you judge her, too, I imagine.

Audience: Well, only in defence.

Darby: Hm, and you don't judge other people?

Audience: Only when they do things badly that could easily be done well.

Darby: And thus is it demonstrated. **Moon in Capricorn** does grow up aware of the rules of the household, and especially those made by its mother. It is sensitive to her need for respect, and it will respect her for her efforts and for any hardship she endures when the Capricorn Moon child is young. This Moon gains control of its emotions young. It cannot bear others having power over its feelings, and it is generally uncomfortable when around those who cannot control their own feelings, either.

Audience: Do you look to Saturn here, too, to find how it reads the laws?

Darby: Nice way of putting it. Yes – you block off certain emotional channels according to where you experience a sense of privation or fear or isolation. Saturn is always where you turn your discomfort and lack of equilibrium into something workable. You make up rules here, and then have to obey them or suffer. Now, when the Moon is in Capricorn, there is always a feeling of isolation somewhere in there, because you are controlling what emotions come in and go out. So you look to Saturn to see where the control is coming from. With Saturn in water and Capricorn Moon, the restriction on one's emotional expression as a child directs the emotional energy into concrete activity which controls, shapes, and establishes something in their personal environment. Their fear of loss of emotional control is a gift – much can be accomplished – and a burden – it is scary to feel outside the proscribed limits of what are "safe" emotions. Do you see how I am working here?

Saturn in air will describe mental or communication restrictions in early years, which form the Capricorn Moon child into an adult whose skills are used to shape their personal environment so that they control the communication and flow of information that comes in. Their fear of being overwhelmed by information or judgements can make them instinctively control other's communication. They will only allow certain information to get through. The rest is emotionally dangerous, or is felt to be that way. Moon in Capricorn will control its emotional environment in one way or another, and Saturn will tell you how and why.

Audience: I am a Gemini with Moon in Capricorn and Saturn in Taurus. From what you are saying, I can look at my childhood's material poverty as a motivation for the way I control my environment. I think that's true. I live alone, although I am in a long-term relationship, and I know it is because I fear being tied up with someone too tightly, both financially and sexually.

Darby: Yes, and if you look again, you can see another layer. The material poverty of your childhood, and the fear it engendered, gave you the motivation to improve your home situation as you grew older, so you now live in that very lovely house on the river.

Audience: And I make mistakes along the way. But that is Saturn and its work, of course. I am aware that the thing I need to watch out for now is that I don't settle so deeply into my controlling nature that I isolate myself. I *am* better than other people at organising people and things. Others agree, but I am beginning to see that is not the point. I feel in danger of closing myself off from life, and I'm trying to see what I can do about it.

Darby: But you are still wanting to control the process of letting go of some of the control. Think of Jung's "earth altar", perhaps, and use the image to "offer sacrifice" to that inner deity of your own land. Because of the urge to control, to colonise, you who have Capricorn planets must understand the role of sacrifice in any developmental process.

Audience: My girlfriend says that, if I met God, I would probably sit there figuring out how I could help improve creation. I can always see how people could improve their lives. I was reminded of this when you were talking about earth and the tendency to improve whatever is there. I haven't thought much about sacrifice.

Darby: Moon in Capricorn can be so organising that it is hard to see what is being sacrificed along the way. It's best when it has a legitimate channel. Otherwise it gets caught in bringing improvement into every aspect of its day and everyone it encounters. Remember the survival drive within Capricorn – the drive to improve things is interwoven with the need to control the environment. You can see how strong this is with the Moon, which is also about survival within its environment.

Now let's look at **Mercury in Capricorn**. This careful and serious councillor will only serve Sagittarius, Capricorn or Aquarius Suns. Its wry, dry humour perhaps masks the seriousness with which it approaches its sources of information. When Aquarius is the Sun, then Mercury seems to screen information in terms of what will support their ideals and ideas, and then it simply ignores the rest. Very clear, very simple. Very little waste. When the Sun and Mercury are in Capricorn there is also very little waste, but there is perhaps more frustration. That may be because the Capricorn Sun takes time to come into its own, and so Mercury gathers all kinds of information that will be useful once the direction is clear. Of course, Saturn dictates what the information will be ultimately used for. A Capricorn Sun and Mercury with

Saturn in Sagittarius might order its information-gathering faculty towards education and the development of earth wisdom. One with Saturn in Leo might take in that which will most surely establish security for their children. A Capricorn with Saturn in Capricorn will also be counselled by their Mercury in Capricorn, which will pick up information that shows them the ways of mastering the world. They need to become useful and respected for their own personal achievements. Other things will tell you what sort of achievements they are drawn to. If any Capricorn finds himself or herself respected and admired only by people they don't respect and admire, they are in big trouble with themselves.

Darby: I am a Sagittarius with **Venus in Capricorn**, and for me love and respect go hand in hand, as you would expect. I notice that I really expect people I love to go on improving themselves endlessly. It seems to me that when you stop improving yourself, you stop living. It is such a waste. My partner is a cook, and he is constantly improving his recipes, so I imagine that I will go on loving him.

Darby: I hope so. Venus in Capricorn is in love with the lines of order in nature, and therefore, when it falls in love, it is falling in love with the most highly developed part of another person, that which has been worked into something fruitful. It is drawn to that which has been carved into grace of form by the vicissitudes of life. It does not reject another person's failures, but it does reject lack of dignity in the face of failure. It loves watching things and people become more themselves, especially when that means they become established in their environment through talent worked into worth. Getting better at things turns them on.

Audience: And what if you won't "improve" according to that Venus' ideal?

Darby: It isn't an ideal. It is clear recognition of what is best developed in you. It isn't a sense of what you "might become". It isn't a potential. It is what is already there. Venus in Capricorn loves your mastery, and it will support your way to that mastery. Venus in Capricorn loves to gain control over chaotic environments, loves to pull the workable out from the unworkable, loves to bring order out of chaos, and, according to the house position and aspects, it will do this wherever it can.

Audience: I have a friend who has Venus in Capricorn in the 12th. He's an Aquarian. He never had any girlfriends until he met a woman who was a political activist. They had a sort of affair, and then she went to jail for six months, rather than betray her colleagues who had committed a "righteous crime". He became her lifeline – he was her constant support outside the wall, so to speak. They got married when she got out, and as far as I know, they still are. We watched him go from a rather solitary individual to a full-on lover.

Darby: Where is Saturn in his chart?

Audience: In Scorpio, in the 11th. Oh, I see, co-ruler and ruler of both Sun and Venus. It must have been her courage to accept isolation for social change. She was in solitary most of the time.

Darby: Very interesting. One more thing about this position: Venus in Capricorn is very pragmatic, and so, not prone to disillusionment. They love those they respect, and they respect those who are working to make themselves or their community a better place. They may discover, over time, that their beloved is not as capable as they would wish – for instance, if Venus is in awkward relationship to Neptune or Uranus. This is disappointing, but its desire is to endure. It indicates that one will work very hard to help loved ones foster and cultivate whatever natural gifts are there. Remember, Venus in earth loves to be used well, and it loves those who use themselves and life well. It is not idealistic. If you are liked by an earth Venus, you can be fairly sure they will see the best and the worst of you and carry on regardless. They may keep trying to improve you, if you aren't actually doing that for yourself, because they love the process of cultivation. You can also be sure that they have become attached to you because they see your ground is worth cultivating. Whether you want it cultivated or not is another thing. They are very aware of hierarchies, for better or worse.

We spoke about **Mars in Capricorn** when we were talking about Fire.[14] Here let me say something about its capacity to improve itself and its life. Whatever draws it into action becomes the focus of a concentration that is extraordinarily patient and careful. No amount of struggle will distract it, once this Mars has found its direction. This may or may not be considered "a good thing" by oneself or others, but it is its nature. Obstacles are like lovers, and the challenge of any obstacle becomes a relationship. This Mars has heroism as its highest goal, and that means winning something that is cherished by the community. Anything less than pure courage is cowardice to this Mars. Whatever else is in the chart, Mars in Capricorn indicates some measure of mastery in one or another area of life. Once excellence is achieved and recognised, it is the nature of this Mars to look for a challenge somewhere else. One of the *sangomas* I knew in South Africa with this Mars had walked more miles, swum more rivers, climbed more mountains in his search for mastery than any of the others. The magic he channeled though their bodies was extraordinary, and the price he paid for it was very high. He once told me that the more powerful the gift, the higher the price, and you must be consciously willing to pay that price because it was

---

14   *Op. cit.,* Note 10.

the shadow of the gift, and the gift was always meant for the use of the tribe.

Audience: And when Mars in Capricorn is square Neptune in Libra?

Audience: Or conjunct Neptune in Capricorn?

Darby: There will be a conflict of interests, or, more accurately, a conflict of dimensions. It is difficult to have Neptune mixed up with Capricorn planets, isn't it? Mars in Capricorn drives directly to where it can develop mastery and, like it or not, it will recognise greater mastery when it sees it. With Neptune's remote and subtle call interfering with the drive towards excellence and recognition, it may slip and slide along the way, losing focus at times, feeling undermined, interpreting the actions of others in a way that undermines their own drive. It usually occurs in the charts of people whose fathers were brilliant at something, but the rewards for it were somewhat dubious. There is consequently a pain associated with excellence, one's own or others'. With Neptune interfering with this Mars' clarity of aim, one might seek escape in all sorts of undermining ways. Or one might become a passionate warrior for something that others can barely see. There is a Holy Grail in the lives of those with Mars in Capricorn when it is connected with Neptune.

Now, there is something paradoxical about **Jupiter in Capricorn** – it seems a conflict of interests. The wide, imaginative world of Jupiter is somewhat constrained in Capricorn. Those with this placement take their social position for granted, but life's adventure shows them it is not enough. They will have to win respect through time and work. And they will have to do it through the dictates of their Saturn position. Wherever there is Capricorn, there is work, and the work here is win some sort of freedom and respect through facing Saturn's wall.

Audience: Have you got an example?

Darby: I am thinking of someone with Sun in Cancer on the Ascendant opposite Jupiter in Capricorn in the 7th house, on the cusp of the 8th. When he was in his early twenties, he got into local politics, and ran for some sort of public office. He was very well connected, through his father, and he was sure he would win. He has Sagittarius Moon in the 6th, and it is square Saturn in Virgo in the 3rd. He didn't think the women in his constituency had much power, and he ignored their issues. I think he even said something about them "staying where they belonged, in the home". This was in the 1970's.

Audience: Big mistake.

Darby: Very big mistake. His opponent won with a huge majority. A few years later, he was invited into a fortuitous business partnership which gave him a good position in his community, and with the promise of increasing his security over the years. This time he paid attention, and when he found himself critical of his partner and especially of his partner's wife, he held his tongue. "I bit my tongue," was how he put it. (And he really had to, because he has Mercury conjunct Uranus in Gemini.) Now, fifteen years later, he owns the business, has earned the social standing he assumed was his by right in the beginning, and shares mutual affection and respect with both his retired ex-partner and his wife. He worked to reign in his critical tongue, and he learned every detail of the business, taking nothing for granted. He also learned to apologise when his tongue got out of control. He won his position. He has become someone whom others admire, although he still overestimates his capabilities and doesn't always judge the reactions of others accurately. But he never stops working at it. Jupiter in Capricorn has to work to win good fortune – it has this contradictory quality. And it has a tendency to colonise, to expand its territory and widen its range of influence wherever it can.

And now we come to **Saturn in Capricorn**...

Audience: ...Where luck plays no part in getting to the goal!

Darby: Precisely. When Saturn is in Capricorn, you must look to the house and aspects to see what it is about, more than with any other placement of Saturn. Saturn in Capricorn simply says that this person is born in a time when the rules and laws that govern things are accessible. The bones are showing. People with this position have to learn the rules of any situation, or they will pay. They can break the rules, they can ignore them, and at some point they may find ways to change them. But they mustn't go unconscious and say, "I didn't know the rules here." Ignorance is not an excuse here. It isn't with any Saturn position, but with Saturn in Capricorn, ignorance reaps a whole lot of trouble. They cannot afford to ignore the laws in any system they inhabit for any length of time. Do you see why the house is so important?

I have a friend who was running guns in Africa in the 1970's. He has Saturn in Capricorn in the 7th square Uranus in Aries in the 9th, and opposing Pluto in Cancer in the 3rd. He went to America to do some huge money deal, and got thrown into a maximum security prison in Chicago. Quite an adventure. His Uranus is conjunct both Sun and Moon in Aries. He got out by some wild stroke of luck and decided his life of crime wasn't a good idea. He'd been married four times. In prison he got religious, came out, married his fifth wife, and went off into the bush, where he built up a new life. Every once in a while we speak on the phone, and I ask him what's happening. "Still legit," he says. The Uranus-Pluto square still goes off periodically – he lives in a very volatile part of Africa now – but he stays "legit" now, with his Saturn in the 7th. It took him sixty years to decide to play strictly by the rules.

Audience: I have Saturn in Capricorn in the 6th, and I have ignored my health all my life. I've never had much energy – it squares my Moon in Libra in the 3rd. Now I'm in my sixties, and I can see trouble starting. I am *so* lazy. But I've taken up yoga, just to get some discipline going. It's very hard starting so late, but I hope it's better late than never.

Audience: I have Saturn in Capricorn in the 3rd, and I get into all sorts of trouble with local authority. My father was a tyrant in our neighbourhood. He thought everybody was beneath us, and we paid for that by being shunned. I have very good relationships with my neighbours – I work at it – but I still get the 3rd house hassle by having to constantly deal with local zoning laws and such. It's such a bore. But better than neighbours who hate you because your father hates them.

Darby: Saturn in Capricorn can transform its life inch by inch. At its deepest, it is seeking mastery of time and space – but it can look like it is simply trying to get some time and space! When someone with this Saturn has a focus in their life, then they accomplish great things. Without a central focus, it can seem like living with a heavy-handed old tyrant. Unrelenting effort produces something that looks like magic, but the magic arises out of the strength of the container that has been built through time. Saturn in Capricorn is a walled garden in which strange and wondrous things may grow. But it has to be built, stone by stone, in all kinds of weather.

Outer planets in Capricorn

We are living in a time during which many of us will experience all three outer planets in Capricorn. We have recently participated in the Uranus-Neptune conjunction in Capricorn, and they were particularly "interesting times" as Saturn joined it for some of the time, as it does every 684 years. I have heard talks, and have given them myself, on the profound cultural and spiritual revolutions that took place around 1307 CE, when the conjunction was in Scorpio; 622 CE when it was in Virgo; and 60 BCE when it was in Cancer. The Cancerian conjunction is associated with the birth of the Greco-Roman empire; the Virgo conjunction with the spread of Islamic culture; and the conjunction in Scorpio with the birth of what Jim Lewis once called the Northern European individualised ego. I wonder what astrologers in 684 years will call this one?

We have all watched this transit through Capricorn, and we have seen so many of the world's established and taken-for-granted structures melt and shape-shift. We were constantly surprised at what was melting down and what was holding together. For those of us who were viewing from the balcony, with our modern astrolabes charting the changes, it was fascinating, even though a good proportion of us were personally experiencing disruptions in our own world-views and our own structures. Whenever we found ourselves in the middle of it, our sense of order and safety in tradition collapsed and fell apart. We disrupted others and were disrupted ourselves, and no one will ever see the world in the same way again. I am sure we still take many things for granted, but Saturn went through Capricorn, Aquarius, and Pisces during the Uranus-Neptune conjunction and we no longer take for granted the earth, air, or water of our planet. We have become collectively aware that the boundaries between safe and unsafe are no longer clear, as they might have seemed to be for some time.

In 1989, Saturn was in Capricorn along with Uranus and Neptune, and I remember noticing that the year began with an outbreak, in the UK, of salmonella poisoning from eggs. It ended with the breaking down of the Berlin Wall. Uranus and Neptune in Capricorn have shaken us out of our collective security. Neither food nor governments are safe. They probably never were for any length of time, but we have become collectively aware of this again. As the old sense of order has broken down all over the world, we stand on the brink of a new world, whether we like it or not.

Now, what about all those Capricorn children born during the conjunction? One day we will be doing charts for those people. They will be informed collectively by the world into which they were born, and they will dream of a world which is safe and organised for the good of the communities they inhabit. They will disrupt any version of it that is not good enough. Depending on which Saturn group they were born into, they will struggle with physical, mental, or emotional discipline, with social structures, ideals, or personal longings. But they will all be part of the ongoing cultural, scientific, spiritual revolution which is touching every part of the planet. Won't it be interesting to do their charts? They will have lines of order and rhythm in them which seek cooperation between such seemingly irreconcilable systems and dimensions. They will, in one way or another, be part of establishing a new sense of order in so many different ways. I wonder what that order will look like to us? Many of us will be quite old then, and so, probably, it will look threatening.

Audience: They also have Pluto in Scorpio.

Audience: And they will begin to come into their power when Pluto is in Capricorn.

Darby: They will. What will they destroy to uncover the lines of a deeper order? We are watching ourselves evolve towards something totally new now. We can communicate instantly from any part of the earth to any other part of the earth. Those who have Saturn in Capricorn as well as the Sun and Mercury will need to feel they are contributing to something that affects the world at large.

Audience: That sounds terrifying.

Darby: Yes, it does, but so did Pluto in Scorpio, to many of us.

Audience: And it *was*, to some of us.

Darby: There *were* moments... Be that as it may, Pluto always pulls us deep into the territory of the sign it is transiting. Something about that sign is always being exposed in such a way that we mere humans find it hard to bear. The corruption that began to surface in Pluto's transit through Scorpio is becoming widely accepted knowledge. In Sagittarius we are being driven to understand and educate ourselves beyond the borders of our known territory, to shape the future by reorienting ourselves. When Pluto goes into Capricorn in 2009, whatever we have learned will start working its way right into the very structure of our societies. We will be taking things apart and putting them back together in a very pragmatic way. The information explosion we are experiencing now will be sifted and strained to see what can and can't be used.

Planets in the 10th house

Planets in the 10th house are aware of "the world" and their own position in it. It is associated with status and honours received through one's professional life. "Good" planets there signify honour, "bad" planets, disgrace – according to the old textbooks, anyway. There is no question that planets in the 10th house *do* drive the person towards the achievement of mastery in some field, even if, as Liz once said, the field is the kitchen sink and mastery is washing the dishes. Planets in the 10th house aim for recognition of what they have worked on. They give us information about how this person sees "the world" and what they will do to find a place in it. Planets here will give information about how you improve your position in your community.

Audience: Is it true about Mars in the 10th being associated with scandal, and Saturn in the 10th with downfall?

Darby: I think **Mars in the 10th** does have to pay attention to that possibility. You have to watch out for "naked ambition", so you have to watch your Mars there, and keep checking that it is connected to the notion of excellence rather than passion for recognition. It depends on the 10th house cusp as to how you "see the world", but Mars there will add a combative, competitive note to your approach to success. **Saturn in the 10th** can give a very secure reputation, but one can get into colonial expansion – the dangerous side of 10th house planets. Then one might "fall from a great height", as did Napoleon with his 10th house Saturn, and Hitler with his.

Mother Theresa has an Aries MC, with its ruler, Mars, in Virgo in the 2nd. She probably does see "the world" as a field which could do with some serious improvements, which she, with her six earth planets, has been willing to take on. In keeping with Mars' association with scandal and controversy, she has had a bit of flack about some of the money she has accepted for her missions. She also has Saturn in Taurus in the 10th, and it squares Venus on the Ascendant and trines her Sun in the 2nd in Virgo. Her order's rituals would demand that she examine her conscience and struggle with her pride as part of her daily life. Perhaps that has kept her from the "downfall" aspect of that position. Anyone with planets in the 10th could use that concept of "examination of conscience". It may not be very fashionable, but it could be the ritual, the rope that keeps you from falling. If you have planets in the 10th, then you will be used by your community in some way, and if you get sloppy, it gets recognised and talked about. Demanding house, great rewards.

I don't go along with the heavy judgements in the old texts, but I certainly find them useful clues. I use charts for navigation. I give navigational advice to my clients. If I see Mars in the 10th house, I hope to bring awareness of its dangers to my client. I don't know what is avoidable and what isn't, but I will assume my client has some power to move within their own fate, and we will work with that. Perhaps some sort of "scandal" is part of that person's fate. We will then work with the results of it and see where we can go from there.

Planets in the 10th house indicate that you have to keep your eye on your need for recognition. **Neptune in the 10th** does not mean that you don't have a need for recognition. It can mean you may deceive yourself about this need. Also, you have the need to stay invisible in the world while being recognised for your subtlety. It puts a strange mist over what you see as "the world". Pluto, Saturn, and Mars have to be watched. If you have any of those planets in the 10th, you can go very far in achieving respect for your position and doing useful work that gets recognised – *but* you must keep an eye, always, on that which grows in the dark.

Audience: So if you have Sun or Venus there, you are safe and can trust your ambitions?

Darby: Any planet in the 10th house will drive to the summit in one way or another. But the **Sun in the 10th** is less likely to fall into the darker shadow side, simply because it is used to being in the light and therefore generally pays attention to the moves it makes. **Venus in the 10th** is used to being liked and appreciated for its gifts by significant people through its life, so those with this placement are less driven to extreme measures, unless Venus is heavily aspected and extreme measures are part of her dance. **Mercury** is always a trickster, of course, and so, in the 10th, it is not completely reliable. By that I mean it throws you around the mountain a bit – and you might do or say things that are not strictly according to the rules. But this is Mercury, and one can get away with things, now and again. **Pluto in the 10th** indicates a compulsion to have the field to itself. Here we are with Nixon again, with his Pluto in 28º Gemini in the 10th opposing Mars and Mercury in the 4th at 0º Capricorn – a great but sobering example of being careful about what you think and say when you know you really want to keep your position and you feel threatened from below.

Audience: And the mother/father debate?

Darby: I simply don't know. If I ever have a clear opinion on that, I'll be sure to tell you.

Capricorn rising

In the mid 1970's, I was visiting London from South Africa and, to my great delight, I happened upon Watkins Bookshop. On one of the top shelves I found a book full of treasure. I cannot re-member which book it was, and have not come across it again. It was too big and probably too expensive for me at the time, so I stood reading it for about an hour. One of the things I read about was Capricorn rising. It said that those with Capricorn ris-ing are either fools or wise people. Their personalities are driven by their need for recognition and respect, and they either falsify themselves to appear wise or make their way slowly, mistake by mistake, until they achieve wisdom and therefore respect. I only knew one person with Capricorn rising at the time – Howard [Sa-sportas]. As I was visiting him, I asked him what he thought. He agreed, and said he hoped he was the latter. Since I had known him in his "foolish youth", we spoke about those early years, and he felt that any wisdom he had came out of those experiences of "excessive foolishness".

Since then, I have known several Capricorn rising people. When they are young, they can appear terribly frivolous. Later on, they can appear severely constrained – look at the Queen! Underneath the frivolous nature is a deeply serious approach to life. When they take on Saturn, they begin to get taken seriously, too. And that is important for them. When I say "take on Saturn", I mean that it shows the area of restriction or difficulty, the area of karmic reckoning, the place where you are most vulnerable to embarrassment and where your deepest work lies.

Audience: Where is the Queen's Saturn?

Darby: It's in Scorpio, in the 10th.

Audience: Ah.

Darby: Indeed. Capricorn rising can struggle between the fool and the wise person. Those who learn to use their foolishness as a path towards wisdom, and those who hide their wisdom under the guise of a fool, are remarkable indeed. They have the strength to work on their own personality expression, so that it conveys their spirit more efficiently and more clearly over the years. But they always have to watch a tendency to rigidity and exaggerated dignity. Saturn's placement and aspects show where rituals and routines are either useful or outdated and useless.

Wherever Saturn is placed, it always demands constant attention. Ignore its law for a moment, and crystallisation begins. With Capricorn rising, the crystallisation shows in the personality expression. When a Capricorn Ascendant with Saturn in Scorpio on the MC tries to control or ignore the sexual or financial needs, demands, and secrets of the world around her, "things fall apart." The world order collapses. And with her Capricorn rising, it is her world order. But because she is Queen, it says something about her country, too. We are in a falling apart time, where chaos and order battle it out on our TV screens and in our lives. But we are also at the frontier of a new time. We each partake in its building with every action we take. We are responsible for our piece in the work. The rest we have to leave to mystery.

TEILHARD DE CHARDIN

We are now going to look at someone with a lot planets in earth signs. In this case, most of them are in Taurus, so we shall get a chance to look at a stellium, too. Some of you have told me that, when you are faced with a chart which has many planets in one sign, you feel overwhelmed – how do you take it apart? This man was controversial throughout his adult life, and is still considered controversial. He may be troubling to some of you here, but not for the usual reasons.

Audience: What are the usual reasons?

Darby: He's not an axe murderer with a chart that has several features similar to your own or that of your best friend.

Audience: So what was he that is so disturbing?

Darby: He was a Jesuit priest – with a vision.

Audience: Oh. That *is* disturbing!

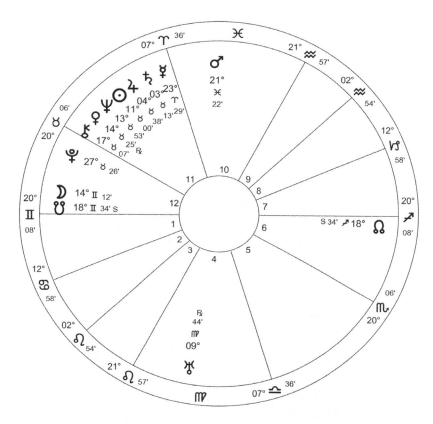

Teilhard de Chardin
1 May 1881, 7.00 am LMT, Orcières, France
Koch cusps; true Node

Earthy roots

Darby: I will tell you something about his origins and his life, and give you quotes from his writings as we go along, so you can see his chart speak. We'll look at some of the progressions and transits that occurred during his early life, so you can see how his vision took shape. Take a moment to study the chart.[15] Gem-

---

15   Chart source: Hans Hinrich Taeger, *Internationales Horoskope Lexikon*, Verlag Hermann Bauer, 1991. Taeger classes this data as Group 1* (reliable).

ini is rising, with Moon in Gemini in the 12th in a T-square with Mars in Pisces in the 10th and Uranus in Virgo in the 4th. Though Mars and Uranus are not strictly in opposition, they are linked through the Moon. Mercury, ruler of the chart, is in Aries, and moving fast by progression. By the time he was five, it was conjunct his Saturn, and for the next thirteen years it progressed over all his Taurus planets.

"Blessed be you, universal matter...you who by overflowing and dissolving our narrow standards of measurement reveal to us the dimensions of God..."
– Teilhard de Chardin

His birthplace was in the Auvergne, in central France. It is mountainous and rocky, with several extinct volcanoes. With all that Taurus, it comes as no surprise to us that this landscape affected him strongly. He was born into an ancient and noble family on both sides, and was the fourth of eleven children. This large family was deeply embedded in an even wider community of uncles, aunts, and cousins. Both parents were devout Catholics. He and his siblings were educated at home by father and mother until each of them was old enough to go to school, about age eleven or twelve. This austere, steady, tradition- and season-regulated life gave him a natural security that served him well through all the years of his adventurous and turbulent life. I don't know how the other children absorbed the dynamics of the large family web. But we do know that, with six planets plus Chiron in the 11th, this large family-clan made a deep impression on him. With his Moon in the 12th, he was more introverted than most of his siblings, and was sometimes teased for being so serious. He adored his mother – not fashionable today in the 20th century West, but not considered grounds for suspicion in his time. His mother was the great-grand-niece of Voltaire.

Audience: Wasn't Voltaire a Gemini?

Darby: No. Voltaire's birth data is controversial, but I was given this data in Paris, and it is generally thought to be the correct one. Listen to this: He was a Scorpio Sun, Aquarius Moon, born on 21 November 1694 at 5.30 pm LMT, in Paris. That gives him 23° 56' Gemini rising. He had Uranus in the 12th at 17° Gemini, and he had Neptune in the 10th house at 21° Pisces. Look at how those planets sit in Teilhard's chart. It certainly seems there was a resonance between these two men across the generations. In the 12th house Gemini Moon, we can see the trace of an ancestral influencing mind – a mind which is not only a personal, maternal ancestor, but a collective ancestor as well. The mythological effect of his mother's learned great-grand-uncle must have exerted an exciting pull on this Gemini rising child. He probably heard much of him in the legend and story told by his mother, and this touched his Gemini Moon soul. The village they lived in was also the home of Pascal, another great collective ancestor. And guess what: yes, Pascal was a Gemini.

The search for the treasure

Teilhard received a deep love of Christ and the Virgin Mary from his mother, to whom he owed "all that was best" in his soul. "To rouse the fire into a blaze, a spark had to fall on me;...[this spark] ...undoubtedly came through my mother to light up and fire my child's soul." This quote comes from the introduction to his most well-known mystical work, *The Divine Milieu,* which was only published after his death.[16]

Now, look at this Moon in Gemini, and let's look behind it to the spark he mentions. Mercury, ruler of his Moon and Ascendant, is in fiery Aries. By the age of five, this Mercury had progressed to Saturn and was beginning its journey to set alight all his Taurus planets, one after another. It began with an incident with his mother, and it set the physical and spiritual direction of his whole life. She was cutting his hair by the fireplace, and a lock fell into the fire. The child was consumed with horror. He suddenly saw that he was perishable. He says that he sobbed "pathetically" and could not be comforted for some time. Mercury in Aries is ruled by Mars, which is in Pisces, in the 10th. His "pathetic" tears led to a heroic quest. When he recovered, he decided he had to find something solid, permanent, in a world of such fragility.

Now, look at the progressions and transits. His progressed Mercury had reached Saturn already, and was nearing progressed Saturn a few minutes away. His progressed, retrograde

---

16   Teilhard de Chardin, *Le Milieu Divin, An Essay on the Interior Life,* Wm. Collins Sons & Co, London, 1960.

Venus had reached back to within one minute of the Sun. I love the mystery of Venus-Sun progressions. It was as if he was in a dream until now, while Venus had slipped over his Neptune; and when it touched the Sun, the loss took light, and consciousness was born in him. And in the sky, Neptune was on his natal Pluto in Taurus, all that year.

Audience: We get transiting Pluto on our natal Neptune, which I think is similar, in our mid-twenties, and it can be fairly devastating, too. It's often accompanied by disillusionment, like a bubble being burst. To me, it felt like a spiritual awakening.

Darby: Yes, it often does. Interesting, isn't it? So now he was on a quest, and he quickly found his treasure. He found iron. He felt secure again – he had found a true imperishable, and he began collecting it. During the next few years Mercury progressed over his Jupiter and then his Sun in Taurus. I don't know what was happening with his father, but he tells us what was happening in his own heart. In his autobiography, *The Heart of the Matter,* he wrote, "You should have seen me as in profound secrecy and silence I withdrew into the contemplation of my 'gods of Iron'...there was nothing in the world harder, tougher, more durable than this wonderful substance..." He wrote that, in iron, "...There was about it a feeling of full personality, sharply individualised..."[17]

However, another crisis occurred when he was ten. He discovered that iron rusts, and so it, too, was perishable. Again he collapsed in what he called "pathetic despair." That 10th house Mars does not approve of his sensitive Piscean response, does it? Was his father something of a sad stoic, perhaps? His progressed Mercury was now on Neptune, and progressed Neptune was closing in on Venus. He looked for a deeper permanence,

17   Teilhard de Chardin, *The Heart of the Matter,* quoted in *Teilhard* (Note 20).

"...Sometimes in the blue flame (at once so material, and yet so pure and intangible) flickering over the logs in the hearth, but more often in a more translucent and more delightfully coloured stone: quartz or amethyst crystals, and most of all glittering fragments of chalcedony such as I could pick up in the neighbourhood." His father told him these were even older than the oaks that stood round the house, and so his young heart was reassured. These stones became a lifetime passion. They drew him onwards into geology and later palaeontology, which is the branch of science that deals with fossils of extinct animals and plants. This obsession with permanence drew him forward spiritually, too, as the permanence in the flame and the permanence in stone came together in his imaginative soul. In his autobiography, he said that the land of his childhood home was where he was first "drawn by Matter – or more correctly, by something which 'shone' at the heart of Matter." How's that for a stunning expression of a ruling fire Mercury setting alight each earth planet, until his whole nature was alight!

His fiery Mercury lit up the earth, one planet, one field at a time. But behind that Mercury we see the Moon in Gemini – his mother, with her brilliant ancestor and her deeply religious nature and all the conversations we can imagine with her impressionable child. He says he got his love of rocks from his father. But I wonder if he received his contradictory love of science and religion through his mother. Mercury was the powerful ignition, but the Moon stood behind.

Audience: But you can go the other way too: Mercury in Aries – Mars ruler; Mars in the 10th in dual-ruled Pisces, with Neptune ruler conjunct the Sun.

Audience: His father must have been Neptunian, with Sun conjunct Neptune and Mars in Pisces. Do you know anything about him?

Darby: Not much. A Neptunian mist surrounds him, of course. He was an enthusiastic amateur natural historian who belonged to all the learned societies of the area. There's the 11th house Taurus Sun. Long walks in the mountains were part of the children's education, and Teilhard says that he did indeed receive his love of rocks, minerals, flora, and fauna from his father. Looking at his Sun, we can easily imagine that he absorbed an almost mystical love of nature from him. We know that the father suffered much loss in his life, not least through the death of many of his children. Yet he never lost his Catholic faith. But I wonder what unfulfilled ambition Teilhard received from him? Would his spiritual and conventional father wished to have been more publicly courageous, even controversial, perhaps? I can imagine that Teilhard felt a Neptune-Sun disillusionment with him at some point, but with his incredibly fixed nature, he never deviated from his loyalty and affection. And it is this fixity, this powerful earth-will, that was his strength, and many would say his weakness, at the same time.

At eleven he was sent off to the Jesuit boarding school at Mongré, some distance away. He was an exemplary if somewhat introverted and serious student. In June of 1897, when he was sixteen years old, he wrote to his parents that God had offered him a vocation, and he was willing, though he would wait awhile – Taurus! – to make sure that he was perceiving this call correctly. Transiting Pluto was on his Moon. Saturn and Uranus were conjunct in Scorpio, opposing his natal Pluto. Neptune was in Gemini, nearing his Ascendant and about to square his Mars in Pisces. His progressed Moon, in Capricorn, was trining his natal Neptune and Venus, and about to quincunx his natal Moon. And progressed Sun was about to conjunct his Pluto, in the 12th.

He entered the Jesuits as a novice on 20 March 1899, after having spent more than a year at home gaining physical and moral strength for his vocation and letting himself deepen into his decision while his progressed Sun went over his Pluto. When he entered the order, his progressed Mercury had caught up with and passed both his natal Pluto and his progressed Sun, and was about to move into Gemini. Transiting Pluto was on his Moon, having passed it once already, and Chiron was opposing it. Neptune had crossed his Ascendant and had squared his Mars. He looked back on the period between school and entering the noviţiate as the happiest period of his life. Interesting – with those progressions and transits, would you predict this as the potentially happiest period of your life? He did have to put up with more teasing from his more extraverted siblings as he wandered around deep in meditative thought, and we have no idea what was happening between his parents, under all the rituals and routines. But this was the last time he was ever to have a real home, a physical, earth-based, deeply familiar home, in his whole long life. And perhaps some intuition of the discomfort to come made him, very sensibly, take the pleasure and comfort of his home routine and rituals deep into his nature.

Audience: The ruler of his 3rd and 4th houses is Leo, and his Sun is not only conjunct Neptune, but also Venus and Chiron. He couldn't help romanticising his family, I suppose.

Darby: Yes, and at least two of his beloved sisters died young, of illness – one a very long and lingering illness, as was not unusual in those times. I have given you these early progressions and transits in some detail, because of the density of the action. By the time he was eighteen, Mercury had progressed over all his Taurus planets. His entire life was set in stone by now, and he made conscious and enduring decisions about his direction in ways that few of us do. He had seen light shining in the heart of matter, and he knew he was called to the priesthood. He also knew his life was dedicated to exploring the material world as a scientist.

His progressed Sun was now in Gemini, and with his Moon and Gemini rising, his twin-minded soul had dedicated itself to the contradictory positions of science and religion. Whether we look at his dual Moon in the 12th or his dual Mars in the 10th, this contradiction was to cause him great trouble throughout his life. Yet it was also the source of his greatest joy. He was a visionary in love with matter, and he was a Jesuit priest. As a priest, he became an obedient servant to an institution which had rejected matter for most of its history, and was certainly not on friendly terms with science. These are interesting contradictions and paradoxes.

Audience: He never rebelled against the Church? He had Moon square Uranus.

Darby: He never rebelled. He went through terrible torments at times, and raged in frustration at those who blocked his writings, but he would not leave the Church. He had made his vows and he must keep them, though being responsible to his vision and to his vow of obedience sometimes almost tore him apart. In the worst crises many of his friends urged him to become a lay priest at least, so he could get his most important works published. But that was out of the question. He despaired terribly at times. He felt like an Old Testament prophet crying in the desert, but he repeatedly renewed his commitment to the Church and to his vision. If he had to die in the desert, he would, but it would be as a Jesuit. The world had called him, and he would not reject it.

However, as we all know with the 12th house, things happen behind our own scenes. He shared almost all of his writing with friends and colleagues through his life, and when he died they were all published by friends. He had been advised by a priest-friend to make sure they were in good hands before he died, and he did that. He never got the seal of approval – the *imprimatur* – from Rome, but the collection of clergy and scientists who gave their seal of approval to his work after his death was formidable. I will tell you about his writings in a moment.

The visionary and the scientist

During his training for the priesthood, he spent three years teaching in Cairo, years where he developed his taste for foreign soil. He spent as much time as he could in the countryside, studying its flora, fauna, and fossils, but he also wandered around speaking to everyone and exploring the religious and moral ideas of the people he met – his Gemini Ascendant with Mercury in the 11th. He was fascinated by the diversity of religions and philosophies he came across. He began to love the world. He loved being in Egypt. He felt completely secure in all sorts of environments, with all those Taurean placements in the 11th. When he returned to Europe, he was sent to Hastings to complete his theological education. Again he explored the land and the people with enthusiasm. His scientific and religious studies were now beginning to come up against each other. The notion of evolution, which was being taught as part of his scientific education, did not sit well with Catholic theology. However, it seemed perfectly sensible to him, and indeed, a magic key "which kept coming back to my mind, like a refrain, or a taste, a promise and an appeal." Then there were the new findings of physics, which were revealing reality in the sub-atomic layers of matter. These findings excited him enormously.

He felt that he was able to love matter even more deeply through knowing it better. I quote here from Nicholas Corte's *Pierre Teilhard de Chardin: His Life and Spirit*.[18] "...All round it [the study of geology] was, almost incidentally, the growing appeal of vegetable and animal Nature; and deeper down, one fine day, came my initiation into the less tangible, but no less tempting, grandeurs revealed by the researches of physics. On each side of Matter stood Life and Energy: the three pillars of my in-

---

18   Nicholas Corte, *Pierre Teilhard de Chardin: His Life and Spirit,* Barrie and Rockliff, London, 1960.

ward vision and happiness." Tricky thoughts for a Jesuit priest in the early part of this century. And yet, it *was* Jesuit, too, in the sense that it was based on the absolute belief that Spirit = Good = God. And for him, this was the realm of Permanence, beyond all change and disintegration.

He was ordained a priest in August 1911. During the years of his novitiate, four of his siblings died, and one had become permanently ill. These sorrows bit deep into his soul. He not only felt the loss of each sibling individually; he also felt the disintegration of his once full and stable family. But at the same time, his world continued to expand.

The war came in 1914, and he became a stretcher-bearing priest. He refused offers of advancement through the war, preferring to stay with the ordinary soldiers – heroic in the old-fashioned way. We would expect that with his Mars in Pisces, 12th house Moon, and Taurean preference for "salt of the earth" collections of men rather than the elite world of officers. He was liked and admired by the men, and was always right in the thick of battle. In Corte's book we read that a friend once asked him how he could remain so calm in danger, and he answered, "If I'm killed I shall just change my state, that's all." This man went on to say, "The conviction and assurance, as well as the simplicity with which this statement of faith was made, gave me quite shock. We were still right in the middle of the war, and God alone knows how much carnage there was. So what he expressed was an attitude of mind quite deliberately adopted and lived out, his rule of life."

Audience: What he expressed was his Taurus stellium.

Darby: Yes, but his friend didn't know his chart, as far as I know. His rule of life may have been deliberately adopted, but it was the most natural thing in the world for him. I like the description of the Saturn-Jupiter conjunction in Taurus as "imperturbable

calm" as a "rule of life". In all that horror, he was able to nourish his vision of the goodness of God. Evil was simply part of the
process of evolution to this God. His powerful earth stellium
fixed on the light that had been set off in his early years, and his
intellect and emotions served this with his whole will. Notice:
one planet in fire, one in air, and one in water. All served and
were served by his fixed earth nature. Physical dangers never
disturbed him. But he did suffer from nervous disorders later in
life, when the strain of constantly coming up against the authority of his Church for the expression of his vision, and never being
allowed to publish his religious works, began to tell on him.

And then there were all those planets in Taurus, and no fixed
abode after the age of eighteen. This "discomfort" was a further
incentive to galvanise his will towards another kind of permanence. Look at Chiron in Taurus. It was natural to deny himself
physical comfort, but Venus in Taurus is a powerful sensual nature which needs a warm stable. Through his Sun-Neptune he
found warmth through his mystical sense, which felt a divine
heat at the heart of matter. But he was always sacrificing more
natural comforts for this. And that was also his strength – he was
willing to sacrifice that which he had no choice but to sacrifice.

And the gifts he received were great. It was during these
years that his vision took the shape and form that would develop
and ripen through his life. He wrote in his autobiography, "Un-
doubtedly it was during my wartime experience that made me
aware of this still relatively rare faculty of perceiving without
actually seeing, the reality and organicity of large collectivities,
and developed it in me as an extra sense." His progressed Sun
conjoined his Moon in 1915, and Uranus in Aquarius was moving through his 9th and squaring his Taurus planets all through
the war years. It was also during these years, living with such a
diverse group of men in such extreme circumstances, that his
personality took its full shape and form, and he lost his earlier
shyness. From now on he knew his own mind. The full weight

of his earth stellium set his heart in one direction: the spirit of matter was divine light, pure, good. Christ was its personality. Nothing else was significant.

For the next forty years he worked around the world, on palaeontological expeditions, and in research institutes and universities. He spent the years between 1923 and 1946 mostly in China during one of its most turbulent phases in history. He was often in great physical danger and great mental and spiritual isolation. Often he was not able to say Mass on his expeditions to remote places. His prayer then became: "Since, Lord, once again...in the steppes of Asia, I have neither bread nor wine nor altar, I will raise myself above these symbols up to the pure majesty of Reality, and I, your priest, will offer You, upon the altar of the whole Earth, the labour and the suffering of the world."

Audience: He was a real romantic. But it does make me uncomfortable.

Darby: It's probably that "pure majesty of Reality" that is uncomfortable. Or perhaps just the word "pure". It is hard for us, in the second half of the 20th century, educated to shadow recognition in one way or another, to listen unblinkingly to those who speak of the purity of the spirit, of reality. Our belief in absolutes has collapsed, and Teilhard, the seeker of permanence, was wedded to the Absolute. And yet, should he be other, with this chart?

Everywhere he lived and worked, he was drawn to diverse societies of people, as they were to him. As time went on, wherever he went, he was invited to teach, lecture, and present study groups to all kinds of people. He spoke about his exciting vision of humanity's potential future. He was certain that we were moving towards an "Omega point", and that all the suffering and torment were part of the process of development. He was certain that it was time for humanity to make a leap into a new consciousness, and that we must now become conscious participants in the evolution of life in the universe. He used all the evidence of his Jesuit-trained and paradoxically scientific mind to back up this claim. Also, he had been moved by the courage and beauty he witnessed in the trenches, amongst his fellow soldiers, and he continued to see evidence of something growing in the heart of matter – a convergence towards a new consciousness. This "naivety" angered some of those he met in the various social worlds he inhabited. He was accused of not taking evil seriously enough, and of not looking at things as they were in what other people called this fragmented and soulless age. Was he looking at things "as they are" deeply in the heart and spirit of our material world, our material selves? Or was he, as even Jung thought, misguided?

Audience: Was his earth deluded by the dream of his 12th house Moon? And fixed on a "comfortable" Taurean view of reality? His life was not comfortable by my modern Taurean standards, but then, we don't have Neptune, Chiron, and Pluto in Taurus.

Darby: He had seen the fire of divinity burning through matter, and he believed that a new consciousness was being born in the modern soul. He believed profoundly in evolution, and wrote and spoke about the developments in the "biosphere" in all species of rock, plant, and animal over the millennia, and the developments in the "noosphere" in our own species. He coined this word "noosphere" for what he saw as our developing collective consciousness. "All around us, tangibly and materially, the thinking envelope of the Earth – the Noosphere – is multiplying its internal fibres and tightening its network; and simultaneously its internal temperature is rising, and with this its psychic potential." Everything he saw throughout his long life deepened his belief in his vision, no matter how contrary looked the evidence. Can you imagine how comforting this vision must have been to many of his contemporaries who had experienced so much collective disturbance? He found comfort and he gave comfort. He saw hope in the future, in spite of the material and spiritual carnage around him. The Pluto in Taurus generation saw their stable world smashed to pieces. Teilhard explained all the destruction in scientific lauguage often enough, as part of the process of evolution towards the next, higher stage of consciousness. He was profoundly aware of how young our species was, and how quickly it had to develop.

Audience: His noosphere sounds like a bit like the World Wide Web.

Darby: That's one of the things I find so fascinating about his work. He was accused by Jung of literalism, and that is certainly true, from the Jungian standpoint. He had too many planets in earth signs not to believe that what he saw in his imaginal mind wasn't literal. He is not like Blake, with all that fire. Teilhard has one fire planet, and its visionary power had to express itself through his earth stellium before it reached his Gemini capacity to express it in words. He brought heaven into earth, the imaginal plane into time and matter. He did not see light and dark as a dance in the imaginal realm. He saw it in the depths of the most material reality, and as we are also matter, so it was being fought in our souls. He saw in individual souls how the will to believe in the future battled with despair. From the evidence of all his senses, he perceived that if we didn't will ourselves to believe and work for the next great stage in our evolution, then we would fall into the dark. Our hold on this life on earth, in matter, would come to an end. And I'll tell you something else interesting. When Jung died, copies of Teilhard's work were on his bedside table. I can imagine the problems Jung had with Teilhard, but in the end, did the mystical heart of the one man speak to the mystical heart of the other, in spite of the different ways they had of conceptualising, of airing, their visions?

Listen to this, from *The Phenomenon of Man:* "The two-fold crisis whose onset began in earnest as early as the Neolithic age and which rose to a climax in the modern world, derives in the first place from a mass formation (we might call it a 'planetisation') of mankind. Peoples and civilisations reached such a degree either of physical communion or economic interdependence or frontier contact that they could no longer develop save by interpenetration of one another. But it also arises out of the fact that, under the combined influence of machinery and the super-heating of thought, we are witnessing *a formidable upsurge of unused powers.*"[19] He says that we don't know what to do with all the time and abundance we have created, and that we are even tempted to "trample this super-abundance back into the matter from which it sprang without stopping to think how impossible and monstrous such an act against nature would be." We needed a new religious form, so that we could move to our next evolutionary step.

Audience: Was he thinking of the violence done to the Earth through chemicals and bombs and pollution?

The Christian Neoplatonist

Darby: He was living through the first part of our century, remember, so all of this was just beginning. But he had a sense of where it was heading. But he was deeply Catholic, Christocentric. You could say he was a Christian Neoplatonist, through his Jesuit education. He saw Christ at the centre of this necessary transformation. He is a spiritual ancestor of our emerging ecological awareness, but with a very Roman Catholic, Jesuitical bias. And in his own time, he was both insider and outsider – the

---

19   Teilhard de Chardin, *The Phenomenon of Man,* Wm. Collins Sons & Co., London, 1959.

outsider who was welcome everywhere with his radical vision in Jesuit mental and physical dress, and the Jesuit whose vision was too radical to be allowed the seal of approval by his Church. He saw no split between the sacred and the profane. He suffered *with* the Earth, in his own earth, in his body, in his heart: Sun conjunct Neptune conjunct the Sun-ruler Venus conjunct Chiron in Taurus, and Moon in the 12th square Uranus in Virgo. He saw his own family suffer through death and disintegration, but with no loss of faith, and he saw the world suffer death and destruction with great loss of faith. His Taurean nature must have been driven to bring comfort to the world he lived in, and he did this through his Mercury-lit Gemini Ascendant.

As I said, his vision, thoughts and ideas were not met with delight in Rome. He wanted his Church to reform, to admit that the Christian era was past and that scientific thought had made much of its dogma outdated. He said we had entered the trans-Christian era, and it required a new and thoroughly modern look at the world and God's inhabitation of it. The Lukas sisters tell us, in their biography, that he saw humanity "...crying for some Absolute in which it could achieve itself. Religion, he declared, must break out of the factious world of 'verbal theologizing, quantitative sacramentarianism, and oversubtle devotional practising', and ally itself with this forward thrust of mankind. 'The time has come', he concluded, 'for us to save Christ from the clerics, in order to save the World.'"[20]

In "Reflections on Happiness", he wrote, "Unless it receives a new blood transfusion from matter, Christian spirituality may well lose its vigor and become lost in the clouds." Like many great minds who are born into times when Uranus is in earth, he turned established notions of reality on their heads and re-visioned matter. Though he published all of his scientific work in his lifetime, he was not allowed to publish any of his spiri-

---

20   Lukas, Mary and Ellen, *Teilhard,* Wm. Collins Sons & Co., London, 1977.

tual writings. Though many got into pamphlet form and were circulated, and though all of his writings were seen by friends and cherished colleagues, they caused so much excitement and scandal that he was eventually permanently exiled from France, where his ideas were seen to be most inflammatory. In spite of himself, his Moon slipped out of the 12th house, and expressed the square to Uranus. He was reworking something previously irreconcilable in his very being, and though he remained absolutely obedient to his superiors and to Rome, he still managed to be deeply unconventional and troublesome.

He was and still is troubling to Catholics, with his matter-oriented, evolutionary ideas and his passionate zeal to reform the Church. And he was and is troubling to non-Catholics and non-Christians, with his absolute belief that Christ is at the heart of creation and is our key to the future of ourselves on the Earth. However, as problematic as he was to his Church, he was respected by the scientific community in which he worked, wrote, and taught. He received the Légion d'Honneur in 1947, for his "outstanding service rendered in the propagation of French intellectual and scientific influence...as one of the glories of French science, the international prestige for which he has done so much, through his personal relations with scientists of other lands, to develop and maintain." He was elected to the prestigious Academy of Science in 1950. Though he was a priest, his work as a scientist led him to spend most of his working life with people who either had no religion or had religious beliefs very different to his. He was fascinated by everything and everyone – endlessly curious, tolerant, and yet rock-solid and even dogmatic in his dedication to science and to God. He was generally liked and respected by men and, as men with lots of Taurus planets usually are, he was loved, even adored, by women. They supported and cherished him in different ways through all of his life.

Taurean celibacy

Audience: Taurus men and their women – a bull in a field of cows.

Darby: But in this case the "bull" was a celibate priest with a calling. Although that was a problem for at least one woman in his life, it was not, in principle, ever a question for him.

Audience: Venus is conjunct Chiron in Taurus. Mars is in Pisces, square the Ascendant-Descendant axis. His choice of a celibate life, with all those planets in Taurus, is intriguing. And Mars is sextile the Venus-Chiron conjunction.

Darby: He was a very attractive man. I have no idea how much distress he caused to women. I can imagine, with Venus in Taurus conjunct Chiron, and Gemini Moon in the 12th square Uranus in Virgo, his notions of chastity, and his capacity for mental and spiritual intimacy, must have caused a few flutters. In an essay called "The Evolution of Chastity", he wrote, "However fundamental woman's maternity may be, it is almost nothing in comparison with her spiritual fertility. Woman brings fullness of being, sensibility, and self-revelation to the man who has loved her." Heady stuff to the women of his time, I imagine.

I know he had a very long, intimate relationship with a sculptress he met in Peking in 1929, named Lucile Swan. After he left China, they only met occasionally, but their correspondence, which lasted until his death, indicates great mutual passion and regard, and also the difficulty of love between a free woman and a celibate priest. She was often very angry with him for what she must have sometimes felt to be his stubbornness. She suffered frustration and jealousy when she knew he was close to other women, and as she was a Sagittarian, she told him exactly how she felt about everything. I wish I knew her exact date of birth, but I don't. In the end, his love had a much more disinterested quality to it. But he gave her credit for much of his soul development, and probably, through her love, he came to understand something fundamental about the feminine, which he then wove into his vision. He certainly did not see the feminine as dark or shadowy. He saw it as the "unitive" – that which bound things together – "...not so much as an element by itself than as a kind of light illuminating the whole process of universal concentration...the spirit of Union." This is from a letter to one of his women friends, written just a few years before he died.

Audience: Did he feel guilty for generating such a physical attraction in a woman, and then not fulfilling it?

Darby: He certainly felt bad about it. I imagine his Venus conjunct Chiron in Taurus, and that 12th house Moon square Uranus, must have sent out the odd crossed signal as he went along. Also, he would have attracted women whose lives had a strong note of suffering and sacrifice woven into their fabric. However, he managed to maintain his friendships with women and with men throughout his life. His friendships formed a web that circled the globe and released his writings when he died. I studied his work at a Catholic university in the 1960's. He was very radical, and we loved him.

That he was a geologist and a palaeontologist cannot surprise you, with his Saturn-Jupiter-Sun-Neptune-Venus-Chiron conjunction in Taurus. That he might be a priest would also not surprise you, especially adding the Moon in the 12th. But that he was a mystic whose vision illuminated his life might not be expected with eight planets, plus Chiron, in earth. I am very interested in how his Taurus planets expressed themselves through the 11th house. I am fascinated by the juxtaposition of all those fixed earth planets in the house associated with fixed air, and with the kinds of struggle an earth mystic might have as opposed to a fire mystic like Blake. Unlike Blake, Teilhard worked continually to see his vision embodied. He wrote papers for UNESCO. To Julian Huxley, his friend, he proposed an "institute for the study of human self-evolution." He may have been accused of taking himself too seriously and being too literal by Jung and the Jungians, but he was more earth than anything, and so he had to be and do what he said and thought. Earth is about maintaining and improving things. It is about manifestation. With Pluto in Taurus, in earth, improving meant transforming, and with all his personal earth, too, it meant here, now.

Audience: His institute sounds like an intellectual version of EST.

Darby: Doesn't it? And all the other versions of it that our generation with Pluto in Leo became so fond of after the "consciousness explosion" in the 1960's. He might have got quite a shock if he had lived then and seen what kind of consciousness burst into flame around the world. I think he would have been excited by much of it.

Audience: Earlier, you said something about Mars in the 10th, and controversy and scandal. His Mars was in the 10th and square his Moon.

Darby: Yes, and it certainly became a thread in the tapestry of his life. He was even involved in a palaeontological scandal – the "Piltdown Man" – through his naivety and trust of someone he liked. I don't know if his close relationships with women caused scandal in some circles. I imagine they did. In 1947, when he was in his mid-sixties, he had his first heart attack. After that, he was not completely healthy again, though he did make a few more interesting field trips. He spent the last four years of his life, between 1951 and 1955, in New York City, attached to the Jesuit house there. He spent his last few months in a hotel near the house, while it was being renovated.

Audience: If the 4th house has to do with the end of life, then Uranus there in Virgo makes sense – and square to the Moon!

Darby: It's perfect, isn't it? During this time he felt very much alone in the world of men, often terribly sad and depressed that his voice could not be heard outside his own circles. He had never won his battle with Rome, and was now truly exiled from France. Saturn was transiting in Scorpio in the 5th, opposing his Taurus planets one by one. His progressed Moon was in Aquarius in the 9th, and it squared Pluto in February of 1955. Chiron had just entered his 8th house and was squaring his Saturn and Jupiter in Taurus. It was a terrible New York winter. He had been feeling the presence of death for a few years now, and he continually prayed that it would be a good death. He felt the sort of death he had would crown his life, and he wanted that crown to reflect his life's work. In his last month, in spite of despondency, he told friends that he had never felt so close to God, so peaceful with God.

He said he hoped death might come on Easter Sunday, the day of the Resurrection. On Easter Sunday in April, 1955, he said his own Mass, then attended Mass at St. Patrick's Cathedral; he lunched with the priests, and then had a meeting with others in the afternoon. He ended the day with several friends who were having tea together. They were delighted to hear him say that he had enjoyed the best Easter of his life. Then, we read in Nicholas Corte's book, "Suddenly, as he was going round the room, he fell, like a tree hit by lightening. They gathered round him. He was dead!" I had to quote that because it was as if he was describing the Taurus stellium with the Mercury in Aries flash at the top. There he was, with friends, in his 11th house, and it was Easter Sunday. He had his good death.

Within a year, his friends had made sure his writings were getting to the larger world. By the 1960's he was being taught in Catholic universities throughout America. He was still very controversial, but the Earth was beginning to be revisioned in so many other quarters, and the 1960's were a time of radical thought even in the Catholic Church. He is, as he would have wished, part of the new voice that is seeking to find again the sacred in matter, in the Earth. How he would have loved chaos and complexity theory in its revisioning of matter, and therefore of reality! In the introduction to *The Divine Milieu,* which was first published two years after his death, he wrote, "This is what I have learnt from my contact with the earth – the diaphany of the divine at the heart of a glowing universe, the divine radiating from the depths of matter a-flame." He dedicated the book, *Sic Deus Dilexit Mundum,* which translates as: "For those who love the world."

And now we come to the end of the day. I trust you all will attend and tend the earth, each in your own way. Whether you have planets in earth signs or not, it is the ground of our being, and each of us has a responsibility to some part of it as long as we are incarnated in bodies on a physical planet. Those of you who have planets in earth signs and houses are directed by your nature to the rituals and routines that will bring your gifts into manifestation. Those of you who have no planets in earth signs or houses are asked to bring your water, fire, and air – your feelings, passions, and thoughts – to the houses the earth signs rule. We are the material universe, and each of us is responsible to matter in some way. As we relate to it, so we are part of the destruction or creation we see around us. Thanks for a very interesting day.

BIBLIOGRAPHY

Baring, Anne & Cashford, Jules, *The Myth of the Goddess,* Viking Arkana, Penguin Group, London, 1991

Bierce, Ambrose, *The Devil's Dictionary,* Oxford University Press, Oxford, 1997

Bly, Robert, *The Rag and Bone Shop of the Heart,* Harper Collins, London, 1993

Carson, Rachel, *Silent Spring.* Houghton Mifflin, Boston, 1962

Costello, Darby, *Water and Fire,* CPA Press, London, 1998

Frazer, James, *The Golden Bough,* Macmillan & Co Ltd, London, 1954

Gettings, Fred, *The Arkana Dictionary of Astrology,* Penguin, London, 1991

Jung, C. G., *Man and His Symbols,* Aldus Books, London, 1964

Jung, C. G., *Psychological Types,* Vol. 6, *Collected Works,* Routledge & Kegan Paul, London, 1971

Jung, C. G., "Paracelsus as a Spiritual Phenomenon", in *Alchemical Studies,* Vol 13, Collected Works, Routledge & Kegan Paul, London, 1967

Lovelock, J. E., *Gaia A New Look at Life on Earth,* Oxford University Press, 1987

Corte, Nicolas, *Pierre Teilhard de Chardin: His Life and Spirit,* Barrie and Rockliff, London, 1960

King, Ursula, *Spirit of Fire, The Life and Vision of Teilhard de Chardin,* Orbis Books, Maryknoll, New York, 1996

Lukas, Mary and Ellen, *Teilhard,* Wm. Collins Sons & Co., London, 1977

Teilhard de Chardin, Pierre, *Hymn of the Universe* (English version), William Collins Sons & Co., London, 1965

Teilhard de Chardin, Pierre, *The Phenomenon of Man,* Wm. Collins Sons & Co, London 1959

Teilhard de Chardin, Pierre, *The Heart of the Matter,* Harcourt Brace, 1980

Teilhard de Chardin, Pierre, *The Divine Milieu, An Essay on the Interior Life,* Wm. Collins Sons & Co. London, 1960

PART TWO

AIR,
the Breath of Life

*This seminar was given on 2 February, 1997 at Regents
College, London as part of the Winter Term of the seminar
programme of the Centre for Psychological Astrology.*

ON THE WING

Today we take to the air. This will be interesting because, although we are incredibly sensitive to its subtle changes, it is the element we most take for granted. Because it is invisible, we don't think about it directly, yet it has to be in precisely the right proportion around us, or we suffer. We seem to ignore it, and yet we talk about it all the time. We notice instantly when the balance is wrong for us; when it is too cold or too hot, too moist or too dry, too still or too active. We notice when there is too little of it around; in a room with too many people and no windows open, or deep in a cave we have been exploring for too many hours, or underwater when our tank fails. We notice when there seems to be too much around; when the mistral has been blowing steadily for nine days and people are jumping off buildings, or when our house is suddenly lifted off the ground and blown across our field of corn into the river. We refer to it constantly as the "weather".

All of which inclines me to notice that we are in a room which is too small for us. In a very short time, we're going to be in one of the conditions I just mentioned – too little air. We're in danger of suffering from air deprivation in the middle of a seminar on air! We need a bigger space. I'll go and see what can be done.

[15 minutes later, having transferred to a large room at the top of the building]

Well, here we are in what seems to be a large eyrie. I think it must be more than twice the size of the previous space we were in, and it has carpets and pillars and windows open to the sky. We can breathe up here. Please feel free to get up and move around if you feel restless – this seems appropriate for this day on air!

Now, we can think about air again. During this day we are going to explore this element in terms of the ideas and ideals which inform us at every level of our lives. We shall examine air in various ways so we have a basis for understanding how it mediates the images of fire and, mixing with earth and water, gives shape and soul to everything we see and everything we are.

Every plant and animal knows how much air it needs to survive. Since we emerged from the ice age and the air warmed up enough to let us begin to think, we have paid attention to the weather. But until recently, we have not thought much about the miles and miles of air swirling high above our Earth, except to fill it with some of the gods and goddesses who personify the forces of nature operating within and around us. Today we see these layers of air with our modern scientific eyes, and we see how it protects us from the life-damaging emanations of the Sun and other stellar bodies. We know that this "aura" around our planet filters the rays of the Sun, allowing in the life-giving heat and keeping out – or transforming – the rays which are inimical to life.

Perhaps there was a time between the death of our old vision and the birth of the new, when the air seemed empty to us. But it is full again, and we are paying attention. The gods may no longer live there, but something is happening. We are noticing that what we send into our local air spaces effects the upper layers of air around us, and that may seriously effect our survival.

Heaven's breath

The other day I came across a book about the wind in my bookshelf. It is called *Heaven's Breath,* written by Lyall Watson. It was published in 1984, and I remember being excited about it when it first came out, as it gave me so much information about wind and air. Ah, I see some of you have read it too. He gave me the notion of air as the "aura" of our Earth, although this may be a early thought. He says that it "serves the same function as the fur on a fox or the shell of a snail, but it is more sensitive and more responsive." It circulates constantly, keeping temperatures right to foster endless variations of life. It is the mediator between the fire of the Sun and the Earth itself. This is an important fact for our discussion on astrological air today.

Heaven's Breath tells us that there are about 5600 million million tons of air wrapping the Earth and moving round it at any time. It is a dynamic system in which we each breathe about ten million times a year, using about five million litres of air a year. He writes:

> All constituents of the free air, including the oxygen we need to breathe, are being constantly replenished. There is an open dynamic interchange between Earth, biosphere and air that stirs things up and keeps Gaia herself alive and breathing...[21]

Don't you like the notion of "free air"? Perhaps this is the only element that is still free, though I have heard of a bar in New York or Los Angeles which sells different sorts of air. You order "Arizona air" or "ocean air" and then breathe it in through a mask! I don't know if this is a real bar, or one that lives in someone's imagination still; it has a real sci–fi ring about it. And good science fiction always operates within a ring of truth. It tells us what we may be about to lose. And we usually only discover how precious things are by losing free access to them.

In his book, Lyall tells us that we are living at the bottom of an ocean of air. I would like to briefly describe these layers of air. Not only do they protect life on Earth, but they also keep it

---

21   Lyall Watson, *Heaven's Breath,* Hodder & Stoughton, London, 1984.

open to the influences of other bodies in stellar space, not least the Sun. It is interesting to think about these layers of air, not only in relation to the Earth, but also, as astrologers, in relation to the element of air. I am thinking here of our three levels of air – Gemini, Libra, and Aquarius. Each has a different role in circulating what we might call the primordial images, born in the fire, through the various layers of thought, from the highest philosophical conceptions to the simple truths that come out of a good gossip over a morning cup of tea.

At the surface of the Earth, air is at its densest. We can feel this in our own lungs when we drive from the sea to the mountains in a day. It literally took my breath away when I first drove from Durban to Johannesburg one day, from the sea to over 5000 feet above sea level. Air gets thinner as it gets farther from the surface and rises to a "natural ceiling" of air which is about eight kilometres above the Earth at the poles and about fifteen kilometres over the equator. Below the ceiling is the "troposphere", where most of the air and water vapours are confined, and where they turn and circulate the Earth. Each layer of air rests on its denser layer, and although most air moves horizontally in its own layer, "There are vertical movements of air, which are vital in shaping climate and in moving things. . ." These vertical movements of air interest me greatly.

Above the ceiling is the "stratosphere", where the air can be seen in layers and the temperature is fairly constant. The stratosphere rises about fifty kilometres above the Earth and gets thinner and thinner. There are layers within layers, of course, and the one we are most familiar in the stratosphere is the ozone layer which occupies the region about twenty and thirty kilometres above the Earth. As we are all aware, this layer of our atmosphere seems to be getting more and more damaged by some of our emissions here on Earth. There is a feeling of imminent crisis in the air. Our collective imagination is horrified at the thought that it may be irreparably damaged. And with good reason: this ozone layer filters out the most damaging ultraviolet radiation from the Sun, and without it we cannot survive.

And beyond the ozone layer there is the freezing "mesophere" where temperatures can fall to -143°C; according to Lyall, "the lowest natural levels ever recorded anywhere in Gaia's being." And above that, another more or less 300 kilometres of air, "...so thin no part of it reaches a density of more than one millionth of an atmosphere." Lyall calls it "...Gaia's first line of defence...Ultraviolet, infrared, radio and X-rays, corpuscular streams from our Sun, similar radiation from other stars, and cosmic rays from interstellar space all buffet the outer edges of the atmosphere. Oxygen and nitrogen molecules are split apart and free electrons gather in electrically charged groups of ions that arrange themselves in belts around Earth." This is the "ionosphere", and it is the region which manifests itself at the poles, the auroras, out of which the imagination of early northern peoples made sense of their reality. The extraordinary drama of these moving layers of light gave birth to the northern myths and legends which form some of the imaginal sediment of our mythical and religious ancestry.

These outermost layers of air receive matter and energy from space beyond the borders of our Earth's atmosphere, and they are exchanged from level to level, interacting with the matter/energy of each layer and changing at each interaction. When they arrive down here, where we live, they are further mingled with all that breathes on the Earth, and then they begin their rise upward, back through the layers towards outer space. We both receive and give out substances through these layers of air.

From our view, on *terra firma*, we can see that the air is filled with natural life, creatures of such infinitesimal size we can only imagine them, up to the giant eagles of remote mountains. The birds of the air are perhaps most interesting to us as astrologers. Not only do they call our eyes to the sky during the day, as the stars do at night, but the rhythms and patterns of their life in the air is part of the root system of our art. For one thing, the origin of the word for "bird" – *avis* in Latin – is connected to the word for "augury" and "auspices." We have literature from early Rome on soothsayers on the reading of omens *(auspicium),* in which the soothsayer read the paths of birds in flight at dawn and dusk to get information which would help the rulers plan their day. The distances between birds and stars may be far in linear distance, but not so far in the imaginal world of our ancestors.

There are many strange and wonderful things about birds and omens which I would love to include in this seminar on air, but I think I must leave them for another time.

A dictionary browse

The Oxford English Dictionary tells us:

> Air is the invisible gaseous substance which envelops the earth and is breathed by all land animals and plants. It is one of the four elements of the ancients, now known to be a mixture of oxygen, nitrogen, carbon dioxide and traces of other gases...It is the body of the air surrounding the earth.

The dictionary describes it as "a medium for the transmission of radio waves.", and later as "a medium for operations with airplanes, aircraft and aerial power." Its mediumistic powers are part of its very definition, it seems. In the last few years we have seen it become a medium for a dimension called cyberspace, which, in part, is carried by air when signals ping-pong up to satellites and then back to earth again. It lives in an "electrical etheric" carried by air.

The *OED* also tells us that air is "a special state or condition of the atmosphere as affected by contaminating exhalations, temperature, moisture, etc. Or as modified by time and place." This connects to something Jung said in his exploration of the imagination and the archetypes which inform us. We will come to this in a minute. We are also told that it is a word for the bearing, disposition or mood of a person.

My crumbling copy of *Chambers Etymological Dictionary* tells us that air is: "The fluid we breathe: the atmosphere; a light breeze: a tune: the bearing of a person." It refers us to the French and Latin *aer.*

In the Latin dictionary *Lewis and Short,* we find that *aer* comes from the Greek αηρ, and designates "the lower atmosphere (in distinction from *aether,* the upper pure air)." *Aether* is "the airy summit," and points us to "the highest point." *Aether is* "the upper, pure air, the bright, clear, serene sky." It is "Heaven." *Aethra* is also a word for the sky, air or heaven, and, coincidentally, Aethra was the mother of that great Greek hero, Theseus.

A*ura* is a gentle breeze, but it can also be used for the upper air, or heaven. We, of course, use the word to describe a light-body which surrounds life forms, and Lyall used that word to describe the envelope of air itself, as it surrounds our body of Earth.

I am interested in the notion of the aura of the Earth being its air wrapping and, here, "gentle breeze" and "upper air". In Africa, when I was working with tribal people, particularly Zulus, there was a word, *moya,* and it was used a lot and interchangeably for breath, for wind, and for the spirit. When I asked questions about why this or that was being done, I was told, "It's *moya Da,* it's the spirits." When a *sangoma* did something extraordinary, they would say, "His *moya* is very powerful." But you would also speak of the wind, *moya.* If the wind was very powerful at a ritual or ceremony honouring the spirits, you would hear someone say, "The spirits are talking. The spirits are very powerful." And *moya* was also the word for "breath". When one died, one's *moya* left the body and joined the ancestors. So the wind, breath, the *aura* and the spirit are all connected here.

Audience: Catholicism has its Holy Ghost or, as modern people say, Holy Spirit. In pictures of the Annunciation, it is depicted as a bird, or otherwise, a flame hanging in the air.

Audience: The Old High German for *Spiritus Sanctus,* was rendered as *Atum,* which is breath.

Darby: Yes. I had a friend in Johannesburg who was a Jungian analyst, and she showed me Jung's exploration of the religious connections between air, breath and soul. He followed an etymological trail from the German word for soul, *Seele* all the way to the Greek *psyche* which was spirit or soul and also, delightfully, "butterfly". In Latin, *animus* and *anima* were later translated as "spirit" and "soul". They were both born from the Greek *anemos,* "wind". And *pneuma* also means wind and spirit, from which we get our "numinous". *Psychein*: to breathe; *psychos*: cool; *psychros*: cold, chill; and *physa* means bellows. And all of them signify spirit. If you want to follow Jung's word trail more closely, look in *Collected Works,* Volume 8, page 345.

In his *Alchemical Studies,* he speaks about Hermes, who was originally a wind god, and he connects him to the Egyptian Thoth, "who makes the souls to breathe." Jung says these two figures are the forerunners of the alchemical Mercurius in his aerial aspect. He says that the ancient texts often use *pneuma* and *spiritus* in the original concrete sense of air in motion: "He [Mercurius] is the...stone uplifted by the wind..."

We astrologers have tended to say that the Sun describes the "masculine creative spirit" and the Moon the "feminine receptive soul". The Moon tells us how we bring into our daily lives the impulses of the spirit-drawn, spirit-driven Sun. But Mercury is also connected to soul, in that it gives us the power to think about and to articulate the connection between our spiritual imaginative aspirations and our instinctive survival-oriented daily behaviour. Mercury moves vertically through the layers of air, keeping the connections alive. What we do with its information is personal to each of us. When there are aspects between the Moon and Mercury, the soul life is very active, because there is direct communication between the Sun's "first minister", Mercury, and the emotional body which carries the rhythms of the soul into daily life. If you want to follow these word trail further, look in James Hillman's wonderful book, *Anima*.

IDEA AND IDEAL

Now I want to discuss with you the idea of air as idea and ideal. I think this is central to understanding the astrological element air. Just as planets in fire work straight from images, planets in air work straight from ideas which convey the images to our understanding. *Chambers'* definition of "idea" is a good summary of all dictionary definitions. It says an idea is "an *image* of a thing formed by the mind: a notion: thought: opinion." It comes out of the Greek *idea – idein,* which is translated as "to see." It says "ideal" exists in *idea*: it is mental. And then it goes on to say an ideal exists "in imagination only: the highest and best conceivable, the perfect, as opposed to the real, the imperfect." And it is "the highest conception of anything."

We consider the element of air "idealistic", don't we? *Chambers* defines this as: "...the doctrine that in external perceptions the objects immediately known are *ideas*: any system that considers thought or the *idea* as the ground either of knowledge or existence: tendency towards the highest conceivable perfection, love for or search after the best and highest." Since Plato, philosophers have grappled with the notion of "ideas". The interaction between the "ideal realm" and the "real" or material realm is a fundamental notion in our Western heritage. You can read almost any philosopher of any age and you will come across the struggle to understand what *is* and our perceptions of it. Emmanuel Kant said that things exist in themselves, but we cannot know them apart from the ideas we have of them, and those ideas are a product of the construction of our very minds.

Audience: Up and up we go until we disappear in the stratosphere and beyond, where we begin to exchange molecules with the Sun and other stellar bodies.

Darby: Exactly. Air directly refers to the realm of the "ideal". Plato's "realm of the idea" and the dictionary definition of idea and ideal are more akin to this numinous realm of images which we reach through our imagination. Air is the element which brings images into formulation; concepts, schemata, maps of reality, thoughts, ideas. If you remember the fire seminar,[22] we spoke about how fiery planets move straight from their images. Air planets translate images. If you are dealing with a person who is primarily fiery and you want to know why they did something, you have know the images which were moving them. Any reasons or explanations come from the air.

From mesosphere to Earth

Henry Corbin says the realm of the idea is the first layer of "almost substance". We might imagine it here as somewhere just beyond the mesosphere, where interstellar rays are about to enter our atmosphere. Once they enter this first layer of air, they begin to take on substance, and by the time they get down to us, they are mediated, translated, conveyed into our living systems. Interactions take place, from the above to the below. The earth breathes – and this includes us and all our chemical outpourings now – and the air conveys the mixtures of all the myriad interactions back up through the layers of air and into the regions beyond. At every level there is interaction and translation.

Audience: It sounds a bit like Chinese whispers. You know, one person whispers something to another and that person repeats

---

22   This seminar is published in *Water and Fire,* CPA Press, London, 1998.

it to another and on and on until, at the end of the game, the original message has been changed out of all recognition.

Darby: That's it! But in this case the Chinese whispers go on and on, and there is a constant flow between the highest and the lowest levels of air. Looking at it this way, whatever idea you have about something comes from an idea behind it, and another behind that, until you get up into the mesophere where the ideas are so subtle and light that the fiery images mix with this rarest of air. As the images descend through the layers of air the mix "thickens" into thoughts and concepts, notions and opinions. When you see two people haggling over the price of a shovel, a painting, or a race horse, you are seeing, right in front of you, a down-to-earth manifestation of all this spiraling air.

Any notion of value is contained in what Jung calls "primordial images". These images are conveyed through layers of atmosphere – modified by time and place – and translated by the most subtle minds of every era, and then retranslated by less subtle but more accessible minds and conveyed through all sorts of air in all sorts of times and places, and everyone who airs their view is part of the constant flow.

Audience: In the beginning was the verb.

Darby: The verb?

Audience: The word. My English mixes up words sometimes.

Darby: It's an interesting mix-up. However: "In the beginning was the word", and the word was written in fire.

Most of us cannot breathe long in the refined atmosphere of ideas that border on the realms of imaginative fire – ideas that reach for God, as someone said to me recently. With words and thoughts we begin to become aware of ourselves. Descartes' *cogito ergo sum* – the meaning of which has been Chinese whispered into something else by now – indicates this self-reflection, this detachment. There is suddenly a space, a gap, a sense of subject and object, and the first time we experience this, we are on our way to thinking.

Audience: You mentioned Jung's primordial images. Are you speaking of the archetypes?

Darby: Yes. He says that the "idea" is "derived from the primordial image. In its formation it is the concretisation of the primordial image, and the primordial image is what we call archetype. He says that the concept of idea is "...used to designate a certain psychological element intimately connected with what I term image...image may be either personal or impersonal in its origin...[in the] latter case, it is collective and is distinguished by mythological qualities...", which he terms the "primordial image." He goes on to say that, even though ideas are expressions of primordial images – they are abstracted or derived from the original images and are a "formulated meaning" of these images – they also have an *a priori* existence in themselves. Though begotten out of images, an idea has its own individual and unique character and its own psychological impact as itself. He speaks of ideas at this level as collective thought-forms. So ideas can be seen both as derivative (originating in primordial images) and *a priori* (describing collective experience).

Audience: This is very heady. Very airy, in fact. I am torn between wanting further elaboration and something more concrete, more personal here.

Darby: For those of you who want to look at the way Jung develops these notions, go to Volume 6, *Psychological Types*. You will see his Saturn in Aquarius trine Jupiter in Libra in action! Very heady, indeed! Delicious, if you have the taste for it.

The idea of beauty

But let's work with an archetype such as Venus. As an image, as a symbol, Venus represents simply that which attracts. We can see it within the polarity of Empedocles' basic forces which rule, or describe, the world – Love and Strife, or Concord and Discord. Let's call it beauty here. Beauty is an idea – we can talk about it endlessly, and we do – but is also an image in the mind. We first expressed it in pictures and carvings. Later we began to articulate the image with words, poetic words. Each era, tribe and person has a particular notion of beauty, but the notion itself is universal: it is an archetype. It is part of our nature to be attracted to some things and repelled by others. At a basic level it has to do with survival – creatures are naturally attracted to that which furthers life, and are repelled by that which destroys life. This is part of its root system. Venus is the name we give to those things that attract us – or rather, Venus is the planet that tells us what sort of beauty we need for our survival.

Venus represents a principle of nature which is also a primordial image, and this image is translated differently in different times and places, ages and stages. Each time and place has its collective idea of beauty and each individual has their version of it. Even weather effects it! People who live in snowbound countries, cut off from other people, will have very different "ideas" of beauty to those who live on balmy tropical islands. In our fast-moving times, notions of beauty change in every generation. From the mesosphere to the troposphere and back, our notion of what is attractive, life enhancing, and what is destructive, life destroying, evolves and changes.

Audience: Uranus is now in Aquarius, and soon Neptune will be there too. It will be interesting to see how the multicultural exchange of ideas and images unifies and individualises our collective and personal notions and ideas of beauty over the next decade.

Darby: It certainly will. These planets which point to collective changes will be in the sign which is collective in nature! What new notions of beauty will be thrown together and thrown apart by the jostling of nation against nation and tribe against tribe? From our daily life interactions to our cultural interactions and up to the exchanges between our civilisations, we are mixing and communicating in a way that is new on the earth. The movements of air seems to be more vertical than they have ever been before.

Audience: So, can I get very personal? I have Venus in Gemini in the 10th house. My brother has Venus in Virgo in the 8th. Both are well aspected. Being human, we both respond to beauty, as it is archetypal and fundamental to consciousness. But our responses become specific through our development. There are three more girls in the family – I think our oldest sister is the most beautiful, and coincidentally, she is the most successful! She writes for television, but she was a writer from her childhood. I have always found her beautiful. My brother thinks the youngest is the most beautiful. She is quiet and shy and kind and secretive – a real Sun-Moon-Virgo. Her Moon is balsamic in this case.

Darby: And how has your mother given opportunity for those Venus images to build?

Audience: Our mother was still working, and loving it, when my sister and I were born – I am the second child. When my brother was born she wasn't working, except for keeping the books for my father. We took our images of beauty from her, at first, and then they got enhanced through our sisters, and now they get modified through various experiences as we go along. My brother and I both love books, but I am more classically snobbish, or conventional about judging a book. He really notices and minds if the print is not well set on the page. I think his taste in literature is a bit obscure, weird. He thinks I just follow the fashion.

Darby: If these planets were squared or opposed by other planets, then your "primordial image" of beauty might be problematic and require conscious work, because it would be negatively attached to other images and the combination would constellate oppressive thoughts and feelings. But even well aspected, it is wise to observe your assumed values, Venus, from other mental vantage points, getting perspective on your own perspective.

You can study mythic systems and see beauty expressed in different times and places. The realm of fire carries the image and the air realm brings it down to a local time and space. Any of you who have moved from a small town to a big city know how the air we all breathe, the thoughts that circulate, change our values – change our sense of what is beautiful. Perhaps not at the highest level of values, where the air is thin and rare, but certainly at the lower "market place" levels where we all jostle with each other, close and dense. Perhaps your Venus in Gemini in the 10th always loved well-constructed phrases, but what you consider well-constructed phrases will change through time and interaction with others.

You can work your way upwards and back downwards with the levels of ideas. Jung tells us that primordial images inform everything at all times, as do the ideas constructed to carry them, although the ideas are more influenced by time and circumstances. The primordial images – archetypes – are subjected to "rational elaboration" which "make it suitable for rational usage." He says, "It is this rational elaboration which gives it formulations corresponding with the spirit of the time." We could translate this by saying that ideas are essentially constructions which carry primordial images to different times and places. But it is also changing times and places which modify and change the constructions, the ideas, which burn with the deeply embedded fiery images.

The need for and love of beauty has always existed. Beauty calls us. Recently, many of us in the Western industrialised world have come to love Nature. There are reasons for that – many of us no longer live close to it, for one thing, and a little distance always enhances appreciation of things. Also, we have begun to feel that we are losing Nature, as we seem to be destroying it in our desire to improve our situation. Or perhaps our desire to improve has become our need to control that which dominated us for so many thousands of years. Our present love of Nature is collective, but local in time to about the last two hundred and fifty years here in England. But love itself, attraction to beauty, is universal.

Audience: I am thinking of times and places where the Church dictated the "ideas" about reality, but then the corruption of its prelates and growing information gave birth to contradictory ideas that seemed to rise out of the ground. The air was disturbed, and something new arose out of the mix. Now science might be undergoing that with the new complexity theories that are arising.

Audience: Taking it to the very personal, I recognise that I have an idea of what is beautiful, and some of it is based on my personal pre-conscious experience. But even that is based on my inner makeup, as represented by the planets and their positions, such as Venus in Gemini in the 10th house. It is my primordial image taken from the prime primordial image, and it is elaborated by my experience and the ideas of beauty circulating before

IDEA AND IDEAL   151

and during my lifetime, based on local and collective changes through time.

Darby: Yes, and you have Neptune in Libra, and your generation's collective notion of beauty is quite different to the group before you with Neptune in Virgo. That "spirit of the times" is interesting – it is back to the definition of air as "a special state or condition of the atmosphere as affected by contaminating exhalations, temperature, moisture, etc. Or as modified by time and place."

ASTROLOGICAL AIR

Archetypes are timeless and eternal, and the ideas we have are their formulations, their substantiation. Planets in air receive and transmit ideas. Any group with, for example, Neptune in Libra will be collectively sensitive to ideas of beauty which embody harmony and balance. However, the generation alive today has notions of beauty very different to those of the late 18th century, the last time Neptune was in Libra. The longing for grace and harmony was there, but idealised differently. A person with a well-proportioned body would have been idealised, but the size and height of the person idealised would have been different then because of all sorts of different conditions. Any group of people born into a time when Neptune is in Libra will be informed by what we call the Venusian archetype, but the ideas about this will be different in different times and places. And each of us will have our own personal ideas, depending on our Venus position. And even our using the words "Venusian archetype" is an "idea" which is modern, too. Without Jung's formulations we would not be using this language to describe what we are talking about.

The sea of things invisible

In Fred Gettings' dictionary, he says that the air element is "all-pervasive, a palpable link between the inner world of man (lungs) and the outer environment." He says air is the element most deeply associated with thought and with volatility. He quotes Philalethes: "Air is the envelope of the life of our sensitive spirit." In other words, we swim in the world of thought, as fish in the sea, the "sea of things invisible". Getting says this bears little resemblance to physicists' air, but astrologers try to connect them.

If we go back to Lyall's book, it seems to bear a lot of resemblance to the biologist's air. This "envelope of the life of our sensitive spirit" and this "sea of invisible things" in which we swim seem very much like our astrological air. Do any of you remember Jung talking about his conversations with Philemon, who admonishes him – Jung – because he treats his thought as if they were his own possessions?[23] When I first read this, I thought of birds. As they inhabit the air, so do thoughts inhabit the mind. Thoughts wing through our minds – they seem to come from everywhere, at times. We often notice them most when we have to concentrate our thinking for a task, or when we are trying to sleep, or trying to meditate.

Air circulates according to laws we only partially understand; ideas do, too. Our thoughts are prey to internal weather. They circulate according to subtle and mysterious laws. They mingle with our emotions, they arise out of our digestion, they stir up our imagination. Our thoughts in our heads are almost always a mixture of elements. Our physical, emotional and spiritual condition effects our thinking. Learning to think properly is not a simple task. Most of us are using other people's thoughts. Sometimes you meet people who join up various concepts and ideas in such a way that you think, "That is an original thinker." But this, like any other gift, is rare.

According to Gettings, air signs are "versatile and dedicated to human relationships", but he says that they get caught up in "superficial and transient matters."

---

23 See C. G. Jung, *Memories, Dreams and Reflections*, Vintage Books, NY, 1989.

Audience: I wrote down the *OED* definition you gave for air. What you are saying now reminds me of a section of it. It is "a special state or condition of the atmosphere as affected by contaminating exhalations, temperature, moisture, etc. Or as modified by time and place." That sounds like what you are describing.

Darby: When those with air planets are not turning to the timeless and eternal verities, or when they are disconnected from the deeper realms of feeling or the harsh necessities of earth life, they get swept along by local and current thought-forms. An airy person gets caught up in fashionable thinking, and that keeps them from finding their true North – universal notions that guide us through life. Air signs need to feed themselves on the best and finest thoughts they can find, if they are not to get lost in the air waves circulating around them. Otherwise, they become simply radio transmitters for various ideas that come through town.

Stephen Arroyo[24] also talks about this tendency of air to be shallow. He says it is because of their power to abstract ideas from experience, rather than live their feelings. But, he also says, they can understand all sorts of ways of thinking and don't need everyone to agree with them. They get offended if their ideas are ignored or disparaged, but they don't generally feel threatened by other points of view. Water and earth need things to be felt or tested against feeling and earth reality, and when they feel or test something and then turn it into an idea, they find it difficult to tolerate the ideas of others. He says that fire excites air but can be impatient with air's need to conceptualise and to understand what fire intuitively knows.

Audience: I have four planets in air, and my mother has four in fire. She says I drove her crazy as a child with all my questions.

---

24 Stephen Arroyo, *Astrology, Psychology and the Four Elements,* CRCS Publications, 1975.

But she drives me crazy because she never seems to do anything for rational reasons. She assumes that, because she feels it, in some intuitive way, it is invariably right.

Darby: That sounds about right. The interesting thing is that, when we lack an element, we invariably attract it in other people. I guess we need the element even if it is there in someone else, although there is then that problem of air getting overexcited by fire, and fire feeling put out by earth, and water being agitated by air, and, well, you all know those equations. Love always demands discipline and self-reflection; otherwise we eat each other up and are left lonely.

Carter talks about the sociability of air signs in his *Encyclopedia of Psychological Astrology.* He says that afflictions in air signs cause disharmony with people. I would also say that difficult planetary conditions in air houses do, too. Air is certainly social, in that its very nature is to circulate ideas, and it needs people for that. It's not going to get very far circulating ideas to cows or sheep. However, people with a strong air emphasis often get disappointed with people, because of their idealism. Their ideas about how people should behave can interfere with their longing for communication. I am thinking of Libran Bridget Bardot, with her five air planets plus Chiron. Her Mercury is in Libra, conjunct Jupiter. I think she prefers cows and sheep to people now, but I imagine she still needs people more than she might admit.

There is a sharp sense of isolation that blows through very airy people at times. It is very easy to see in someone with lots of air planets and one element missing. For example, an airy person with no planets in water signs finds themselves periodically isolated, feeling exiled, cold, and cut off from their common humanity. An airy person with no fire feels cut off from human warmth, from inspiration; all the thoughts go round in the head but they feel no central heat, no excitement, no passion, and that feels like exile and is very lonely. An airy person with no earth gets cut off from their own substance, their bodies, the struggle, toil, and comfort of ordinary earth life. They lose ground when they are not in physical contact with the earth or with others.

Air planets operate directly from ideas which are a combination of something eternal and something local in time. It always depends on which sort of mental nutrients you feed on; airy people can find universal truths in trashy novels, but if that is all they read, then part of their airy life is starved of nutrition. Air planets mediate ideas, thoughts, experiences in their interactions. Gemini planets, ruled by Mercury, gather and disseminate these ideas according to the wind that is blowing. This air simply keeps the air circulating. Libra planets, ruled by Venus, use information to move in and out of equilibrium on various inner and outer levels. They bring warm air to cold environments and cold air to hot environments, always shifting their position to accommodate what is out of equilibrium. And planets in Aquarius bring in ideas from that which is emerging, and work to integrate them into present time systems, no matter how awkward that might be. With Saturn and Uranus as their rulers, they are moved to bridge the gap between the potential and the actual.

Missing air

Audience: But what if there is no air in the chart? Does that then mean that there is no rational derivation? That there is no way to bring these "primordial images" into being? That would mean that people with no air cannot mediate these images. And I seem to remember that many people we consider "great thinkers" had no air, or hardly any at all.

Darby: Well, "no air" and "hardly any" are very different things in my book. If you have six daughters and one son, it is very different to having six daughters and no sons. But let's speak about that in a minute. What do you think about the question of "no air" in a chart – I mean no planets in air signs?

Audience: Space – its a question of space, I think. They get very close to things. Sometimes it's hard to breathe around people with no air – I don't think I mean that literally, but as an airy person I seem to need more mental space around me than my friends who have no planets in air. And it hasn't got to do with the houses. It's just the planets I am talking about. They can have all their planets in air houses, but if there are none in air signs, there is this intensity. They experience their thoughts in such an intimate way.

Audience: It certainly doesn't mean lack of intelligence, but perhaps lack of detachment about ideas. Ideas are *felt,* ideas *burn,* ideas *burden* one with no planets in air.

Darby: Ideas inform and are taken more seriously, perhaps, the less air one has. One's own ideas are taken more seriously. They are not just birds in the inner sky – they are my birds in my sky. The water or the earth planets seem to take possession. That can happen in a chart where there are air planets too, but it rarely lasts for long. They notice when their ideas get shot down. They may not like it, but it clears the air, too.

Let's explore this notion that great minds are airless! Most of the great philosophers I have studied have at least one air planet. Perhaps because of this, they get less entangled in cross-currents of air – they don't approach reality with many levels of ideal constructs. They look at the air, they examine the ideas and ideals around them, and they show us how, and sometimes why, we are thinking in this or that way. They show us the constructs that inform us. They get right up close and they see these constructs in great detail. I don't think you'll find a great philosopher with no planets in both fire and air – it takes only one fire planet to be full of enthusiasm for "eternal truth". That backdrop of fire, with no air and lots of earth, will create a hard-working observer of the airy realm – the realm where ideas circulate, the realm where the fiery images at the heart of reality are translated into every-day thinking.

Audience: But that doesn't mean that people with no air planets are automatically philosophers.

Darby: No, just as it doesn't mean people with no water automatically understand human emotions. It does mean that you might have some distance on an element if you don't have planets in that element. But whether this distance is disassociation or understanding depends on other things. It is certainly true that many English philosophers have little or no air, but little air is very, very different to no air. Bertrand Russell had lots of planets in Taurus in the 7TH and one planet in air – Moon in Libra in the 11th. That air Moon held his idealism, but all the earth finally had its say and he had to give in to seeing things "as they are".

Do you know the story of Helen Keller? She was one of my heroines when I was young. She had an extraordinary lack of air in her chart – no planets in air, not even air signs on the MC or ASC, and only one planet in an air house; and that was Pluto in Taurus in the 7th. Her Mercury was in Leo, in its detriment, and square to Saturn in Aries, in its fall. Her Sun conjuncted Venus in Cancer in the 8th, and she had Moon in Pisces in the 4th. How about that for the least airy chart imaginable?

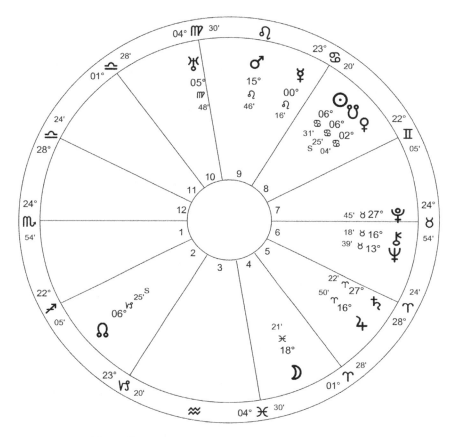

Helen Keller, 27 June 1880, 4.00 pm, Tuscumbia, Alabama
Koch cusps; true Node

Audience: It sounds incredibly un-airy, but who is she?

Darby: She was born in America. When she was a year and a half old, she got ill and lost her sight and her hearing completely. Her parents loved her and kept her at home, even though every-one thought she was retarded and mentally disturbed – you see, no one could communicate with her, or teach her anything. They had no idea how to deal with her, and she grew up as wild as a wild animal until she was about seven. She had a string of nurses or nannies who all left after a short time, until Annie Sullivan came along and persevered until she found a way to communicate with the child. She taught her to speak, to read Braille, and to write. She got a college education – *Magna cum Laude* from Radcliffe College – became a journalist, lecturer, and educator, and became an inspiration to people everywhere.

Her Mercury was in Leo in the 9th, in an out-of-sign square from Saturn in Aries in the 6th and an out-of-sign sextile from Pluto in Taurus in the 7th house. Annie Sullivan was a Taurus. Isn't that neat? But can you imagine the intensity of their relationship? She was all fire, earth, and water – passion, endurance, and feeling. She did not have ideas about herself or the world which informed her actions. Yet she was an ideal for many people whose lives she touched in one way or another: the idea of what she had overcome motivated others so powerfully.

Singleton in air

When any of the outer planets, Uranus, Neptune, or Pluto, are in air signs, then that group of people is mediating the heat of primordial images to the time and space in which they live. For example, those with Neptune in Libra are attuned to imbalances in the air around love, justice, fashions of relating. They long for a life which has grace and harmony and proper relationships, and many of them have found ways to get this for themselves, if not for the rest of the world. Those who have not found relationships which give them a sense of imaginative or spiritual sustenance feel a disquiet that causes them to search for "something more." If this is the only air planet in the chart, it will be a strong and subtle drive, and dominates the chart in some way. It will be the one access to air, to collective ideas and ideals which can give reasons for this person's motives, particularly in relationships.

As I have said before, having one planet in an element gives great energy to that planet. Einstein is one of my favourite examples of this. He had an air singleton, Jupiter in Aquarius in the 9th. He was a Pisces dreamer, and he had Mercury conjunct Saturn in Aries. It is said that one day, when he was shaving, he began to wonder whether he would be able to see his own image in the mirror if he was shaving while travelling at the speed of light. With his Jupiter in Aquarius in the 9th, he roamed the upper reaches of air, using various mathematical methods as vehicles, and one day he found the right vehicle. If I remember correctly, it was multi-dimensional non-Euclidian geometry. That did the trick. He was able to bring down the answer in mathematical language. Others then translated this answer further downward through denser layers of air until the very heart of the atom was touched and the atomic bomb was created and exploded.

Einstein was horrified at how his "discovery" was used, even though he worked on perfecting its use. He imagined energy and then translated his imagination into the highest form of language, the mathematical language, and the densification of that translated image was the bomb. That Jupiter in air dominated his life, and it was the ruler of his Sagittarius Moon in the 6th. He practised mathematics daily. Jupiter, its ruler, was square to Pluto in Taurus in the 11th house. His daily work, for which he had great enthusiasm, was moved by something beyond him – Jupiter in Aquarius in the 9th – and it turned out to have powerful consequences for humanity. Matter was annihilated through his translation of an image into language.

GEMINI

If thoughts are internal weather, then the weather is variable in Gemini's country. With planets in Gemini, thoughts circulate quickly – they "change their minds" frequently. It is a volatile climate. The weather vanes keeps turning, turning, all day long. Thoughts fly in and out through the medium of Gemini. They are local, immediate, often glittering; a grab-bag from which you can snap up a bargain in a minute, but if you wait too long, they may be gone. Gemini is the *marketplace* of ideas. All sorts of ideas are thrown together on the stall. Sometimes they fall into an easily perceived pattern, and sometimes you have to get some distance away before you see the pattern. But in the midst of the marketplace you can usually find something for yourself – something to brighten your day, to give you a message, a clue, to unlock your imprisoned thoughts and change your perspective. There is something for everyone who is willing to pause and look.

Gemini is the mutable air sign. It is the sign of the Twins. Fred Gettings says that Gemini's mutability shows itself as "in constant motion, an untamed wind, blowing in many directions".[25] He says Gemini tends toward Platonic relationships. He obviously does not mean "Platonic" in the Ficinian sense, which would be uniting through something two people find "good, true and beautiful." He means it in the modern sense of "no sex". But that is not the point with Gemini. Whether there is physical sex or not, Gemini looks for conversation in all its relationships.

---

25 Fred Gettings, *The Arkana Dictionary of Astrology*, Penguin, London, 1991.

It looks for dialogue, exchanges of information which touch the depths while flashing across the surface at the same time. It is looking for conversation which will satisfy both twins: the one hidden in the dark, without a day voice, and the one on the surface, giving air space to all sorts of ideas and opinions as it goes about its business.

Audience: Perhaps that is part of the restlessness. Conversation and information need to reach both sides of the Gemini nature.

Darby: Yes, I think so. Those with planets in Gemini are always seeking to nourish both the unspoken and the spoken parts of its nature. If there is a strong water bias in a chart with Gemini planets, then the unspoken part may live in the feelings, and these feelings need words which touch them. If fire planets dominate a chart with Gemini planets, then the inner images need ideas which will articulate that vision, bring it to light. If there are strong earth positions, then they need ideas which will bring a plan to get the earth manifesting something useful and perhaps even beautiful.

Audience: You have been saying that air is the element of idealism, and Gemini is air. Is it an idealistic sign?

Darby: It is not as obvious as it is in Libra or Aquarius, but it certainly operates from ideas rather than feelings, passions, or practical considerations. Gemini's idealism often manifests in curiosity, an instinctive belief that there are interesting people everywhere, and disappointment when people turn out not to be interesting. Geminis can become cynical very young. It is the teenager's defence against disappointment in people, and it is the mark of an idealist afraid of being tricked again. One half of the Gemini is always expecting that something interesting is just about to happen; someone interesting is just outside the door.

There is endless curiosity, and it is this curiosity which keeps it going, even when things look gloomy and dark and the Gemini appears to be most cynical. Even the most upbeat and brightest of Geminis suffer bouts of depression. No matter how much they seem to dislike being bored, people with Gemini planets will put themselves into situations which seem to offer no exciting ideas at all. They starve themselves of stimulating ideas, and so have to turn inward and begin to listen to their inner other. In spite of surface evidence, they are always attracted to the depths in themselves, which they can only reach through sometimes depressing the view of all the upperworld glitter. In this way they can connect to what really interests them.

This leads me to think about the Gemini split. We can see how people with planets in this sign flit back and forth between one region of themselves and another. Everyone has different sides of themselves, but it is highlighted in Gemini people. In this field all sorts of opposites are clearly polarised, and they can seem like "two different people". In old textbooks, you always had the idea that Gemini was two-faced. Mars in Gemini can fight for one idea in the morning and another in the afternoon. Venus in Gemini can love two people from two sides of their own nature. Gemini cannot live on only one kind of air – it needs to fly up and down. It is endlessly passing across the borders of various layers of air – that up-and-down vertical motion that Lyall was talking about. Mythologically, it is the Twins story that explains this.

Audience: When I was a child and I got into trouble, I used to say, "It wasn't me, it was the other one." When my mother asked me, "What other one?" I would say, "*That* other one." I couldn't explain it further. Later I realised I was looking for this "other one" in all the people I met.

Darby: Yes, there is always this notion of twinness. Gemini circulates ideas by picking them up here and putting them down there, and it can seem random, undirected. But if you remember the twin, then the restless seeking is not so unreasonable. The other is in the dark, the unreachable, and Gemini looks for a reflection of it in other people. It speaks to other people so that the twin might hear. It speaks so that it can reach the hidden part of itself, and it listens so that it might hear the voice of this lost twin. This is perhaps why people with strong Gemini planets can be impatient in conversation. Without knowing, it is sometimes using another person to have a conversation with its underground twin. And so it moves from subject to subject, trying to catch a word or phrase that might settle inside. It is moved by the idea that somewhere there will be a connection – a magical word will be spoken – and the sense of separation will end. It seeks a trace of its twin in everyone: "When I find you, there will be perfection."

Audience: But it must not be trapped. No matter how good the conversation, no matter how satisfying, it must be able to get away.

Darby: Yes. There is the imperative here that ideas must be circulated, must keep moving around. There can be moments of complete satisfaction: reading a book which gives an idea that touches both inner and outer self; having a conversation with someone that touches the heights and the depths. But people with Gemini planets have to keep moving their attention because this is mutable air, and it is in charge of tracking, touching, expressing ideas, and translating them according to whatever language the local inhabitants speak.

Audience: I have several planets in Scorpio, and my father has several planets in Gemini. Just when we begin really talking about something, he gets up and ends the conversation. I wonder if he begins to feel trapped by my intensity. I know that the astronomical Mercury orbits the Sun with one side of itself always facing the Sun. So one side of Mercury is always really hot in the light, and the other side is dark and cold. Always the same side faces the Sun. It's as if he turns the cold side to me just when I begin to feel the heat in what we are discussing.

Audience: Yes, we feel trapped by too much intensity. We seek the depths, but then, when we get there, we need to move upwards again, into the bright air. We need to feel free to keep moving from one perspective to another. We have "messages" to pass on from one place to another.

Darby: Hermes is the one Olympian god who can move between high Olympus and deep underworld Hades, from the mesosphere to the lowest part of the troposphere, the dank air of underground caverns below the surface. With your planets in Gemini, you may never feel secure for long, or sure in your ideas about things for long. But there is always something to be learned, another conversation, with yourself or someone else, which can come at any moment to change your perspective. In a moment you can go from the most mundane to the most sublime, and the conversation goes on as long as you have breath in your body. Planets in Gemini need to keep moving. The individuation process for a Gemini has to do with recognising and acknowledging their own light, bright side and their own dark, lonely side. It has to do with recognizing that no idea of reality will ever keep you safe because you cannot hold ideas fast. They change and slip away before you know it. And it has to do with being willing to be one thing one day, and another the next – one thing to one person, and another to someone else – to see things one way today and another way tomorrow, next week, or next year.

Audience: Somebody once said to me that when Gemini learns to get into better communication with itself, it loses some of its communication skills with others. Can that be true?

Darby: I think it can be. When Gemini sits alone and has no one to talk to, it talks to itself. If it starts nourishing itself with good ideas, and begins to enjoy its conversation with these ideas, it can lose some of its hunger for constant, unnourishing conversations with others. It may lose some of its facile conversational skills as a result. Yet Gemini is safer in the world when it has time for conversations with itself; when it has lain by the tree that guards the entrance to the underworld and spoken with its twin hidden below. It is less restless, less hungry, less frantic. It enjoys life most when it can be in touch with the inner *and* the outer conversation.

Audience: I have been thinking about Castor and Pollux, the stars in the constellation of Gemini.

Darby: Yes! Their story is a beautiful metaphor for what I was trying to say before. Castor and Pollux are two brothers, very close. One day in battle, Castor is mortally wounded. Pollux – Polydeuces is his Greek name – begs Zeus for the life of his brother. He offers his own life in exchange. Zeus grants his wish, but even he cannot transgress nature; Castor is already in the underworld, and cannot be redeemed except with another life. Castor agrees to spend half the year in the underworld and half the year in the upper world, so that his brother does not have to be in perpetual darkness while he is in the light. They will never meet again, but they will share one life, one fate. And so they live like that, each one in the light half the time and in the dark the other half. When they eventually die, they are made into a constellation, presumably so they can now be together. This brings me back to the notion of individuation. With Gemini, it is not so much about healing the split as recognising the split and bearing it, because it has its place in the scheme of things. Planets in Gemini seek out those who will reveal the split. And Geminis often reveal the hidden, split-off parts of other people, whether they mean to or not, bearing information from the dark side to the light.

Audience: This reminds me of Gemini's mimicry. I am thinking of the court jester who makes a joke out of the king's grandiosity, imitating all his big gestures and words. I am Aquarian, and I notice that Gemini can show me how split, how unconscious I am of big parts of myself. Because one of the twins is in the underworld and they cannot get at it, there is something in their tendency to unconsciously imitate that makes me see hidden parts of myself. When I see a Gemini coming along, I think, "Oops, here we go again!" I know I am going to be tricked into seeing something I don't consciously accept in myself or the world. It is often the other side of my high-minded principles.

Audience: For me, it's the opposite. They make me see that I do have ideas, because they bring out my capacity to articulate them. They can show me my own unconscious idealism. That is good for me, because I have so much water and earth.

Darby: People with a strong Gemini emphasis who have learned to listen, have found the key to enjoyment of life. Otherwise they are caught in their own untidy aviary. But going back to what you said, Gemini often learns by imitation. As it travels up and down through the layers of air, one of its ways of gathering data is by imitating the source of the data. Then it passes on the data, by imitating the receiver. It's a way of translating.

Audience: I once had a friend whom I constantly accused of inconsistency. By the end of our relationship I had been shown the amazing amount of inconsistencies in my own position. If you decide to fling accusations at a Gemini, you'd better be prepared to have the inconsistencies in your own ideas about life flung back at you.

Mercury

Mercury, as archetype, has such a wide range of ancestral images. The field of Mercury is filled with some of the most interesting figures in all of mythology. We have Hermes – not only the Greek god, who Jung said was originally a wind god, but also the original god of crossroads, market places, trade, and exchange. Then there is thrice-great Hermes Trismegistus, and all his alchemical associations. In Egypt we have Thoth in his role as regent of Osiris, bringing agriculture, writing, mathematics, music, and culture to the kingdom. As assistant to Osiris, he is in the underworld, where it is his task to weigh individual souls against the feather of truth before they are judged worthy to go into the hereafter. And that brings us to Hermes the psychopomp, able to travel between the highest and the lowest realms of the earth, from Olympus to Hades and back. And finally, in our extremely brief survey, we must never forget the great Trickster archetype, perhaps the oldest representative of all, who seems to be embedded in every culture's mythology, no matter how isolated or remote. It seems we discovered very early that no matter how you figure things out, no matter how you sew them up, there is always something subtle and mysterious about reality – or something inherently elusive in the gap between external reality and our perceptions of it – and the more seriously you take yourself, your own notions, things, or people, the more likely you are to be tricked.

And all of this is somehow contained in the field of our little planet Mercury, never more than 28° from the Sun and "neutral" in colour and character, only being defined by its sign, house, and aspects. The sign, house, and aspects of Mercury will tell you what sort of information this messenger is gathering, where and how it is being gathered, and where the Sun and other planets must go to pick it up. When the Sun is in Gemini, Mercury will be in either Taurus, Gemini, or Cancer, because of its physical proximity to the Sun. So you might say that there are three types of Gemini. There are those who are attracted to information because it might improve or enhance their situation at any time. This Mercury seems closest to Hermes Trismegistus with his magical and alchemical associations. Then there are those who gather and use information because it fits the needs of their information-bearing destiny, and this Mercury plays with and is played with most by the great Trickster archetype. It knows how to find treasure by glancing sideways at things. And there are those who seek and absorb information which feeds their need for security on whichever level their Moon demands. Of course this Mercury is still gathering information for the Sun's use, but it must listen to the Moon's needs on its way. Doesn't this sound like the Mercury of Thoth's lineage? They each partake of Hermes as psychopomp in their own way. Each Mercury travels vertically, through the layers of air, as high and as low as the person's spirit will entertain.

Mercury in Taurus is said to be slow to absorb information, and to resist learning anything that does not aesthetically please them. This can be a frustrating Mercury for Gemini, whose spiritual character requires it to be in touch with every aspect of its environment, and yet it can find comfort in information where others might find disturbance. When Mercury and the Sun are together in Gemini, there is always this sense of information being gathered which perfectly suits and fits exactly the direction that the Sun is heading. It picks up and drops whole packets of information if they no longer suit its direction. And the Gemini with Mercury in Cancer holds information close, not liking to let it go, because it may come in handy for one's personal use one day or another. But remember, Gemini is always very immediate, no matter what the Mercury position. They need to respond to what is in front of them, and to forget what or who was in front of them yesterday or last week, if it no longer serves their purpose. Mercury in Taurus or Cancer finds places to store old information, but generally Mercury in Gemini knows it will come across what it needs when it needs it.

Mercury is ruler of Gemini and Virgo. It is in detriment in Sagittarius and Pisces. It is exalted in Aquarius, and in Leo it falls. This tells us that it is constrained by religious, philosophical, or even emotional or empathetic ties and considerations. It needs to gather information from all sorts of *different* market places if it is to be truly helpful to the Sun. It is best when it can go outside the walls of the town and take in even contradictory information, and listen to news that would be considered strange in its local environment. It is hampered when it is proud, easily offended, or seeks credit for itself.

It is generally said that any aspect to Mercury is better than no aspects to it. It seems, according to our tradition, to need to be in contact with other planets. It is considered neither feminine nor masculine, but neutral, and any planet aspecting it gives it a "colour". The more aspects it has, the more territory it can explore and gather information from to offer its king, the Sun. Aspects to the Moon keep it close to home, in the sense that it receives and gives out information that brings the past up to date and is connected to currents of feeling that inform its environment. Aspects to Venus sweeten the tongue or the pen and make communication a joy. Aspects to Mars sharpen it and bring it a "fools rush in" approach to information and communication, and they also add a heroic note to its method of gathering and giving data. Aspects to Jupiter widen its territory to an impressive degree – sometimes sacrificing the usefulness of its information to the adventure of finding it. Saturn steadies it and draws it repeatedly into the same territory, deepening and limiting its range. Uranus brings it into contact with information that is barely translatable, and it makes ordinary information seem strange and partial. Neptune brings it messages from regions that can only be expressed through metaphorical language; otherwise it comes across as tricky, confusing, or deceptive. Pluto drives it into dangerous neighbourhoods of thought that are considered "taboo" or perilous because they somehow threaten the kingdom and even its safety. And Chiron connects it to information that reveals the gap between who we are and who we could be "if things had been different".

Do you know about the gift of prophecy given to Hermes by Apollo? On that first day of his life, when he was getting up to so much mischief, he discovered Apollo's oracle at Delphi, and he ran to his brother and said, "I want one of those." Apollo couldn't give him an oracle of such power and depth, but he was so charmed by his young brother that he gave him one more suited to his nature. And this is how it works: ask the god a question, and then go into the busy market-place. The very first word or sentence you hear will be the answer to your question.

Audience: We still use a version of that. I'm sure lots of people have, at one time or another, pondered a question or a problem that seemed unanswerable. And then, while you are reading a book, suddenly a sentence leaps out at you. Or you even go to your bookshelf and randomly open a book to see if the answer will be there.

Audience: My grandmother used to do that with her Bible. My sister uses the *I Ching* like some people use a therapist or, as she says, a wise grandfather.

Audience: How does the depth and range of Mercury's mythological ancestry fit the small neutral Mercury of our astrology?

Darby: I would ask you all to think about that whenever you are looking at Mercury in your own or someone else's chart. And I promise I will give a seminar on Mercury one day soon. For now, bear in mind that there is a good chance that absolutely everything we see is perceived according to how we see, and not according to how it is in some objective realm. Our ideas "create" our reality in this sense. Some of these "ideas" are collective and inherent to the survival nature of our species. They are environmentally determined. Some are culturally determined and some are personally determined by our psychological background. Understanding this deeply is perhaps the first step to freedom, but it is a very hard step to take because we have to see how very determined we are, to begin to find freedom.

Audience: What about an unaspected Mercury?

Darby: Liz once said that an unaspected planet is like a relative living in some part of your house which you seldom visit. The people I have known with Mercury unaspected are very active mentally, gathering all sorts of information, full of ideas, thoughts, and opinions. But it is somehow disconnected from the mainstream of their life. They may enjoy knowledge and information, but it does not feed into the mainstream of their lives. It seems as though, in the larger scheme of things, an integrated system of ideas is not deemed necessary for the development of their natures and their function in the world.

Planets in Gemini

With planets in Gemini, everything depends on Mercury. Of course, this notion of the ruler always being behind the planet is true of every sign, but perhaps it is more obvious with Gemini.

A **Sun in Gemini** child once told me, "I have a flock of birds inside me. They are all different colours, and when something is exciting, then my birds start singing. I love it when they sing, and I love listening to them. And I try to tell everyone the songs." When the Sun is in Gemini, millions of people are born who carry a flock of birds in their heart. At different times in their lives, different birds are fed by thoughts circulating in the air, and then these birds fly out to pass their information on to others. When they are aware of the thoughts that are feeding them and a notion of what information they are to circulate, they feel as though they are in touch with their destiny. If their Sun is strongly aspected, then they often feel as though the information they gather is to be conveyed to others. Mercury in their chart will tell us, by sign, house, and aspect, how that information will be conveyed. The best thing you can do for Gemini Sun children is to give them an environment where the information flows around them. You have to watch them, though, because the rate of information can be disturbing if it is too slow or too fast, too dark or too light. They need to know as many sides of the stories as they can handle – for if they get only the dark side, they will be burdened and their wings will not unfurl properly. On the other hand, if there is only "light entertainment" around, light conversation, then they will not develop enough *gravitas* to feel safe.

Audience: My Gemini daughter was always demanding that I tell her the part of the story that was not in the book. I would finish a story at night and she would say, "But *why* didn't Cinderella just tell her father how mean they all were to her? Why didn't she have the mice take a note to the prince and explain everything? Why...?" So many why's.

Darby: A Gemini client once told me that curiosity was the only thing that kept her going in the darkest times of her life. She just couldn't close the door on life because something really interesting might happen just the minute after she had. **Moon in Gemini** also has a curiosity that keeps it going. It gathers emotional information from two very different sides of its female ancestry and it longs for a life which will satisfy both sides. When people with this Moon naively trust other people, they usually gets tricked after a time. When they retreat into cynicism, they trick themselves into a lonely corner. Every Gemini Moon goes through periodic attempts at being cynical and worldly. They grab modern ideas in an emotional net and try to settle themselves with ideas of what life is really about. Satisfying conversations are their emotional nourishment. Good conversation satisfies emotional needs. Aspects to the Moon tell us which realms nurture and disturb their capacity for emotional sustenance. For instance, if it is trine Neptune in Libra, it is fed by any stories that express its generation's notion of good relationship. If it is square Neptune in Virgo, it is fed by that generation's notion of sensible living, though the reception can get scrambled.

Audience: I'm not sure what you mean there, but my older sister has Moon in Gemini square to Neptune in Virgo. She is pretty chaotic in her communication. When I was away at college, she used to write to me, and several times she put a letter to someone else in the envelope addressed to me and the letter to me in the one she was sending to her pen-friend in Hong Kong. It was really weird. She was very regular in her writing – our mother had died when we were young, and she was very conscientious in writing to me – but she kept confusing these letters. Also, she was always sending me articles about what I should be eating, and sometimes they contradicted each other.

Darby: Where is her Mercury?

Audience: She has Sun and Mercury in Cancer, sextile Neptune.

Darby: Hence the good motherly intentions, but the confusion in mothering her sister.

Audience: You said a Gemini Sun has a flock of birds in its heart. Well, I have **Mercury in Gemini**, and I think I have flocks of birds in my head. I'm a Cancerian – it is probably easier with a Taurus, or even a Gemini Sun, but I find I am all over the place with my ideas and my feelings.

Darby: Yes, I have seen that in Cancerian friends who have planets in Gemini. Birds who live in and around seas and lakes and rivers are gliding and feeding on particular kinds of watery currents of air. I imagine you are fine if you are left to move in and out of thoughts and feelings. It must be very difficult when others want you to be solid and stable and reliable according to their earthy standards of usefulness, or according to their imaginative fiery images of your "potential".

Audience: I have just understood something about my mother's **Venus in Gemini**. It is her only air planet. She is almost all earth and water, one planet in fire, and this Venus in Gemini. Our father died years ago, and now she goes along day after day, working hard and being serious and good, going to church and taking care of everyone. Then, suddenly, she brings a rogue into the house. I don't know where she finds them! They arrive from Australia, New Zealand, Canada: "The son of Molly, you know your father's great aunt's godchild; you remember..." They stay for weeks and drink endless bottles of whiskey, and she stays up until all hours laughing and talking and God knows what else. I'm sure she gives them money. We all disapprove madly. Then they leave, and she becomes "herself" again.

Darby: Are you afraid she will make over her will to one of them one day?

Audience: My brother once said that, in jest, but we wondered. I suddenly think it is rather mean of us to mind that she "falls in love" with these young men we think of as "tricksters". She is also quietly writing a book, which none of us ever sees. Again, it

makes the rest of us very nervous. I guess it is this singleton quality that makes everything to do with it so nerve-wracking.

Darby: Venus in Gemini is in love with the conversation, up and
down the air waves, tasting all the different notions. Keep the stories coming and Venus in Gemini will keeps listening; listen and
it will tell you such stories. Other things in the chart will indicate
its capacity for fidelity to an intimate lifetime conversation, but
even when constant, it cannot be shut in. It needs to fly about a
bit, if even in the most innocent ways. Mercury will tell us what
sort of interchange is most satisfying for any Venus in Gemini.

Audience: I think that is what worries us, or me, actually. She
has Mercury conjunct Pluto in the 7th house in Cancer, and she
is a wonderful storyteller herself. She remembers all the details
of peoples' stories, and when she tells you what is going on with
this neighbour or that cousin, you wonder how she finds out all
those things. They are always compelling and scandalous. What
on earth is she writing about *us* in her book, and will it be found
after she is gone and shock us about each other? There is that
quality about her, a sense that, for all the morality and upright
citizenship, there is this Venus in Gemini grinning somewhere.

Audience: My mother has Venus in Gemini, conjunct Jupiter in
the 5th house. She is eighty-five and the most delightful and irritating charmer you ever met.

Darby: And I wonder what she says about her children? I know
at least three of you in this room have **Mars in Gemini** – so I'll
have to be careful here, as saying anything about it will get your
minds firing at me.

Audience: We're fast on the draw – so watch out!

Darby: Yes, and as you move forward into one point of view you constellate the other view right before your eyes, either in your own head or through encounters with others. Two swords at the same time, always ready for a duel, defending the territory with its fast tongue and opposing-thumbs thinking. It becomes heroic by pursuing and defending ideas and ideals that are not generally accepted or known.

Jupiter in Gemini is traditionally its place of detriment. The domain of Gemini is supposedly too busy and too distractible for the high aims of Jupiter. However, people with Jupiter here do enjoy gathering all sorts of information, which they delight in handing around to others. There is certainly a mental restlessness that can distract themselves and others from getting down to the practicalities of work, but those who can work give us things that certainly excite our minds. Alexander Graham Bell had Jupiter in Gemini on the cusp of the 3rd house (Placidus). He was a 12th house Pisces Sun – I wonder if he invented the telephone to bring himself out of a feeling of loneliness and isolation?

Audience: He did, actually. He was somewhat deaf, and he was trying to make a sort of hearing aid.

Darby: And then, Fred West, the horrific contemporary London serial killer, also had Jupiter in Gemini, with a Libra Sun in the 12th. Venus and Mercury were in Scorpio, but not conjunct. The kind of information he was interested in does not bear thinking about. You can always learn something unusual from Jupiter in Gemini – though you may not always want the information.

Serial killers apart, some of the most interesting people around have Jupiter in Gemini, as you would expect. You can't get information in the order you necessarily want from them, but you never go away empty-minded. Their joy is in making connections – receiving and passing on information that brightens our days and nights. Sorting and sifting the information for practical use is the function of other placements.

Audience: I have two friends with Jupiter in Gemini, one as a singleton in air, and the other mixed up with other planets in air. One of the things I have noticed with both of them is that you rarely get a direct answer to a question – it's a matter of, "Do you have this information I want/need?" And the answer is something like, "Let me show you what I do have here."

Audience: The two people I know with that position are what I call cynical idealists. They both believe that their ideals can be realised, but they are often disappointed. But they turn away from their disappointment as quickly as they can and get involved with something else near at hand.

Audience: And so, then, is **Saturn in Gemini** the true cynic?

Darby: Not necessarily, but there is a note of mistrust when they encounter ideas that others believe in strongly. If someone takes for granted that this or that is "true", then Saturn in Gemini gets nervous, suspicious, careful. There is also something about the rules of conversation. There is a necessity to learn the rules of what can and cannot be said in different times and places. When a person with this Saturn position ignores these unspoken laws, they pay the price of being feared, disliked, misunderstood, misquoted, misread. They learn the rules by coming up against walls when they ignore them. They then have to be careful not to be enslaved by the local rules, because that, too, harms their capacity to think for themselves. You must learn the rules and then be willing to pay the price for what you do with the knowledge. This is always true with Saturn aspects. Learn the rules and then decide what course to take, but know and accept the price. With

Saturn in Gemini, learn the rules of your time and place, and then decide how far to go in saying, or not saying, what you think.

The longer or harder it is to learn something, the better, according to the Saturn in Gemini rule book. And you know the old rhyme, "Sticks and stones can break my bones but words can never hurt me." Not so for Saturn in Gemini. Other placements may demand that you break out of traditional ways of thinking, but this position demands that you learn to express yourself "properly", according to the ideas of your environment. Of course, one has to learn that through experience – this is Saturn's way. With Saturn in Gemini, you develop discrimination about what ideas you will and won't entertain. But you have to pay attention. If you cut off too much information, you get circulation problems, in your mind if not your body. Saturn in Gemini is a demand to learn continually how to deal with information, not to simply build walls against it. One's ideas need to be continually updated, or they get stale. Ideas are updated through allowing circulation to flow from the outer reaches of one's time and place – the realm of what we are calling the archetypal ideas – to the layers of air in which local gossip circulates, then back up again.

I have a friend whose chart illustrates to me something central about Saturn in Gemini. He has Sun conjunct Saturn in Gemini, late degrees, and Mercury conjunct Uranus in Gemini, early degrees. He is a doctor and holds the secrets of many people in his community – all these planets are in the 8th house. There is something careful and guarded about him, and yet he will suddenly come out with something intensely personal, or outrageous, or shocking. He is both intensely moral and amoral at the same time – he recognises that the laws of society and the laws of "the universe" are often at odds, or seem to be, and so, although he obeys the laws of his community, stated as well as unstated, he will persist in breaking through convention, shocking, or surprising perhaps, the butcher, the baker and the candle-stick maker as he goes along. He is a well-respected, eccentric member of his community. He knows the most extraordinary things, but he is totally uninterested in what is commonly held to be interesting information. He is very much a loner, and also fascinated by people and their peculiarities and their conversations.

Audience: Many people living now have it conjunct Uranus – those born in the early 1940's. And then there is the generation born in the early 1970's who have it, too, many trine Uranus in Libra.

Audience: Billy Connelly has **Uranus conjunct Saturn in Gemini**, and Saturn is conjunct the Moon. They are all in opposition to Mercury in late Scorpio, which is conjunct the Sun and Venus in Sagittarius, early degrees. He has the most extraordinary way of expressing himself – he's both a vulgar and deeply moral comedian-teacher.

Darby: When Uranus is conjunct Saturn in Gemini, the traditions have to be broken if the emerging patterns of thought are to break through. Through Uranus, ideas from other cultures, times, systems begin to slip through the outer layers of air around communities. Cultural boundaries really begin to wobble. All sorts of juxtapositions of ideas break through various layers of thought, and those with Uranus in Gemini pick them up in bunches. This was happening in 1942. Odd bunches of ideas got circulated by the disturbed atmosphere of war, and yet, at the same time, there was heavy censorship on information – Uranus and Saturn together. Codes and code-breakers battled it out for information riding the air waves. The people born during Saturn-Uranus times feel the weight of the responsibility to say things correctly, and yet to break through traditional thought systems.

Audience: There's a kind of "Learn the rules, then break them."

Darby: Or break them and then learn them and then break them again. **Uranus in Gemini** experiments all the time, with words, with ideas, with half formed notions. It indicates a group of people who found a new way to play with each other, and are still doing it. Most of the people at Woodstock in 1969 had Uranus in Gemini. A lot of the people who gave us those songs were from the Uranus in Taurus group, but we were the ones who made them our stories. Neither Neptune or Pluto will be in Gemini during our lives, nor our children's, nor their children's children, as far as we know. Of course, genetic engineering might extend everyone's life so much that this won't be true. But most of us remember some of the people from the early part of the century who had **Pluto in Gemini**. These were our grandparents and their generation. Most of the ones I knew were "sharp as a tack" with their tongues in their old age, even when they were half asleep.

Audience: And what about **Chiron in Gemini**?

Darby: You tell me.

Audience: I have it, and I sometimes feel that words hurt, ideas burn, thoughts bleed. A poem or a random phrase can cut me like a knife. I'll never feel anything but stupid, but your notion of "Mind the Gap" with Chiron speaks directly to me. Through the gap I feel things in words that transport me from heaven to hell and back.

Darby: I'm not sure I could add anything that would come near what you have just said here. Let's allow this Chiron in Gemini to have the last word.

Audience: And Gemini rising? The ones I know are all very restless.

Gemini rising

Darby: If the Ascendant generally says something about the goal of personality development, then Gemini rising aspires toward freedom of speech and movement. It indicates a natural urge to get free of anything that keeps them fearful or constrained or unable to be in touch with all sorts of things in their environment. They need to be able to whiz around, knowing the streets and the places where people gather, and having friendly relationships with the locals. Mercury, ruler of the Ascendant, will tell you what they think of as freedom, where they seek it, and, perhaps how.

Gemini rising always has a youthful approach to life, no matter how old the person may be. It describes someone who seems to have lots of open windows in their approach to life. They are generally very aware of their environment, wherever they happen to be. They notice things all the time. You cannot spend time with a Gemini rising person without getting to notice things around you. Go for a walk with Gemini rising and you will talk to people, smell flowers, stop and look at trees and houses, stop in the middle of the pavement or street, carry on several conversations at the same time. Even the most introverted people with this Ascendant seem to become extraverted in a new environment. Whenever they go anywhere, they seem to open all their windows, to see what is going on or flying by. Curiosity is a powerful drive in this person's life. Friends with this Ascendant have told me it is hard to say no to invitations, because "you never know what might happen".

Planets in the 3rd house

Planets in the 3rd house do not carry the marketplace within them – it is more that they are drawn to it, again and again, wherever they can find it in their daily lives. Their early relationships with siblings or cousins or neighbours – all those 3rd house things – develop in them a natural curiosity about their neighbourhood, their local environment. If they have no siblings, no close cousins, then it is their sense of isolation which draws them to explore and gather as much information as they can about the world around them. They seem to need to find the world a friendly place.

People with planets in the 3rd house are often information junkies, but as I say that, I hear my 3rd house friends protesting. They are fascinated by the kinds of information that suit the development of their planets. If they have several planets in air as well, then they will be drawn to information that will feed their minds and their intellectual development. If they are not airy, then the information will be to support their feelings, or their work, or the images that drive them.

I know several people with **Pluto in the 3rd** in Leo. They are all hungry for information that might offer transformation of their sense of themselves, and they are also frightened of such information or, at the least, wary of it. **Saturn in the 3rd** demands ongoing mental development and a great sensitivity to feeling a fool. They grow up in environments where information is limited to certain kinds of knowledge, and later they often work to overcome the experience of that limitation. They usually only accept information from those they respect, or in less happy cases, those they fear. **Venus in the 3rd** will naturally love information, but not necessarily their siblings, oddly enough. They might "adopt" friends as brothers and sisters, because the need is to love their kin, so they make siblings of their friends. Often this is the case when the outer planets are involved. Look at the planet, its nature and sign and aspects, to see the sorts of information, the sorts of neighbourhood, bookshops, and libraries these people hang around in.

Audience: I have Venus in Sagittarius in the 3rd opposite Uranus, and I wanted so much to love my older sister. But she bullied me, and I finally gave up. I am thinking now that, with Venus there, I must have carried an image of her in my mind, from my mother, and it took me years to realise that she wasn't at all like that to me. She was, in fact, the opposite. I am certain she was jealous of me, and I am now seeing that I was jealous of her too. But I have not got over her bullying, and I stay away from her, even though she would now be friends.

Audience: I have Mars conjunct **Neptune in the 3rd** house, and one brother is an alcoholic and the other a priest!

Darby: The important thing with planets in the 3rd is to see how you make connections with other people, and how your sibling situation affected this. Planets in the 3rd can make the whole world a local habitation. People with placements here are seeking to heal an early isolation from siblings, cousins, neighbours. I know a few world travelers with Sun and other personal planets in the 3rd, and wherever they go, however long they spend there, they end up knowing the place as if it was their own neighbourhood. And that neighbourhood reflects their early relationship to their childhood locales, more often than not. They are great letter-writers, too, when they are not too distracted by what is going on around them, or too self-conscious because of early inhibitions. I always ask clients with 3rd house planets, "Have you written a book?" So often, those who haven't laugh or sigh and say, "I have been working on one." This is the house where we work out our ideas from all the conversations we hear around us. Planets in this house lead people to always "figure things out".

Planets in Gemini are about the conversation that is going on in their heads, and how to get it going with others in a satisfying way. Planets in the 3rd always seem to be practising how to express themselves and their ideas, and they are drawn to environments which will give them the chance to do this in words and gestures – in all sorts of ways. Whether you have air planets or not, your planets in the 3rd house take you to places where you seek to make a world in which you can move and speak freely, where the world becomes your own neighbourhood.

LIBRA

The air space of Libra is filled with birds that glide and swoop and sail with dancing sky-grace that can lift your heart out of the mire of its terrestrial cares. Or it can be a place to which you escape in order to rationalise your bad behaviour in personal and social relationships. It is the air space where clouds make slowly changing pictures in the sky, which you can watch all day as you walk through the autumn beauty. With planets in Libra, thoughts have a direction – they are heading someplace. They are moving toward an ideal that will bring them closer to equilibrium. They are moving towards their idea of a more beautiful world.

With Libra planets, everything is done deliberately – nothing is random, everything is considered. Even when it looks spontaneous, there is an underlying reason, an underlying order. Whatever images inform these people's lives, the images are translated into reasons and then followed as law. If they have strong fiery planets, and are significantly Libran, they will believe that others will know that they are doing this or that for good and appropriate reasons. When they come up against incomprehension in others, they are moved by their inner law to explain their reasons as carefully as possible. If their Mercury is "good", then they will be able to give you "good" reasons. If not, the reasons they give might not match their intention. When they act, their intention is very clear; everything is done so that what is chaotic or disruptive or superfluous or misguided, too much or too little, will be reorganised, in such a way that those with whom they identify will feel more at ease, and be able to live a more beautiful life. When Libra planets are crossed by other planets, this natural inclination to harmony gets thrown off course, and the ensuing disruptions are disturbing indeed.

Fred Gettings says that Libra is "establishing unity through discovering harmonies, shared experiences, and communal responsibilities." He says that Libra is about the bonds of sex and business partnerships. He is speaking about the notion of contracts, which we associate with the 7th house. It is also true that planets in Libra move toward or away from other people, according to some sort of inner, and often unstated, contract they have made with themselves about the other person. Others are either potential partners of some sort, or they are not. If those with a strong Libran emphasis strive to be considerate in most circumstances, this consideration is an atmosphere which is cultivated for a specific idea – the idea that attractive environments and behaviour foster interactions between people which lead to a better life. This "better life" is, of course, conceived according to the Venus standards of the Libran person. You can see that this can lead to all sorts of misunderstandings for the one with planets in Libra and the one being drawn into their spell. But it can also give rest to someone struggling wearily with the harshness of their emotional or physical life, a respite from all the strife, and a real place of recuperation. Those who cannot find solace in grace and charm are indeed made weary by their own ideas of life.

Audience: I am suspicious of what you are calling grace and charm. I think it is manipulation.

Darby: Yes, that is common today, and I notice it especially here in England; much less so in France or Italy. A very charming person has great seductive power, and many of us fear being seduced. We also *know* that there is some intention behind the charm – and we fear being taken in. Don't you think it is interesting that the flower used by Hades to seduce Demeter's daughter into becoming his Persephone is often said to be the narcissus? Getting seduced by another's charm does often lead to all sorts of experiences one later might regret, in one way or another. But it may also lead to experiences that make up a rich part of the tapestry of one's life. Plotinus said, in the 3rd century, that Soul puts lures in things. These are the things, people, and circumstances which give our lives food for the development of our soul here in time and eternity. You might say that planets in Libra, Venus-ruled, send one's soul hunting treasure in other people. They give a charm that conveys the message, "Let's dance." Because someone is charming, we cannot assume they are ethical. Not every graceful person is living to the highest ideas of the Good, the True and the Beautiful. But isn't it sometimes better to accept the grace and beauty on offer, and then learn discrimination, rather than rejecting everything that comes in on a sweet breeze? Plato thought we loved beauty because it was another aspect of the Good and the True – of God.

When I was young, I had a friend who said he thought that physically beautiful people were more highly evolved than ugly people. I was completely outraged and shocked that a friend of mine could even entertain such a thought. He had Moon conjunct Jupiter and Neptune in Libra, and Sun in Pisces with Cancer rising. We discussed it years later and he laughed, saying it was an idea he was experimenting with. He had been reading Plato and applying it in all sorts of ways. But do you notice how extraordinarily beautiful people set off all sorts of reactions in other people? Everything from hatred and envy to desire and longing – and sometimes it is hard to sort out one's feelings. To be given great physical beauty is a strange gift of the gods, because it will definitely fade and you will have to watch it go day by day. It must be quite a task to keep your soul engaged with the eternal, when time is working so powerfully right in your face. But I would say, if you are wary of charm and grace, be wary of your own fear of it. Hunt and find your own unconscious pull towards being seduced, so that, in recognising it, you may be able to navigate the impulses towards it and ride the whirlwind, rather than being simply lifted up off the ground and then dropped unconscious on the hard ground.

Audience: It's so exciting taking off into the air, and so hard hitting the ground. It's not fair!

Darby: And then one has to go back up into the air to get a larger view of what happened. Remember, there are layers of air – mostly the molecules interact on their own level, but there are movements of vertical air too. When you have experiences that just don't fit your map, you may have to go up a level of air to see it all from a wider perspective. And if you naturally live in those upper atmospheres where ideas of reality are more real than what is happening around you, then you may have to come down a layer or two, now and again. Simply put, life does not generally allow us to hold onto the same perspective through its course. If we are very idealistic about life, our experiences will bring us down to street-level thinking at times. If we see life only from a personal level, then life will seek to pull us up to a wider perspective. With planets in Libra, one is finding a balance between the upper and lower reaches of air. Get too abstract in your ideas about life, and you'll get dragged into your emotions and hard material realities. Get too involved in local gossip and in current fashions of any kind, and you'll get entangled in social nonsense and nightmares.

I had a beloved friend who died at the age of eighty-four, some years ago. She was a painter, a Sagittarian with Moon in Libra in the 12th and Mars in Libra on the Ascendant. She told me that one of the only things she liked about old age was that she could let herself be completely charmed by beauty in any sort of person. She no longer had to be "wary of charm" because she was beyond seduction. Actually, that wasn't quite true, now that

I think of it. Each stage of life presents different lures, I guess. She was remembering the physical seductions – in her old age the seductions were more subtle, still causing her trouble, but keeping her fully engaged with life and other people, still engaged in the conversations that seek understanding and wisdom, very nearly to the end of her life.

Ethical behaviour and fair play are underlying themes in any action that involves Libran planets. All interactions are measured internally against some idea of what is right and just. This ideal of justice probably has a natural base, an organic base in the "laws of the universe". It certainly does in nature as we know it on this planet, which is so delicately balanced for life to be sustained here. These ideas are partially universal, partaking of laws that are inherent in the very nature of life, and partially local to both time and space. Libran planets are informed by fashions in behaviour, perhaps more than any other of the air signs. Through their relationships and the interactions they have during their lifetimes, they are made aware of the underlying laws that govern the movements between things. Empedocles said that everything was an interaction between Love and Strife, and for those with planets in Libra, love and strife are constant themes. There is a kind of aesthetic imperative to which they are attached, and they seem to have to keep adjusting their position in relationships to keep this imperative in sight. They seem to be seeking peace at all costs, but they often go about it in a way that creates discord.

Whether their actions are ethical in the highest sense depends on how they nourish their minds and thoughts. Ideas of justice and fair play can be distorted by local interference – air signs are very sensitive to local winds. Every culture and every class has its own politically correct ideas, and though some of the larger ones last for centuries, others come and go within a lifetime.

Audience: You mentioned fashion in regard to Libran planets. Is that what you mean by "local" ideas of what is right and good?

Darby: Yes. Libran planets pick up the fashions of the times or, we might say, they reveal them. They fashion themselves in accordance with the values around them to a greater or lesser extent. Someone with a strong emphasis in Libra will dress and speak according to the fashion of the people they are cultivating. Of course they can have planets crossing the ones in Libra, and then you get mixed messages. I am always aware of the group with Uranus in Cancer, because they are close to my group in age. If there are planets in Libra squaring Uranus, then you get conflict between the natural Libran instinct to act with grace and clarity and the Uranian urge to experiment with emotional expression in such a way that harmony is disturbed. We shall speak of the groups with Uranus in Libra, Neptune in Libra, and Pluto in Libra later on. It's interesting that all the outer planets move through Libra during the second half of this century – in fact, since the mid-1940's. The images of the atom bombs that went off in the 1940's must have swept ideas through the collective mind and psyche that had a profound influence on many levels of thought. So many people horrified by the destruction must have yearned for a peaceful world.

One more thing about fashions: this notion of individuation that we take from Jung is interesting in terms of Libran planets. Individuation, for Libra, has to do with separating itself from fashion – it does not mean that one must ignore fashions in thinking, dressing, reading, and art. But at some point one must break away and judge one's behaviour, one's ideas, and perhaps even one's costume against ideals that show themselves to be universal in content. It is Libra's idea that it is operating out of truth, beauty, or goodness, that has to be broken if any individuation is to take place. Recognising one's bad behaviour, one's areas of lack of integrity, false ideas, unbeautiful perceptions or unbeautiful ways of expression are necessary for those with strong Libran ideals. One must recognise one's vanity. I am not speaking simply of physical vanity, but about their attachment to their idea of the good, the true and the beautiful; that's where the real vanity lies. The first step on the path to the Libran "good" is to recognise this vanity.

Perhaps more than any other sign, planets in Libra prosper by reading philosophers and authors of other ages, other cultures. They prosper through conversations with those of very different ethical ideas and codes of behaviour. Let me quote Fred Gettings again: Libra is cardinal, "blowing in a purposive single direction, and therefore capable of establishing specific relationships." This air sign, more than the others, needs the air that is circulating below and above them. Their tendency to want a steady, smooth course can stultify their air and render their notions of right balance and good behaviour stale and lifeless. Libran planets need the strife if they are to continue their journey towards Love. The loss of harmony and balance galvanises them to go for the ideal again and again. If their ideal is to grow in depth and beauty with the years, they must accept and, at least intellectually, welcome strife in their interactions. This is perhaps easier for those with Uranus in Libra than it is for those with Neptune in Libra!

Venus

Venus is the name of the Roman goddess of Love. She represents Beauty in the chart. She is associated with a huge extended family of mythological beauties that arise as figures from all cultures and all times. They are all goddesses of Love, and they all have stories that tell us about the nature of love in all its diversity.

In Hesiod's *Theogony,* he tells us of her birth from the sea. Her father Kronos (Saturn) had attacked his own father Ouranus on behalf of his mother (Gaia), who was oppressed by her husband's misuse of her and their children. In the course of the great battle, Kronos had cut off his father's genitals and they had fallen into the sea where, mixing with the sea, they had produced a wondrous beauty:

> Eros is her companion; Fair Desire
> Followed her from the first, both at her birth
> And when she joined the company of the gods.
> From the beginning, both among gods and men,
> She had this honour and received this power:
> Fond murmuring of girls, and smiles, and tricks,
> And sweet delight, and friendliness, and charm.[26]

This was Aphrodite, whose constant companion is Desire. Without her, without the idea she represents, our perceptions would not register things as sweet, delightful, joyous, or beautiful. She is the representation of the primordial idea of the power of attraction that brings things together – atoms, elements, molecules, flowers and bees, and all creatures. It is she who symbolises the connections between the stars in our sky, formed as patterns in our minds. She loves joining things up in such a way that connections are made between humans and their universe. She is the pleasure we take in feeling reflected in the dance of the Sun, Moon, and stars.

She is charm, she is grace and allure, without which we would never be attracted to a thing, a person, or an idea. She is what Plotinus is speaking of when he says, "Soul puts lures in things," so that we will want them and, through them, eventually discover eternal beauty. Plato says that it is this beauty we love when we fall in love with a beautiful face – we seek the eternal in the temporal, and once we understand this properly, love is for

---

26   Hesiod, *Theogony,* trans. Martin Litchfield West, Oxford University Press, 1988.

us. In many of her ancestors, she is the goddess of generation –
nothing would ever desire anything else without her presence,
presumably because the fruits of desire are often so difficult to
bear. Have you ever seen what penguins have to go through,
once their moment of attraction has produced an offspring?

Audience: Have you ever seen what humans have to go through,
once their moment of attraction has produced an offspring?

Darby: Point taken. It does seem that what or whoever is behind
this extraordinary experience of life had to factor in something
called Beauty, to which we will be helplessly attracted at times
in our lives. As most myths and stories and legends tell, and as
most of us experience, we are lured and ensnared and bound to
the task of creation in one way or another, and it is that which
we find beautiful, alluring, that ensnares us so that life will move
and evolve through time, rolling forward on its mysterious path.
   The astrological Venus is never more than 48° from the Sun.
With a Libra Sun, Venus may fall in Leo, Virgo, Libra, Scorpio,
or Sagittarius. Look to Venus in one of those signs to find a Libran's informing notions of beauty, truth, justice. When Venus
is in the sign of Leo, then this Libran will be attracted to proud
bearing, drama, and excitement. They will seek those who make
them feel their own vitality and creative juice. When the Sun
is in Libra and Venus is in Virgo, there is a sense of fragility in
this person. Things must be *just so* for one to find peace. They
so much admire those who do things well, and are so critical of
those they love, often for the "best possible reasons". If they are
unconscious in this and therefore cannot navigate their urge to
be useful by criticising, they can become seriously irritating to
others, which sabotages their need to be loved. Of course, it is
more interesting if we go further and look at Mercury, behind
the scenes of this Venus in Virgo.

I have a Libran client with Mercury in Virgo in the 11th house. It is well aspected, but Mercury is in an earlier degree than the Sun, and it is square Pluto. It sounds to me like her friends are always giving her disturbing information about her other friends, "just to be helpful". She goes round and round trying to deal with information that throws her off balance about the friend she is about to see, who will then give her information about the friend whom she just saw. She lives in a very gossipy world, and we have started looking at her place, her role in this world. She has Pluto in Cancer and so, of course, the most disturbing information she attracts is that which concerns her family. She has several children whom she cannot control, and she cannot help trying to help them get "right" so she can feel at rest. It's interesting when we get into these mutual receptive corners of the chart, isn't it? She is quite delighted that she has begun to spot the pattern now. She has even begun to track it back to her childhood and the tight social world of her parents, particularly during the war, when her father was a general and so much happened behind the scenes that was potentially dangerous.

When Venus is in Libra, along with the Sun, then the Libran is drawn to those who will support their need for a well-proportioned life – a life where harmony and reason are the guiding stars. Venus will attract what the Sun carries in its heart. According to how beauty and justice are conceived, this Venus will resonate with people who agree with these conceptions. However, with this position, there is often strong resentment when life does not bring fulfillment of their ideals. And there is something in the nature of life which ensures that, when you get what you want, your wanting goes off searching for something else to want. This combination is a real hunter, though often in disguise!

When Venus is in Scorpio, she fights for balance and she fights for what she wants – her wanting is fierce. And when she is in Sagittarius, the Libra Sun is drawn by images from the potential future and she loves the images of freedom, beauty, and truth that she can see ahead when her sky is clear.

Venus is ruler of Libra (and Taurus). She is in detriment in Aries and Scorpio. She is exalted in Pisces and falls in Virgo. What is interesting here is that, of all these signs, Virgo is the only one in which Venus can occur if you are a Libra Sun. The trail of these categories might say: Venus works best when she is alluring and attracting beauty of mind and body to herself. She also loves to attract things which are lasting and furthering of peace and security. She does not like martial situations and suffers in competitive or harsh climates (whether that be harsh weather or harsh emotional situations). She expresses her highest principle in selfless love, and she is least able to enjoy herself when hampered by duty, ill health, or mundane service.

Planets in Libra

Sun in Libra carries an image in its heart which is beautiful. Its beauty is based on proportion. That which is well–proportioned is beautiful, whether it be a face, a concept, an artifact, a room, or an idea. This sense of proportion is partly universal and partly personal. Not all people with planets in Libra will like the same painting or building or idea – each one will have their own personal notion of beauty – but they will perceive "right proportion" in what they find beautiful. The sign of their natal Venus, its house and aspects, will give you information about where this sense of beauty speaks to them, and from where they convey it to others.

Audience: Margaret Thatcher is a Libra Sun, with Venus in Sagittarius in the 1st house.

Darby: And Jupiter, ruler of that Venus, is in Capricorn in the 2nd house. We can assume that she carried an image of balance and right proportion in her heart, and that her Venus in Sagittarius had a heroic image of herself as the one who could bring the potential into life. With Jupiter "behind" that image, she would do it through the organising of the material world, and with Saturn in Scorpio on the Ascendant, it would be very hard work. She would be misunderstood and derided in doing it, but she was prepared for that, with the optimism of her Venus in Sagittarius leading her onwards.

Audience: Following those threads one more step, she has Mars in Libra square Pluto in Cancer. With the two rulers of her Scorpio Ascendant locked up together like that, no wonder she came across like gangbusters in a neat hairdo.

Audience: Ghandi was a Libra Sun too, and he had Venus conjunct Mars in Scorpio, in a T–square with the Moon in Leo and something in Taurus – Jupiter conjunct Pluto, I think.

Darby: Yes, I think you are right. So we might read that his image of beauty and peace and harmony was built on hard struggle and hard battles with himself and with others – those oppositions and the square to his Moon. He battled for and against the people of his own religion, and for and against the people of the "opposing" religion. What an opposition that is between Scorpio and Taurus! – a warrior of peace. And by the way, when Mars is conjoined with Venus in the chart of a Libran they have to fight for their notion of perfection.

Audience: Sarah Ferguson is a Libra Sun. I saw her chart the other day, and it has Venus conjunct Pluto in Virgo on the MC.

Darby: To make her life work, she has to destroy her own public image? Well, that would be one way of saying it. Fortunately for her, she has Moon in Aries, so she probably doesn't stop too long to be hurt by this image that has become her reputation.

Audience: She also has Mars conjunct the Sun. But the Venus in Virgo is pretty sensitive to the opinions of others.

Darby: Yes, it is, and another example of it – in fact I have two in my head – are Luciano Pavoratti, who has Venus conjunct Neptune, and Eleanor Roosevelt, who had it conjunct Jupiter in Leo. Both of them were (are) striving for very high versions of beauty, Pavoratti in his singing and Mrs. Roosevelt in her life and work.

Audience: You said something about Sun and Venus in Libra together, a few minutes ago. Have you got an example that we might know?

Darby: The only chart I can think of at the moment is such a perfect example I almost hesitate to use him: T. S. Eliot. He had Sun in the 12[th,] and Mercury conjunct Venus on the Ascendant in Libra, too – though not conjunct the Sun in the 12th. He was the quintessential fire-air poet – not a drop of water or a clod of earth to be found. He was exactly the sort of man to write the sort of poetry that he wrote. His manner and demeanour and behaviour were congruent with his poetry in a way that only Venus in Libra with Libra Sun could be. There is no discrepancy there. When Venus is in Libra along with the Sun, the values and ethics support the way of life. It does not mean the person is free of personal weakness – the combination may be cold and unfeeling in some ways. The need for harmony and balance can make people very selfish at times. But the Sun and Venus both in Libra do say that who he is and what he values make a kind of internal sense.

And remember that Heinrich Himmler also had Sun in Libra. Just because someone is informed by an image of beauty and right proportion, we mustn't assume this will necessarily lead to humanitarian behaviour. He worked to get rid of a whole lot of people so that he could bring forth the image in his heart of a beautiful world. That he was a thoroughly nasty man made him work to create this world in a thoroughly nasty way.

There is an internal spirit level in Libra, and nowhere does it show more clearly than with the **Moon in Libra**. The desire for peace, grace, and harmony is so strong, and it seems to take constant work to return the feelings to balance. The very nature of the Moon is to react continually to the environment – to be in constant response. With this Moon, the desire for peace is absorbed from one's mother, but it becomes one's own desire over time. The instincts are to be gracious, accommodating, considerate, but they become cold and warlike if pushed too far out of equilibrium. There is a feeling about people with Moon in Libra that they are continually adjusting their inner balance – they retreat in the middle of activity for a moment, while they seem to retreat internally to adjust the inflow and outflow. Then they come back to the conversation or activity.

Audience: It's hard to get close to them, in fact.

Darby: It depends on what you mean by close. There are all sorts of ways of being intimate, and everyone has their own sense of it. The private world shared with a Libra Moon may be perfect for those who need space to breathe and a touch of formality in their dance of intimacy. And remember, always look behind the scenes of any planetary position to where Venus is in the chart of this Moon in Libra. Aspects to the Moon will tell you something about what facilitates or impedes this person's capacity for finding peace in relationships, but Venus will tell you what is attractive here. Sometimes the sort of person who is attractive to them is not the sort of person who offers a peaceful life. Moon in Libra works to find a peaceful life, and it has to use whatever its soul attracts, to find and lose and find again the intervals of grace that nourish its soul.

Mercury in Libra will never serve anyone but those with Sun in Virgo, Libra, or Scorpio. When the Sun and Mercury are both in Libra, then there is a constant intake of information which tells whether things are appropriate or not, according to that which Venus values. So if Venus is in Virgo, for example, everything and everyone has a place and a use, and it is disturbing when someone or something is suddenly out of place. This can operate according to the highest ideals of virtue, or it can operate in a mean and picky way. That depends on how the person nourishes their mind and soul. When Sun is in Scorpio with Mercury in Libra, there can seem to be a conflict of interests.

Audience: Yes, the Sun is demanding that the house be totally renovated, while Mercury in Libra is bringing in the paintings to put on the walls that are being torn down.

Darby: The Sun is looking for places where the work of transformation can take place, and Mercury is bringing in information that says, "Well, you could do this, but then that would happen, or you could do that, but then, this would be the result. On the other hand…" They have to weight all the information before they can move, but when they move, they have a whole range of considerations sorted out already. Mercury has to have reasons why this transformation must take place, and it finds them. When well educated – either by the street or the university – it can be a powerful combination in its own right, emotional power informed by clear reason. But again, you have to look behind Mercury in Libra to see where Venus has turned her gaze, because she is the one who chooses the information centre for Mercury here.

We already spoke about **Venus in Libra**, but I can't resist saying something more about it here. Venus is ruler of Libra, so the placement of Venus in Libra signals a great love of grace and beauty. No matter what else is in the chart, this person is constantly moved by beauty and hunts for places and people where they can perceive the lines of perfect proportion under the surface of appearances. They work for beauty – they are informed by beauty, they are seduced by it, and they seduce through it. They are offended by discord, and even when they create it themselves, it offends them. It is *very* hard for them to see that they are generating the discord when they do. They have to really work for objectivity here, though they certainly have it when it comes to judging art or artifact of any kind. Often it indicates physical beauty, but even if the person with this position is not physically beautiful, they certainly have a magnet in them which attracts others to them. This Venus is informed by the ideal of perfect proportion and grace, and it suffers when hit by ugliness and ill proportion. Remember, this is beauty and ugliness according to the time, place, era, and depth of mind of the person with Venus in Libra. The deeper the values, the deeper one finds beauty. The more one is connected to one's own fashion environment, the more superficial one's notion of beauty.

Audience: What about **Mars in Libra**? I have a client with it on the Ascendant, and she tells me all the time how people are fighting with her and she has no idea why. I think Mars on the Ascendant is very contentious – as Aries rising often is. But Mars in Libra on the Ascendant is paradoxical.

Audience: They *are* contentious, but they *think* it's other people. I have a friend with that combination, and she is what I would call passive aggressive. You start out all calm, and then find yourself furious at either her or something on her behalf within an hour of being with her.

Darby: Remember that Libra has a concept of justice and fair play which informs its actions. It fights for peace and has a concept in its motor which contains the rules of social order. And Mars is always where the most heroic and crudest parts of ourselves live in uneasy alliance. With Mars in Libra, you will get both – the heroic warrior for the just and the true, and the indecisive victim of others' injustice. Mars on the Ascendant in Libra will either be fighting ruthlessly for its own or someone else's rights, or it will be unable to act because it is feeling unjustly treated. Most of us are light and shadow from minute to minute, or day to day. Mars in Libra can be so infuriating, because when it is good it is so very good, and will fight for your rights and your space. But conversely, when it operates from its uncultured, uncultivated side, it is very noticeable. And Venus will tell the nature of the rights it fights for and demands.

Audience: The present Dalai Lama has Mars in Libra in the 1st house – he fights for peace with his whole life. But you can also see something of the detrimental nature of Mars in Libra, even in his chart. And his Mars is square to the Sun in Cancer, too. It's impossible to win such a battle as his.

Darby: Yes, and his Venus is in Leo in the 11th house – his battle is on behalf of his people, but also humanity. He cannot fight so much as stand for the idea of justice, peace, good relationships. His battle is at the level of social issues. Perhaps that is a clue to its being in detriment in Libra – a warrior who must stand for an idea rather than fight for it. It is hard to defend yourself and others when your weapons are ideas and ideals. It is the middle, impersonal, cultural range that is occupied by Libra air. This Mars position operates better when fighting for social rights than when fighting for itself personally.

People with **Jupiter in Libra** find their spiritual home in beauty. They crushed by ugliness. This is Venus' airy domain.

Those with this Jupiter would find it very hard to believe that they could ever act from sleazy motives. They might admit to being ruthless, hard, or even unkind – but sleazy, never. If Jupiter is where we are prone to identify our best qualities, then Jupiter in Libra might identify its finely tuned sense of order and balance as its essential virtue. People with this position believe in justice and beauty, and are more secure when they are in its presence. They recognise it, even if it is covered over or hidden under a rough surface. They have an eye for good proportions, on all levels.

Audience: And yet they can be tasteless. Peter Sutcliffe and Denis Nilsen both have Jupiter in Libra.

Darby: Yes, they do – both very tasteless serial killers. Why one person becomes evil and another not is ever a mystery. Jupiter is not what we are, but what we imagine ourselves to be. With Jupiter in Libra, other people will shatter this conception, and we will have to build it up again. Those with whom we do the dance of partnership are the ones who shatter our ideas, either about relationship in general or about our own capacity for relationship. And yet, besides poets and writers, it is also our partners who give us the ideas that allow us to construct this other map. Always look to Venus to see from where the map is written, smudged, and rewritten. Both of these men had a harshly aspected Moon and Venus, but not everyone who has that ends up killing other people. Many people struggle through, seeking to find ways to believe in their ideals and living with their own personal sorrows. This brings a nobility and charm to their character, and times of grace in relationship where the ideal does seem to be real. Jupiter in Libra's idealism has a greater dimension and becomes even more demanding when either Uranus, Neptune, or Pluto is also in Libra. It is then attached to a collective current which has its own voice, and the two can merge in such a way that someone with a weak ego-self will be filled with the idea that they *are* Jupiter in Libra – they are the wise judge, the true arbitrator of what is just and true.

And so there is a danger of vanity as moral superiority, with this position. However, there is moral danger everywhere when we are trying to develop consciousness. The work of separating our consciousness from our own instinctive reactions, even our best reactions, is fraught with all sorts of inner perils. The house and aspects of Jupiter will tell you where the ideal of wholeness expresses itself most clearly. Venus and its sign, house, and aspects will tell you what fuels the image of oneself as just and ethical in general.

Audience: My daughter has Jupiter conjunct Saturn in Libra, trine her Moon in Gemini. I have never, ever known anyone who is more considerate in her behaviour. She agonises over the slightest imbalance in her relationships. But I tell her that, when she is older, she will do it beautifully, with ease. She is nineteen now. I worry because she seems to express herself with such care – there is something almost too careful.

Darby: We would have to look at the whole chart, of course. But she certainly carries that as an ideal – and, as it is connected with her Moon, some of that ideal comes from you. But **Saturn in Libra** is a very strong factor in any chart. For those who were born with the Jupiter-Saturn conjunction in Libra, the ideals of social justice and personal happiness are interwoven. You would naturally encourage these ideals – but don't forget that ideals are ideas that inform life. We are rarely able to live up to them perfectly. They can keep us conscious and conscientious in some ways, but they also change and grow as we do. Also, doing relationships perfectly is almost an oxymoron!

With Saturn in its sign of exaltation, there is a constant reckoning of accounts in all transactions and interactions with other people. Saturn in Libra demands a great deal from its disciples in the dance of *eros*. Those who have this placement find the chaos and mess of relationship life distressing; they have an idea of relationship, and something tells them that nothing less will do. Saturn is exalted in Libra, and through this we can understand that, if a relationship is to endure, the ideals that inform each person must complement each other, especially their ideas about relationship.

Saturn in Libra has to develop consciousness around their informing ideals, as they were picked up in childhood from their parents' marriage and they limit the person's capacity to enjoy partnership – *as long as they are unconscious.* Those with Saturn conjunct Neptune in Libra have an interesting time with this. Neptune draws them to a kind of imaginative exaltation of the dance of love. But with Saturn, every step has to be learned, almost in a contrived way. They are driven to learn through deprivation, and this deprivation is absolutely unacceptable to them. They cannot ignore *eros,* and yet their dream is beyond the possible, except in moments of grace. And so they have to work to create a life in which these moments of grace can enter, and those who are willing and able to do that are blessed in their relationships. The gap between the two planets is bridged through willingness to learn to love – and that means overcoming the longing to be loved.

Audience: They have to give up being loved?

Darby: No, I said the *longing*, the *desire* to be loved. Being loved is something that happens beyond your will and cannot be controlled. The desire to be loved is the obstacle to love here. Learning to fashion a field in which love can develop and grow is the work here.

Uranus was **in Libra** from the end of 1968 through some of 1975. The group of people born during this time picked up the energy of the experiments in values, relationships, and art that were going on during that time. This group is divided into two parts – the people who were born while Pluto was still in Virgo, and those who were born with Pluto in Libra too, though Uranus and Pluto were never conjunct in Libra. Uranus seems to act like a voice from the future. It calls for new forms to begin developing. The relationships of this generation are different. They cannot follow the formulae of their parents' generation with any sort of conviction. Those who have Uranus connected to personal planets have to find new ways to dance together. Perhaps they are more interested in the differences than in the similarities of each other. They get restless when the wind blows in the same direction for any length of time. They want to move vertically with ideas, rather than horizontally. They are experimenting with the spaces between things and people in relationship.

I have a friend with Uranus and Pluto in Libra in the 4th, and Venus in Gemini in the 11th. Almost all her friends, from the time she was about eight years old, have been foreign. She feels very foreign herself, even though she was brought up in a very English family. She left home at about sixteen, and has lived in rooms here and there ever since. She is looking for something. She carries a strong idea which she cannot articulate, and the only thing she knows is that she cannot, under any circumstances, follow her family's tradition. And so she keeps watching and listening to people who are as far away from it as she can get. It's as though she should have been born into another culture or another time, perhaps the future. I am very interested in seeing what the creative people of this generation will do in shaping the world. At present, there is a lot of breaking apart of ideas and values – what will be created?

The **Neptune in Libra**, Pluto in Leo generation burst onto the scene with their "flower power" statement in the 1960's. Now they are deep into their middle years, and those who are representative of their generation – who have personal planets involved with Neptune – have either learned to create their dreams of love and beauty through appropriate sacrifice, or they are suffering from finding the sacrifice they have to make for beauty or love unacceptable. Neptune represents a leak in one's defences – in this case, one's mental defences. One's ideas of love and beauty and justice make one vulnerable, and that keeps one's soul alive, but not necessarily at rest. Of course, there are people with Neptune in Libra who are fine and dandy, and all's well with the world. But I guess I think they are simply ignoring the call to attend the battle between harmony and discord that Empedocles said ruled the world.

Audience: My daughter has Pluto conjunct the Moon in Libra. So does one of my nephews. And several of their friends have Venus or Mars conjunct **Pluto in Libra**. What on earth is that all about?

Darby: It's not on earth. That's the point. The people of that generation have grown up in a world where peace was an underlying obsession, and where war – those waged in many countries, those they experienced between their parents, those they saw on TV, those they saw or experienced in the schoolyard – have significantly affected their ideals of "the good, the true, and the beautiful". Pluto describes a collective urge to purify and transform the qualities represented by the sign. The Pluto in Libra group are under pressure to transform notions of beauty, truth, and justice. Each individual has a part in this, designated by aspects to Pluto. Every Moon in Libra person is constantly adjusting their inner emotional levels as feelings are absorbed and expressed through their Moon. Those of this Pluto in Libra generation will do this more fiercely, more extremely than those of other generations. Your daughter absorbed from you the extremes you went to in seeking peace and harmony in her infancy and early childhood. How she uses this information in her own daily life has more to do with her than you, though you will deeply recognise some of her habits of response.

Whenever a personal planet is attached to this Pluto, they will have picked up ways of seeking peace by extreme methods. This is a mental, moral, intellectual sign, and it is concept-driven. They are looking for ideal ways in which to live. They are moved by ideas that come from somewhere beyond conscious experience. As a generation, they are seeking a quiet life in a world they perceive as madly out of balance. This is part of their generation's function – to find a quiet place in a time when all the rules are changing and relationships at every level are breaking down and seeking new containers in which to develop. Remember, too, this generation came into their sexually active years when AIDS was a dominant feature. For them, the dance of partnership is shadowed by the presence of death. That gives it a weight it did not have for our generation. But then, we were developing something else.

Libra rising

If you are wary of charm and grace, then be wary of Libra rising. I suppose you might meet one that is deeply uncharming, but it is not their natural demeanour. They enter situations with an idea of cooperation and the creation of harmony. There may be many things interfering with this ideal, but it is always there as a constant and recurring theme. And it is certainly their initial approach to any situation or person. If they are inspired by grace or beauty in others – and their Venus will decide what sort of beauty inspires them – then they will go all out to charm the one that attracts them. When they are not charmed themselves, they can be very cold and indifferent. Air goes cold quickly, when the heart or the feelings are not touched. And this air needs warmth from others if it is to show its own beauty for any length of time.

Audience: Libra rising is noted for being charming to strangers and selfish with intimates. It certainly seems that way to me.

Darby: There is something to that, but it is a two-way street. When the intimate starts to assume that Libra rising will automatically continue to be charming, then the heat goes out of the dance and the light goes out. Libra rising can only be charming as part of a dance, and the dance must have its reasons. It is noted for its ruthlessness, and that is the counterpoint to its charm. When the dance goes sour, the ruthlessness appears. It *can* be very self–serving, but when the partner attends the heart and feelings underneath the smooth exterior, they continue to benefit from the charm. Look to Venus to see what turns this person on or off. Look to Venus' ruler to see what reasons drive the personality.

Planets in the 7th house

Planets in the 7th house are said to be "projected" onto other people. This is one of those words that really opens up a door to understanding when it is first used, and ends up a cliché that concretises a rather subtle and complex process. Planets in the 7th house do describe the general tenor of your partnership life, and they can also describe how you describe those with whom you enter into partnership. But it is not as simple as it may seem. If you have **Venus in the 7th**, you will bring out Venus in your partners, and that will be happy or not, depending on what aspects of Venus you draw forth. You will find those clues in Venus' sign, aspects, and her ruler, of course. If you have **Mars in the 7th**, then by entering into partnership, your Mars is activated, according to its sign and aspects and ruler. I have had several working partnerships with people who have had **Jupiter in the 7th**, which is really nice, because they bring out the very best in their partners, as long as they leave them room to move.

The difficulty with planets in the 7th is seeing how you bring out those planets, and then discovering that you are "in effect" of them, if you do not pay close enough attention to your interactions. That is the key with 7th house planets: to deal with what you bring out from your partners, and to find your responsibility in that part of it. Planets in the 7th house have their "reasons", and the clue is in finding the reason behind the attraction to that kind of energy. You must, as psychological astrologers, help your clients track their 7th house planets down through the layers of their childhood. You will find the reason behind their attitudes to marriage and partnership in the ruler of their 7th house, and you should be able to discover how that attitude developed when they were young by listening to what they say, in light of the ruler and the planets there.

But there is another thing, too. When you are doing a chart for a client, this is a partnership, at least for the time of your session. Pay attention to their 7th house, as they will call for the qualities written there from you, in one way or another. And you will put them in your 7th house, too. The more conscious you are of this, the more you have a chance to work with it. I don't mean that you must stay conscious of it all through the session, but keep a tiny eye on it, especially if you have problems with one sort of client or another, or if someone has a problem with you. I remember, when I was beginning to practise, a client complained to a friend that I "wouldn't tell her what to do", and she found this unsatisfactory. My 7th house is Uranian; hers was Saturnian. However, she kept coming back to me, and eventually we had to address it. We worked out something between us. I'd say, "Oh, I can give you a rule here if you like," and she would say, "Yes!"

AQUARIUS

Aquarius is, by nature, a paradoxical sign. Ruled by both Saturn and Uranus, any planets there tend to be pulled back and forth between the two rulers. There is always a tension between the two principles the rulers represent, and so planets in Aquarius always express a tension, a discontent with things as they are, as opposed to things as they "should" be. On the Uranian side, planets in Aquarius operate from a set of laws that emerge as we develop understanding about the interface between large and small systems.

It is probably true that "there is nothing new under the Sun", in that every new law we uncover has already been expressed by other peoples in other times. This has been a century in which we really have begun to unearth our past. We find new meaning in old rituals and old mythologies as we uncover or reformulate new understanding. Uranus was the first planet we discovered with our telescopes – it is the gateway to "beyond", but beyond often turns out to be very intimately embedded in our own world, in our own interior perceptions, in the "ideas and ideals" that shape our species' perceptions. Aquarius is informed by the shape of things emerging that have to do with groups and individuals. They are idealist by nature. But Aquarius is also ruled by Saturn, and so they cannot simply hang around at the edges listening to strange voices from beyond. They have to be part of community, and they are deeply sensitive to what the community considers "right conduct" and "wrong conduct". They are "ruled" by the laws of convention which have become tradition – Saturn – but they are also "ruled" by the principle of disruption

– Uranus – which is inherent in systems, in nature, if you like, so that the ways things are is not the way they will always be.

The rarefied atmosphere – the high, thin air of the upper realms, the air that protects the Earth from dangerous emanations from "outside" and conveys "good information" down to the Earth – is the air from which Aquarian planets receive their notions. Let me say this another way. That air space is a metaphor for the thoughts that light up those with Aquarian energy. They seem to be both ahead of and behind the rest of the crowd, group, family. Groups are where they develop their ability to express their ideas, yet groups are often not the easiest place to be. The generation with Uranus in Libra and/or Pluto in Libra probably find groups easier than those with Pluto in Leo or Neptune in Scorpio. However, they are a necessary part of development for those born to bring new ideas and ways of interacting into the traditional sections of society. They feel protective of humanity and righteous about how people should and should not behave. They have a strong sense of guardianship and are extreme in their tolerance and their intolerance.

Aquarius is attracted to the "fresh unexhausted air of the outer atmosphere as opposed to that in confined spaces". Remember that part of the dictionary definition? More than any other air sign, it needs to retreat to the outer atmosphere – it needs *space*. That notion of needing space came from the generation with Uranus in Gemini and Pluto in Leo. But older Aquarians suffered from claustrophobia, too, if they were confined too tightly by their cultural norms, or by the ideas of their families or spouses. They usually found their freedom in their friends and mental companions.

Fred Gettings says, "Fixed air: air under pressure, which tends under certain conditions to explode outwards in rapid dispersals of energy." Now, that is interesting, in that it tells us how Aquarian planets express themselves. It is true, people with Aquarian planets go along quietly for periods, and then suddenly burst forth with the expression of their ideas and ideals. This explosion seems to be the result of a gathering feeling of mental claustrophobia. The air gets too heavy, too dense – and the Aquarian swings out and flashes their lights. The Aquarian field is alerted by thoughts which are circling round in such a way as to be in danger of self-closure. No one else in the room may feel claustrophobic, everyone might feel just fine, but the Aquarian-driven person must speak out. They suddenly release "packets of air" into the conversation.

It is not because the Aquarian is more individualised than other people, but because the birds that land in their heads come from afar, from the territory outside the group's boundaries, outside the village, the class, the business. Sometimes they come from the very edge of collective thought, where ideas are just emerging. Planets in Aquarius mean there is an experiment in progress, and they are duty-bound to bring in what they are discovering. This is experienced as a pressure when too many people are agreeing with one particular idea. The weight of collective agreement forces them into contradictory expression.

Audience: I'm an Aquarian, and I get edgy when people start agreeing with a particular definition. The other day we were talking about Jupiter and its benevolent action. I kept thinking of times when its aspects coincided with nasty events. I felt the pressure of a responsibility to turn the ideas of Jupiter on their head. I did, not being a shy sort of Aquarian. The discussion got more interesting. The information field had been expanded. I could breathe again.

Darby: And others were annoyed or excited about the new direction the discussion had taken. For the one with Aquarian planets, the air gets heavier and heavier with the weight of a particular perspective on things. They either have to leave the discussion or express their own perspective, which is partly created from the idea being expressed and partly from something more subtle and emergent. That's why they can seem awkward. It is their role to constellate edges. Whether you like that or not depends on how attached you are to your own ideas.

With planets in Aquarius, thoughts are under pressure. Storms arise, rage, and disappear, leaving the air clear again. I am not suggesting it is a violent sign – not at all – the violence is almost always in the *mind* of the one carrying planets in this sign. Their inner air might be quite still; then, suddenly, a gust of wind throws the resting ideas every which way, until the pressure is released and the air is still again. Ideas arise, and the thoughts connected to those ideas show the inner and outer landscape in a particular light – bright and clear. Then a cloud passes, and the light changes. The ideas collapse and reconfigure according to new experience. People with Aquarian planets are constantly updating their information. Gemini is gathering information all the time. Libra is assessing and weighing information for its value. Aquarius is updating its information. It has a sense of duty about this. Its information feels heavy, and it must be passed on to others. It feels the weight of Saturn in its sense of responsibility and its desire for respect for its ideas and ideals. But its receptivity to the Uranian impulse keeps it slightly wrong-footed when it is trying to be most respectful. Uranus won't ever let it feel complacent in its knowledge or its social position – not for very long. It might try for complacency in its idealism, thinking it always acts from the highest ideals. Well, almost always. But, of course, this has its own problems.

Where there are Aquarian planets, we can become enthralled by our own "uniqueness" and our own high intentions. Individuation is born out of the recognition that one's ideas and behaviour are as conditioned by the times in which one lives as everyone else's is so conditioned. Aquarians have to navigate between collective notions and personal needs and desires – and that is difficult for any true idealist. And they sometimes mix up their ideals with their own behaviour, not liking to admit base motives. When this is not true, it's a hard fact to face for those with any planets in Aquarius. So a boring Gemini, a badly behaved Libran, and a self–serving Aquarian are people who may be just that, but they may also be on the path toward finding what is true in themselves.

Audience: I met a young lass at a party just recently, and whatever I said to her, she kept saying, "Oh, Aquarius, Aquarius!" I was furious.

Darby: What's the worst thing you can say to an Aquarian when they tell you something? "Oh, all you Aquarians say that!"

Saturn and Uranus

Darby: When I was studying astrology in America in the 1960's, I was taught that Uranus ruled Aquarius. Something was mentioned about Saturn being the "old ruler", but not much, as far as I can remember. When I came to England, I noticed that the old rulers were still considered important, and so I started looking for their action in their signs. After years of doing charts, I now cannot see Aquarius planets without looking at Saturn. It tells me how this person is working to integrate themselves, through their Aquarian planets, into their communities, so that they can get recognition for their unique contribution. If there is a relationship between the two rulers in the chart, then it is easier to see how the struggle to interpret new ideas – represented by Uranus – is connected to their search for self-respect and the respect of others. When Saturn and Uranus are not connected by sign, house, or aspect, then it is not so easy to see, and their detachment may seem more like disconnection. Saturn and Uranus come together through Aquarian planets. There is always a trace of the old war between them. The border between the realm of ideas represented by these two ancient Titans is not easy to pass. The notions that reach us from the Uranian dimension have to be eventually realised in the bone and blood of our world if they are to nourish our development, our spiritual evolution as a species. Even if you have no planets in Aquarius, the house that contains the sign will be where you experience the challenge of barely conceived ideas breaking through traditional ways of thinking. Then look at Uranus and Saturn, to see where these ideas burst through and where they are tested.

Audience: I have Aquarius on the 6ᵗʰ, and whenever I get ill I become mad trying to figure out which method of healing to use. I fear medical science, yet don't trust the still too untried alternative methods.

Audience: I have it on the 5ᵗʰ house. My kids go crazy because I veer between being really conservative about their upbringing, and then really "out there". They like the combination, but they say they can't tell when I'll be one or the other.

Planets in Aquarius

People with **Sun in Aquarius** are carrying an ideal in their hearts for which they feel responsible. They often feel a sense of mission quite early. But it can take many years and many experiences with all sorts of groups before they begin to formulate and then articulate this idea. It takes others to awaken the idea, yet they have to think it through themselves. So they are both gregarious and loners at the same time. They usually venture beyond the confines of their families quite early. They are especially attuned to the ideals carried by their father, and are sensitive to his behaviour with other people; they are sensitive to his ability to relate to people cleanly. They try to ignore any moral inconsistencies in him. They keep him at a slightly remote distance because what they are interested in spiritually is not his mundane side, but his ethical side.

It is hard to conceive of an amoral Aquarian – they may rebel against the mores of their tribe, but they have good "reasons" for it. They have other rules they are following. They almost always say that they feel uncomfortable in groups, and yet they cannot do without them. They are informed by the positions of their Saturn and Uranus, and so, although they feel like outsiders often enough, they are only outsiders in relation to one or another group with which they identify. I see the Aquarian heads in the room rise to challenge this statement. You may not wish to admit that you identify with one or another group, but if you are in rebellion against its values, then you are identifying with it. You can't be an outsider if there is no inside. You can't rebel unless you are rebelling against something, and this something is the group that carries the values and customs that you are rebelling against. Or perhaps you will prefer it this way: you are connected to a group, the tribe, or a social world where you feel something of a mission to enlighten them in some way through making some positive contribution in the world.

Many Aquarians of the Pluto in Leo generation are trapped in a hall of mirrors by the opposition, which comes out as self-obsession. When their world is too narrow, they go a bit mad. They need the access to the upper air. You could say they need to feel they are bringing into their local space something from beyond the limits. They warm up in the high atmosphere where interstellar matter begins its descent through the layers of air. They feel connected to something abstract, an idea of the way things could be if only people would behave as they should. They carry an ideal picture of humanity in their hearts, and they suffer when people don't act as they "should". If their range of activities is not broad enough, they experience air deprivation. And we all go a bit odd when we don't have enough air.

Audience: In what way do they take in interstellar matter? I mean, how would you say that psychologically?

Darby: They don't necessarily relate to things as they are. They relate to things as they could be, if certain conditions were in place. It's not like the fiery person's seeing the potential in people and then relating to that, to the image. With an Aquarian, it is this sense of something that could be, *if* the conditions were right. That is why there is so much discontent in Aquarian planets. Uranus can see the shape, the pattern, the template beyond the visible reality, and Saturn sees that something has to be reshaped here on the ground if the Uranian ideal is to happen.

When **Moon in Aquarius** people are good, they are very good, and "when they are bad, they are horrid". This Moon has absorbed so many different ways of constructing reality that they can lose themselves when they spend too much time with other people. Their emotional nature allows them to tune into the unusual aspect of others' minds, delighting in their own and others' originality and forgetting the other sides of the personality waiting in the dark to return. When the Aquarian Moon begins to air the less ideal side of themselves, they seem suddenly awkward and unpredictable. They get emotionally trapped in their own or other people's ideals, then fight for their freedom to be as they are.

Moon in Aquarius takes from its mother erratically. They can see themselves as victims of her erratic behaviour – or they can see themselves as feeling edgy and uncomfortable around her. They usually admit she is interesting, but they tend to need a lot of distance from her.

Mercury is exalted **in Aquarius**. This is the most interesting of all exaltations to me. It tells us that the upper air is Mercury's finest home. It tells us that Mercury is working at its best when it is able to take in different points of view, when it is able to encompass radically different perspectives. Its natural inclination is to filter what comes into its group, keeping out the harmful rays and conveying the life-giving rays to those around it. An Aquarian with Mercury in Aquarius seems to contradict what I've just said about encompassing different perspectives. This combination finds information about the ugly side of life almost unbearable. It does its very best to see the very best in those around it. It seems to feel duty bound to take in and give out information that will increase the amount of good will around.

You can see that this can make these people seem naive, and they do suffer from shock when other parts of their nature draw them into circumstances that show people as less than the ideal. I remember a very fine woman I knew in my twenties, with Sun and Mercury in Aquarius and Moon squaring them both from Scorpio, telling me that she didn't want to know anything bad when I looked at her chart. She did suffer betrayal in her emotional life soon after. I think that the shock of having to allow in the knowledge – that those she loved were not as she thought – was too much to bear at the time. She was unaware of how her own behaviour attracted betrayal of her ideals. She wanted to learn astrology so that she could understand more about human behaviour, but I hope her studies led to her understand herself better too.

A Pisces Sun with Mercury in Aquarius has an interesting time – fixed ideas in a romantic spirit. The image in the heart of a Pisces has to do with melting or diffusing fixed notions, feelings, ideas – melting the boundaries between things and people. This Mercury looks for information which will create a map of the world which can operate as a guide towards clarity and understanding. It is a combination that makes a surprising person, unpredictable and idealistic in their thinking and speaking, of course, and oddly tolerant in their actions. I think it is always concerned with the best way to melt the boundaries between itself and the members of any group it belongs to. It looks for information that will help it melt the boundaries between people, but also between dimensions. I had a client with this some years ago, with Saturn in Cancer, who impressed me because she said, "I sometimes wonder if I am censoring all kinds of information to keep the world of my family sweet. I am often shocked by information I receive from others, and sometimes I can't think where I should put this information."

Audience: What about Capricorn Sun with Mercury in Aquarius? My son has that combination, and he is very clear about what he wants and very judgmental of those who have fuzzy thinking.

Darby: Both Sun and Mercury are Saturn-ruled, though Mercury gets its deeper impulses from Uranus, of course. The Sun is conservative, wanting respect and recognition from others for its excellence. Mercury gathers its information from all kinds of odd sources. So it is both old-fashioned and up to the minute. Mercury's fixed ideas both hold it back and bring an unusual array of friends and acquaintances to help it fulfill its purpose. A Capricorn with far out ideas, he has to bring something new into his world to secure his place in the community.

Audience: He's only eight, but he has the most extraordinary way of explaining why it is important I keep current with his generation's music. He told me, the other day, that you can tell the future of a society by listening to young people's music. He might have picked the idea up from someone else, but he impressed me with it. I told him I'd remind him of that when I was ninety-four and he was struggling with his grandchildren's music. He said he'd already thought of that. I thought to myself that only a Capricorn would already be thinking of his old age at eight.

Darby: How delightful to have such an articulate child. He must have experienced a future vision of his whole life in his first Saturn square. Let's go on to **Venus in Aquarius**. This position has a kind of quirky steadiness to it. It is steady in its relationship to an ideal of love and friendship. This ideal can act as a barrier to closeness, but it can also be a binding idea in a relationship. These people are attracted to all sorts of people who have very different ways of seeing things – an unusual network of friends and acquaintances. Like any personal planet in Aquarius, it quickly finds what is most interesting in another – and then, aspecting planets decide what happens next. This Venus cannot bear being bored in relationship. It needs to be surprised by loved ones who must also have ideals, even if the ideals are different. Those who are working to become more than simply a set of reactions work to see through their own "idealism", with Venus in Aquarius. There is nothing more dangerous to a relationship than being unconsciously dominated by the ideas we have about how other people should behave, unless it is being unconsciously dominated by ideas of how we should behave ourselves. Venus in Aquarius struggles between the best and the worst that it sees in humanity – and it depends on the consciousness of the person as to how that struggle takes place. Periodically, those with this Venus are forced to reconsider its idealism, lest they become tyrannical – Saturn and Uranus behind the scenes.

Audience: If the other person can't keep some part of themselves free and detached, then Venus in Aquarius gets trapped, and so they push the other person away.

Audience: And it is very difficult to be detached from someone who is detached.

Audience: Two Venus in Aquarius people would have endless detachment competitions, but they wouldn't believe in competition in love, so it could get fairly complicated.

Audience: Unless they were born when Uranus is in Aries – then competition could be their ideal.

Darby: Speaking of Aries, let's speak of Mars. **Mars in Aquarius** fights for its ideals, according to the information received from Uranus' sign and position, and what they can work into their systems of responsibility *via* Saturn. This is a passionately idealistic position for Mars and, when activated by their ideals, they can appear rigid and cold in pursuit of their ideas. There is a cold logic that accompanies their arguments. I have a client with Mars in Aquarius, who recently discovered her father had been unfaithful to her mother when she and her brother were children. She had always admired her father because he was a good man who had been kind to them, and had been a well liked and respected member of his community, for good reasons. Now she has found out that he had a mistress for many years. What an icy wind came off her when she spoke of this! Underneath her cold anger, there was grief, of course, but it was her anger that showed. She had six other fixed planets in her chart, and she absolutely refused to understand how he could have been so dishonourable.

I once had a client who was a Pisces with Mars and Venus in Aquarius, and when her husband had an affair, she said she felt absolutely bound to not punish him for that, as it was his right to decide such a thing. She said she only asked him to be discreet. The affair ended after six months, and she said she worked through her hurt with a trusted older friend, and the friendship between herself and her husband was deepened by it. They had been married thirty years already. I saw her when I was young, and at that time I didn't believe her. Now I would be more inclined to. She was, of course, a remarkable woman. She had Uranus in Aries, and Neptune in Leo opposing her Venus. Her husband's brief affair led her to the study of astrology. She had been a country club type – that level of Aquarius – and this experience drove her into the upper reaches of air, where she really belonged. She still had some of her country club friends, of course, but her interest in astrology and other related thought-worlds had changed their conversations to some extent. She was too discreet to be ostracised, and so that created a fascination in others for her interest in "way out" things.

Audience: How did her husband feel about all that?

Darby: He was "tolerant". But then, she did have Mars in Aquarius – her husband would either be rigid and authoritarian, or tolerant.

Now let's think about **Jupiter in Aquarius**. It gives the capacity to see huge potential in things. It is naturally idealistic, demands leaders and gurus with high ideals, and passionately believes in its own idea as received from Uranus and worked into life through Saturn.

This is an interesting and paradoxical place for Jupiter. It gives an inclination to create an entire world for itself, in which everything that does not fit the picture is kept at a distance. People with Jupiter in Aquarius almost manage to ignore those who do not live according to congruent mental structures. When you spend time with them, you are brought into their world – and it is often a very interesting world. But it is always a shock when either of you realises you are not operating from the same ideas. It seems to me as if they are informed by notions of emerging patterns and conceptions, but they translate this each according to their own intelligence and also, of course, their own pathology. They often act as though the world they believe in is already here. The shadow of this is that they fall into huge holes when, suddenly, something shocks them out of their belief. The light goes out, and they cannot see the pattern or the map on the ceiling, and they lose all hope. Then their belief system is reconfigured somehow, and the cracks in the ceiling suddenly have pattern and meaning again.

Audience: You mentioned Einstein earlier. Her certainly lived in his own mental world, but it was shattered by his extraordinary e=mc² leading to the construction of the atom bomb. His vision destabilised the future of humanity. I am thinking of his Jupiter in Aquarius in the 9th house, square Pluto in the 11th.

Darby: When that Pluto-Jupiter square was activated in his life – and I am thinking of the moment when he discovered that his mathematical insights were about to be used to build a bomb – it must have blown his inner map off the wall. And even after everything that happened, he still said, "God is subtle, but not malicious." I think there were a fair number of people around thinking that, if any gods existed, they were certainly not benevolent.

Have you read Eve Jackson's excellent book, *Jupiter*?[27] She has Hugh Hefner in there. He is an Aries with Jupiter in Aquarius conjunct Mars in the 5th house. They oppose Neptune in Leo in the 11th, and all are square Saturn in Scorpio in the 3rd. He certainly has an idea of the best of all possible worlds, though it may not correspond with the ideals most of us in this room cherish. And he has managed to create a bubble for himself in which he lives out his idea. Imagine how messy it gets when the lights on his inner picture go out.

Saturn in Aquarius indicates a person who is aware, often painfully so, of the difference between the way things are in society and the way things "should" be, and this awareness is not something they can ignore. What they do about it depends on other things, of course. They get the message, from obscure sources of knowledge, that there are inner laws which, if adhered to, will profit humanity. Saturn in Aquarius clearly sees the injustices in social life, and unless they do something about it, they become pinched and cramped and bitter. Remember William

---

27   Eve Jackson, *Jupiter,* The Aquarian Press, Wellingborough, 1986.

Blake's chart from the fire seminar?[28] A singleton in air, Saturn in Aquarius in the 8th opposed his Mars in Leo in the 2nd house. And then, all that fire – a furnace heating up his idealism – abhorring and even rejecting money; a mystic who saw heaven and hell in the world around him and who, fortunately, had the power to express it artistically. Saturn in Aquarius gets its high-minded ideas from the individual's natal Uranus. (Blake's Uranus was in Pisces. He was painfully aware of suffering humanity, particularly those who were victims of mental and spiritual oppression. One can only imagine the spiritual realms from which he was receiving his "higher ideals".) One is then under obligation to bring these ideals into the community.

Oddly enough, Saturn in Aquarius can become decidedly autocratic through its efforts. Idealists are notoriously autocratic – their ideas can become more important than the people they are serving – because they feel they are serving humanity itself, even though that means pushing around those near them who do not see how important their task is. The controversial Albert Schweitzer had Saturn in Aquarius as a singleton in air, square his Mars in Scorpio. Community life is very important for Saturn in Aquarius. It needs the jostle of human life to keep it from rigidity. It is a very serious position for Saturn, because it carries the high, barely traced notions of Uranus into the density of the work in the world, Saturn's realm.

It is not easy for us to separate our experience of **Uranus in Aquarius** from our experience of Pluto in Sagittarius, since they both changed signs in the same year. Cyberspace has opened up a dimension that was not inhabited before. Technology has created a space in which individuals from every group and tribe on earth can connect across the planet in a way that has never happened before. When Pluto was in Sagittarius and Uranus in Aquarius in the early 16th century, the printing press opened up

---

28   See Darby Costello, *Water and Fire,* CPA Press, 1998.

information and connections between people that revolution-ised the world. Today it is happening again. People between the ages of seven and ninety-seven are speaking to each other through a new medium and in a new way. There is a frenzy of activity in a new dimension, and whether we are playing or not, we are affected by it. And this is not the only new technology we are encountering. How about genetic engineering? We are just beginning to become aware of this "advance" in science, and most of us have no idea how powerful an idea it is and how pro-foundly it will alter the planet we live on.

All of the new technology holds a fascination, compels atten-tion, and inspires fear. Beware of being sucked in, and beware of your disapproval and negative ideas around it. It is very hard not to lose yourself in collective opinions on the ideas they represent. It is important to stay conscious – not to fall into "group think" unless you *choose* to do that, then be willing to take responsibil-ity for that. Stay conscious and keep awake to your animal in-stincts, too. Wherever Uranus is transiting through your chart, keep an eye on that area for introductions to new technology or new groups which challenge your fixed attitudes. When Uranus touches off personal planets, we have to open up new ways of thinking about things. We have to experiment and keep awake to the air currents we inhabit, but also to other air currents we might not wish to acknowledge, from people and thought forms. During these transits, everyone of us is moved into unfamiliar territory, whether we know it or not. When the house Uranus is transiting has Aquarius on its cusp – and so one tends to be experimental here anyway – this turns up the voltage. If there are planets there, in Aquarius, then it is as if those parts of your-self wake up from a long sleep. For some, this is very exciting. For others, who dislike excitement, it is annoying. But through Uranus you are brought into the dimensions where life is experi-menting with emerging patterns that are forming, whether you like it or not.

We are on the brink of **Neptune in Aquarius**. When it first goes in, we shall have to watch it for some time to see what arises. Last time it occurred was between 1834 and 1848, for those of you with a historical mind. From here, it looks like we will be led forward, in the usual Neptunian way, by dreams of a new world in which everyone will be fine and dandy, and we will be disappointed and disillusioned each time we are forced to see that it isn't happening like that. Where we are most idealistic and have the strongest fixed ideas is the place where new, barely perceptible notions will begin to melt and reconfigure our ideas. Strange connections, often not noticed until much later, will begin to occur.

When personal planets are touched by Neptune in Aquarius, the ideas already contained in that planet's field are either melted down or intensified. Disillusionment occurs with community and technology and friends – and also new connections, new worlds. Neptune always operates out of the light of our personal awareness. We can see it more clearly as it sweeps through the collective. This time it might be just visible to our personal and inner eye. If we keep an eye on the dreams and disappointments revealed through the larger body – as expressed through art, poetry, theatre, dance, and through the types of idealistic groups that form and dissolve around us – then we might get a sense of how it is working in our own personal lives. One thing is for sure: if it touches a personal planet, we will be brought into the new era forming in a personal way. Whether it be through technology or groups, art or science, we will connect strongly with what is happening "out there".

Pluto will enter Aquarius in around 2024. It was last there from 1777 to 1798, for the historians in the group. Uranus was discovered during this period, if you remember. Many of us will still be around then. Some of you will be going through your Pluto trine Pluto, and others will be experiencing the Pluto opposition – an unusual experience in our human history. We will have gone through Pluto in Capricorn by then, and I wonder how the shape of our world will have changed? Pluto in Aquarius will give birth to a generation of people who will have the "evolutionary task" of transforming and purifying collective notions about ourselves as a species. Old ideas are blown away to give space for the new.

Groups of people will probably feel the struggle between holding onto their collective identity and letting themselves be integrated into a larger group. While Neptune is in Aquarius, a generation will be born into the dreams and ideals for a new world that will be circulating. They will carry this dream, and because Uranus will be there too, they will experiment with it. When Pluto goes into Aquarius, they will work their world with these dreams and ideas. By this, I mean that, when they are adults, this generation will work to transform the ideas of who we are in the wider sense. For those of us with Pluto in Leo, it might look pretty strange, as we were working together – whether we were conscious of it or not – to transform the notion of individuality and individual rights.

Aquarius rising

There is an aura of electricity around people with this Ascendant. Some of them you recognise immediately as unusual, but others seem very ordinary, at first. Saturn and Uranus vie for rulership here, and so, whatever your first impression, be prepared for a surprise the second time. Sometimes they have a distinctly unusual look about them, but not always. Surprise is the key here. Neither you or they can ever predict what will happen next. At each stage of life they suddenly discover a new idea, which leads to the next stage. Just when they seem to be settled, something arises to send them into a new air space. They have a disconcerting effect on their environment, which, in part, they enjoy, but it depends on other things as to whether they can accept the surprising effect the environment has on them.

The one with Aquarius rising, and anyone who comes within their personality field, will be driven to bring an "outside" idea into manifestation through Saturn's demanding rigour. Each time they become involved with a new circle of people, they awaken high ideals in anyone who has an inclination towards idealism. Whether the ideals are dashed on Saturn's rocks or realised through Saturn's work depends partly on their willingness to work in whatever way is demanded, and partly on whether the idea is right for the time. One way or another, people with Aquarius rising will challenge the traditional expectations of whatever worlds they inhabit.

Planets in the 11th house

People who have personal planets in the 11th house are drawn out of their own tribal group and brought into contact with others whose lives and collective notions are very different to their own. It is said to be the house of groups and hopes, dreams and wishes. It points particularly to the hopes, dreams and wishes that you can achieve through the networks of people you know. I think it has more subtle layers of meaning, too, but for now, let me explore the more obvious one.

The sign on the cusp of this house, and its ruler, say something significant about how you conceive and create your community life. They give information about how you meet and encounter the groups you belong to during your life. Personal planets contained within the field of the 11th house tell you something significant about what is activated, once you are contained within the field of a group. We were speaking about the

Dalai Lama before, who has Leo on the cusp of his 11th house.[29] So we assume groups and organisations are central to his spiritual fulfillment. If we look to the Sun, which is in Cancer in the 10th house, we interpret that by saying his position in the world is such that it brings him the groups and networks which offer him the possibility of achieving his hopes and wishes. He has **Venus** in Leo in the 11th, and so we can say that he is looking for personal heart connections and loyalty from those he associates with, and his hopes and wishes are that those he loves are well and fulfilled.

We can also look back at his Sun in Cancer, ruler of the 11th house, and back to its ruler, the Moon in Virgo conjunct Neptune in the 12th house; we can see the monastery there, the self-sacrifice and the sense of sorrow which moves him to use his position in the world to spread his Cancerian net wider in the fulfilling of his vocation. This has to do with touching groups of people in a very personal, Venus in Leo way. We can also see his mother's self-sacrifice in giving him to his vocation when he was so very young – Moon-Neptune in the 12th – but also the generosity he got from her, which he expresses with others through his Venus in Leo in the 11th. Do you see what I am doing here?

---

29   More than one set of data is given for the Dalai Lama's birth. The Dalai Lama gives 6 July 1935 in his autobiography, *Freedom in Exile*. Lois Rodden's *AstroDatabank* source note quotes a letter from Pema Dorjee at the Dalai Lama's office, giving "between 5.30 and 6.30 in the morning", and adds, "Note: by Eastern tradition, holy men are always born at daybreak. Abayakoon gave 18 December 1933, 00 41a, AQ Fall/1959. AQ Summer/1962 same, adding, 'The overshadowing took place June 6, 1935, 10.10 am, Amdo, Chinghai.' Jim Eshelman quotes George Cecil Nixon in *Raman's Astrology Magazine*, that the 13th Dalai Lama died 17 December 1933. An auxiliary clause in the Official Lama Rule Book states that the soul goes to dwell in a sacred lake for forty-nine days before reincarnating."

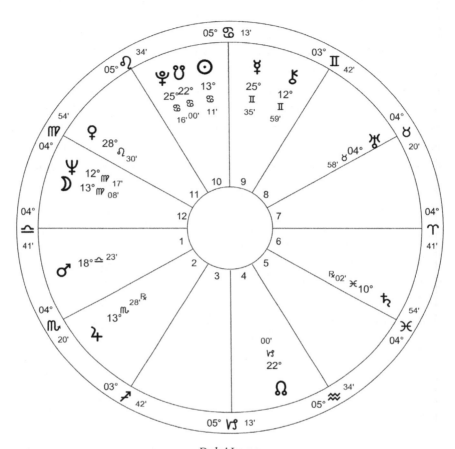

Dalai Lama
6 July 1935, 11.45 am LMT = 4.45 am GMT, Takster, Tibet, 36N32, 101E12
Koch houses; true Node

Audience: Yes. I have just realised that, each time you start any-where in a chart and follow the trails, you end up repeating cer-tain themes over and over. Of course you end up with planets in rulership, or if there are no rulers, then you end up with one or two planetary duets again and again. But I wanted to ask you about **transpersonals in the 11ᵗʰ**.

Darby: When anyone has planets in Scorpio, Aquarius, or Pi-sces, I follow the trails using both traditional and transpersonal rulers. They tell you about two different dimensions of a person's life. It is interesting that we are discussing this here, in the 11th house. This is where the most complex connections are made with people. Everyone you know knows other people, and when you are with a group of people you are in contact with the webs they inhabit. Sensitive people often find groups troublesome. I wonder if this is partly because they get entangled in the complex lines of these webs, and lose their own inner place for a time.

When you have transpersonal planets in the 11th, you are particularly sensitive to the potential of all those connections when you become part of a group. In Johannesburg in the 1970's, I did a chart for one of the musicians in the orchestra there. Then several more came to me, and I remember being fascinated that so many of them had Neptune in the 11th. They each said, in various ways, that they were always waiting for that magic moment when the whole orchestra became one and there was nothing but the music. But they could not make it happen and, more often than not, it didn't happen. Ah, but when it did! With transpersonals in the 11th, there is the knowledge that what happens in groups is beyond your control. You either connect or you don't. You slip through groups with Neptune, often feeling invisible; you feel and behave like the outsider with Uranus; and you feel threatened with Pluto, until – and this is the key – until you happen upon the group which resonates with the planet in your 11th house. Then a whole dimension of yourself opens up, and you are connected on levels you only imagined before. Whether this is happy or not, of course, depends on other things!

WILLIAM BUTLER YEATS

Let's look at the chart I have to show you today. This is the chart of William Butler Yeats. As you can see, his chart has Sun conjunct Uranus in Gemini in the 5th house, in a grand trine with Saturn in Libra in the 8th and Moon in Aquarius in the 1st house. The 3rd, 7th and 11th houses all have planets in them. Mercury is right on the IC. It seems alone down there, but it is moving towards the midpoint of that fire trine, and is in its own sign and Sun ruler, so it has a lot to say in this chart. The two rulers of his Aquarius Ascendant, Saturn and Uranus, are both in air and trine to each other. This is an extraordinarily coherent chart.

Audience: Do you mean that it's all joined up?

Darby: It's all joined up, and each configuration reinforces and embellishes the meaning of another. Themes repeat and are deepened throughout the chart. There are two areas of action and even they join up. There is the grand trine in air connected to the opposition of Sun and Jupiter. The Moon is part of a T-square with Venus Pluto and Mars, which is then trine Neptune. There is a sharp pattern between 10° and 20° and then 20° and 30°, and the Moon joins the two patterns at 19° 46′. Mercury alone is outside of all this interweaving, but heading towards the dance in his early years and joining it all up in the end.

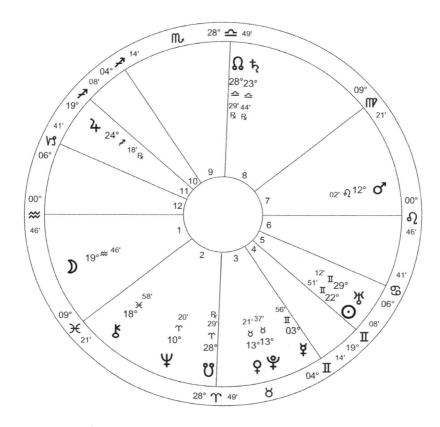

William Butler Yeats, 13 June 1865, 10.40 pm LMT, Dublin
Koch houses; true Node

Audience: Only an air sign could be so fascinated by the patterns themselves. What I want to know is, what does all this connectedness tell us? What does it mean?

Darby: We will have to see what it tells us as we go along, but for the moment it does give us a sense of order. There is beauty in order, and so, for those who love the airy spaces, it shows us something beautiful. Perhaps it shows that the soul who incarnated into this time-space knew how to order his inner world. He could certainly translate the images that arose in his imagination into mental constructions that speak very powerfully to all sorts of people, although we may not always understand them. Some of his structures were pretty far out. And I keep noticing Mercury down there at the roots, in Gemini – a little bit disconnected from the rest and therefore free and a little bit lost in this otherwise highly organised pattern of interactions. And yet, at root, it is the key to his life and work. Let's explore this life and his work in light of his chart.

A biography

"...Always it is an impulse from some Daimon
that gives to our vague, unsatisfied desire, beauty,
a meaning, and a form all can accept."
– William Butler Yeats, "Anima Mundi"[30]

---

30   William Butler Yeats, *Mythologies,* Collier Books, New York, 1959.

Yeats was many things in his life: artist, dramatist, critic, social historian, politician, theatre manager, mythologer, philosopher, occultist, and mage. But above all, he was a poet. Every aspect of his life, every mask he wore, was brought to his poetry. He was born into the Pluto in Taurus generation of the last century. Those who lived past middle age saw the peace of their known world shattered beyond recognition, and the resultant profound change of values affected all of them. His Venus conjunct Pluto seems to act almost like a singleton, in that its elemental voice is very strong in his chart. Venus is in its own sign, and the planets are only a few minutes apart and in the 3rd house. The transformation of himself and his world, and his search for what was truly real underneath all the Mercurial tricks of light and the Plutonian upheavals, were themes he returned to again and again through his life. He had no planets in water signs.

Audience: You haven't mentioned Chiron, which is in Pisces.

Darby: Yes, but Chiron is always another thing. I do not treat it like a planet because it isn't a planet. It describes something other than planetary influence. But yes, it is in Pisces. Chiron in Pisces, and Neptune, are in his 2nd house. When this man was mining his resources, we can barely imagine where he went inside himself – but we can see the results in his poetry. Chiron is square his Sun in the 5th. His father, John Butler Yeats, trained to be an attorney, but gave it up to become a painter shortly after his marriage. He had a very great influence on his son. He had strong opinions on many subjects, and was dogmatic, unconventional, perceptive, intensely social, and conversational. He was a Pisces who read poetry to his children, painted pictures, and was financially irresponsible, which was very difficult for his family. We can see Yeats's Sun Uranus conjunction in Gemini in the 5th square to Chiron in the 2nd and opposing Jupiter here.

We can also see Neptune in the 2nd trine Mars in Leo in the 7th. Some time after his mother died in 1900, his father moved to New York and never came back. Yeats sent him money, even when he didn't have much himself. It was a very close, difficult relationship – the weaknesses and wounds of father and son entangled with each other. J. B. adored his son and demanded much of his dreamy, timid first-born. Yeats suffered from not being able to live up to his father's expectations, until middle age. He responded powerfully to his father's strength, as he did to all dramatic and powerful people throughout his life, with his Mars in Leo in the 7th. He resented his father, but loved and admired him too. But it was only late in Yeats' life before his father returned the compliment. The physical distance between them created a greater closeness, as is often the case with Uranian people. The senior Yeats wrote, in his later years, "Old Priam was not much in himself, but then, Hector was his son."

The two voices of Yeats' Gemini spirit were naturally activated by his father, as the Sun was there. From a very early age he was intensely self-critical. We can imagine he took this in from his father's unconscious self-criticism, which was then turned onto his son. Yeats says of himself, "Because I had found it hard to attend to anything less interesting than my thoughts, I was difficult to teach." He complained of having a short attention span throughout his life. He could not learn to read, until his father took it upon himself to conquer "my wandering mind", sometimes with such impatience that he would throw the lesson book at his son's head in anger. J. B. Yeats was a Pisces, with Moon Venus and Pluto in Aries opposite his Moon in Libra. A complex man full of wisdom, self-delusions, passion, selfishness and intelligence.

But the opposing voices of Gemini took root from other sources too. He was born in Ireland but he spent a lot of his childhood in London and was educated in both countries. He spent his holidays in Sligo with his grandparents and yearned for it when he was in London. He was lonely and isolated in London and suffered the feelings of the outsider in the school yard. "I was divided from all those boys, not merely by the anecdotes that are everywhere perhaps a chief expression of the distrust of races, but because our mental images were different." This is air recognising itself.

He says little about his mother, but it was from her that he received his love of myth, legends and folklore. She was from an old, established family, and had little liking for society, much eccentricity, and some madness. She comes across as a sensitive, religious woman who hated the social, artistic world of her husband and preferred Sligo with its local stories, legends, and folk tales. She was always thought to be odd. She became deeply disillusioned with her marriage, and was depressed, ill, and somewhat mad through all her later years. She had been apparently very beautiful and confident as a young woman. Yeats was the eldest of six children, two of whom died, one at three and the other at just a few months old. Four of the children had Moon in Aquarius, *all* square Pluto, and another had Moon in Libra, probably square to Uranus. Three of them had Venus in Libra, all heavily aspected. We can see his beautiful, idealistic mother in these placements, but also the pain that each inherited through her. Willy was often separated from her because she disliked coming to London so much. His relationship with her seems to have been quite uncomfortable. He remembered his childhood as full of torment and sadness. He was convinced of his sinfulness.

Audience: Irish Catholic.

Darby: No, Irish Protestant on both sides; but his father had turned from his background and become a fierce religious sceptic. This was another way Yeats's divided spirit was energised. Every thought brought opposing thoughts, and they spurred him on to more opposing resolutions. He saw himself as divided, always struggling to bring his opposites together, unable to see or be or believe one thing without seeing or being or believing its opposite. And this, instead of reducing him, drew him forward into greatness. This is partly because he took responsibility for his nature very early on. He wrote: "Indeed, I remember little of childhood but its pain. I have grown happier with every year of life as though gradually conquering something in myself, for certainly my miseries were not made by others but were a part of my own mind." His Saturn in Libra, trine both Sun and Moon, gave the feeling of steady progress and certainly endurance in the pursuit of resolution. Mars in Leo in the T-square offered endless conflicts as a spur to self-conquest, and this was his path to mastering his mind. Saturn is always where we seek mastery, and in air it seeks mental mastery. There is such a strong link between his Saturn in Libra in the 8th and Venus-Pluto in Taurus. We see them speak together with different voices throughout his life and work.

The houses where Yeats and his siblings grew up were filled with painters and actors and articulate men and women full of passion and ideas – his father's friends. The children were expected to be articulate, interested and interesting, and so they turned out to be. With all Yeats's air, the conversations and characters around him activated all layers of thought and fed his dreams and reveries. Very early on, he recognised in himself a fascination with passionate men and women, feeling so timid and sensitive himself. We can see the Moon in the 1st opposing Mars in Leo in the 7th again here. He was highly sensitive to dramatic and energetic personalities, and he was inspired by the images and thoughts of visionaries. He was impressed first by his father's energy and power (and by his maternal grandfather and uncle), and later by the passionate old republican, John O'Leary. In a period of disillusionment with the world, in the early 1900s, he wrote, "Romantic Ireland's dead and gone, / It's with O'Leary in the grave."

The ruler of his 3rd house is Aries, which points to Mars in Leo in the 7th, which looks back at the Venus-Pluto conjunction in the 3rd. All his siblings were creative. His younger brother, Jack Butler Yeats, became a very great painter. His brother Robert died when Willy was seven; his sister Jane died when he was ten. I wonder about that Pluto in the 3rd. He never gave the impression that these deaths touched him deeply on a conscious level, but whether through his mother's suffering or his sisters, they certainly touched him at a deeper level. There were two sisters, Lily and Elizabeth, who grew up to design good hand-printed books and broadsheets from their own press. I know little about his relationship with his sisters but that they were artistic and energetic, and at least one of them was very psychic, often dreaming true. As far as I know, they never married. To a large extent, Yeats's father concentrated on his education to the exclusion of the others. We could look at that Venus-Pluto conjunction for a long time here. As far as I know, the siblings were a close and argumentative family – rows were frequent, but they never lost contact with each other throughout their lives.

Though he was a sensitive and introspective child, he openly admired the heroic and despised timidity. And yet, he did not admire bombast, in himself or others, and he often chastised himself for it. He once said that although he could do whatever he told himself to, he lacked real courage, which he described as "self-possession in an unforeseen situation." During his mid-forties, when transiting Pluto was conjunct his Sun – years of intense self-scrutiny aiming towards self-reformation – he wrote: "It is always inexcusable to lose one's self-possession. It always comes from impatience, from a kind of spiritual fright at someone who is here & now, more powerful even if only from stupidity. I am never angry with those in my power. I fear strangers, I fear the representatives of the collective opinion and so rage stupidly & rudely, exaggerating what I feel & think."

Audience: You can hear that T-square speaking.

Darby: Yes, he is describing one way in which that T-square pulls him out of shape; when he was not able to hold the tension. The tense frustration and pressure of that configuration had to be brought to balance over and over through the hard work of Saturn in Libra, and he worked very hard through his life, in spite of accusing himself of idleness. But also, he had the natural inclinations of an idealist. How could he not, with all that air? The Venus-Pluto square Mars drew him down deep into a Plutonian world where violent forces made themselves known to him. He searched for symbols which could contain and express these forces, and he was fascinated with the notion of consciousness as conflict. Don't you people with strong air planets feel driven to bring your earth and water conflicts into your consciousness? Don't you try to construct, or at least discover, a map that will make some sort of sense of the struggle and conflict beneath the surface?

Audience: I have a lot of air planets, and I have always tried to escape from conflict into my head, as I think most airy people do. I even try to use astrology to get away from it, though that's becoming more difficult as my perspective on the planets change. But I keep thinking I will be able to find a way of thinking that will resolve the conflict. I imagine if I understand myself enough through therapy and self-examination, inner conflict will melt away.

Darby: You sound a bit doubtful of this, at the moment. Perhaps a new perspective is taking shape. It sounds as though you are looking for another flight path, a new way to conceive of yourself.

Audience: I am, and I am interested to see Yeats's chart. What you just said touched a chord. But he was a creative artist, a poet.

He had talent. Perhaps we normal people have to suppress intolerable conflict, because we can't make it tolerable through art.

Darby: I don't know – I just don't know. I naturally believe and willingly choose to believe in the mystery of real choice, somewhere in our souls. Was it William James who said his first act of free will was to believe in free will? Perhaps some of us choose to suppress the intolerable for some sort of peace. But the point here might be that if your map of reality does not take in what you experience, then it is too small. If you are living with a map that does not account for whole chunks of yourself, then you need to go to another level of air and see yourself and your map from a broader perspective. Those with airy charts need to open windows a lot, because our living experiences are always making bits of our maps obsolete.

Audience: Why not live directly from experience, and throw away the maps?

Darby: Yeats did try to do that, again and again. He first sought a home in abstraction, and later struggled to get out of abstraction and into his passions and feelings. But telling an airy person to throw away constructs is like telling a water person, "Get rid of your emotions," or a fire person, "Don't follow your heart," or an earth person, "Ignore your senses." It's a much better idea to get to know what sort of maps you are constructing, and learn to recognise when to adjust or even change them. But get rid of them? Not an option.

Mapping reality

At each stage of his life, Yeats found new maps of reality, and he incorporated them and the vision they represented into his work. And so you see an extraordinarily wide variety of symbols appearing through his poetry, as befits a true Uranian whose writing will be strained through Pluto's deep earth realm. With Mercury at the roots of his chart, he was interested in his own ancestry, but also in the notion of past lives. He was fascinated by cycles and spirals. He didn't find spiritual sustenance in conventional religion – he explored ancient systems and esoteric doctrines from an early age. He found resonances in Irish myth, legends, and stories that came out of the old and ancient earth – his Taurus conjunction again. But he could not rest with only those images. His vast capacity for contradiction meant that any imaginal system, once familiar, opened the way to a search for something completely different. This is partly the Aquarian discontent. When you find the very thing you are looking for, it opens up a new dimension which asks to be filled with something that is absolutely not available in present time-space. You cannot stop developing, even if you try. Realms of air keep appearing above or below your head. Finding ways to navigate the old and new worlds is the trick here.

He developed himself through getting to know the people he admired, either in person or through their work. Gemini imitation, Uranian style: finding the odd kernel in the work, then making it his own by developing it according to his own unique perception. He became a disciple of Blake quite early on. At some point, look at his chart with Blake's, and you will see why the earlier visionary poet had such a powerful effect on the young Yeats.[31]

Blake was the true visionary, uncluttered by anything like the need to order or construct a system in which to place his vision. He was much less complicated than Yeats. He had one air planet through which to build a construct for all his direct fiery experience. Yeats was called to express himself through all levels

---

31   William Blake was born 28 November 1757, 7.00 am, London. See pages 160*ff* in *Water and Fire, op. cit.* (Note 7).

of air, and even through the air houses. He had very few directly mystical experiences, but those he had lasted his lifetime. He received most of his experiences from the spirit world through others – a 7th house fire planet – and then he had to order it in his airy Uranian way, finding earth symbols to give it flesh. The struggle to do this made him both very human and also remote from most people's daily concerns. If he had a problem, he often went to mediums for guidance. In his twenties he joined the Order of the Golden Dawn and the Theosophical Society. He admired Madame Blavatsky, though he was critical of her lack of self-criticism.

One of his maternal uncles had his astrological chart done when he was born, and astrology seemed to be an intrinsic part of his thinking. Listen to this, from his *Autobiographies:*

> There is an astrological sense in which a man's wife or sweetheart is always an Eve made from a rib of his body. She is drawn to him because she represents a group of stellar influences in the radical horoscope. These influences also create an element in his character, and his destiny, in things apart from love or marriage. Whether this element be good or evil, she is therefore its external expression. The happiest have such horoscopes that they find what they have of good in their wives, others must find what they have of evil, or a man may have both affinities. Sometimes a man may find the evil of his horoscope in a woman, in rescuing her from her own self may conquer his own evil, as with Simon Magus who married a harlot. Others may find in a woman the good that conquers them and shapes them. All external events of life are of course an externalization of character in the same way, but not to the same degree as the wife, who may represent the gathering up of an entire web of influences...We are

mirrors of the stellar light and we cast this light outward as incidents, magnetic attractions, characterizations, desires...[32]

Plato and the Neoplatonists were a most powerful influence on his mind, first through Blake and later through his own reading. He was naturally an idealist who felt at home with the notion of hierarchies and spirals, and so when he finally read Plato and the Neoplatonists for himself he felt very much at home. And yet he also embraced much from Eastern mysticism and Western occultism. He did not try to resolve antithetical conceptions so much as free own understanding with them. His biographer, Ellmann, says: "No sooner had he pulled himself into two parts and set them at odds than he wanted to make peace between them, seeking the centre that he fled from in a continual competition with himself."[33] He could not put one thing on the scale without having to put on another, and so we see him juxtapose images and experiences, hardly ever pausing for rest. There were times when he complained, as in *The Fascination of What's Difficult*: "The fascination of what's difficult / Has dried the sap out of my veins, and rent / Spontaneous joy and natural content / Out of my heart." But soon he was called to another adventure, into another juxtaposition, as he tried to "hammer [his] thoughts into unity".

His responsiveness to fiery visionaries drew him forward all his life, continually burning up his previous conceptions until a new scaffolding began to appear and the process began again. He might look like he was contradicting himself, but in fact he was simply terribly alive. This aliveness expressed itself through warring thoughts, none of which he would, or perhaps could, give up for peace. For a time he became obsessed with Nietzsche, and the place of power and violence in evolution and creativity. He was fascinated by the urge to power and by the role

---

32   W. B. Yeats, *Autobiographies,* Macmillan Publishers Ltd, London, 1955.
33   Ellmann, Richard, *Yeats: The Man and the Masks,* Penguin, London, 1979.

of violence in creation. This is from *A Vision*[34], in which one of his characters says:

> Dear predatory birds, prepare for war, prepare your children and all that you can reach, for how can a nation or a kindred without war become that "bright particular star" of Shakespeare, that lit the roads in boyhood? Test art, morality, custom, thought, by Thermopylae; make rich and poor act so to one another that they can stand together there. Love war because of its horror, that belief may be changed, civilisation renewed. We desire belief and lack it. Belief comes from shock and is not desired. When a kindred discovers through apparition and horror that the perfect cannot perish, nor even the imperfect long be interrupted, who can withstand that kindred? Belief is renewed continually in the ordeal of death.

And again, from *A Vision:*

> What if Christ and Oedipus or, to shift the names, Saint Catherine of Genoa and Michael Angelo, are the two scales of a balance, the two butt-ends of a seesaw? What if every two thousand and odd years something happens in the world to make one sacred, the other secular; one wise, the other foolish; one fair, the other foul; one divine, the other devilish? What if there is an arithmetic or geometry that can exactly measure the slope of a balance, the dip of a scale, and so date the coming of that something?

That idea or construct must have momentarily satisfied his grand air trine's demands.

As Saturn is exalted in Libra and co-rules his Ascendant, our astrological eye returns to it often, there in the 8th house. It

---

34 W. B. Yeats, *A Vision,* Collier Books, New York, 1972.

also speaks of his sexual frustration, which is further underlined by the fixed T-square. This is the pathological mulch in which his spirit was nourished. In it we find the bundle of frustrations, inhibitions, and sublimations which could have reduced him to a self-pitying bore, but seemed to be the painful grit which spurred him to creation. Seeing its muddy tracks through his life helps us understand him, his work, and his art. Of course it also helps to have a broad understanding of Irish myths and legends, Greek and Roman mythology, and Eastern religious symbolism. Look at that opposition to Jupiter in the 11th house from the Sun-Uranus conjunction. Can you imagine a more restless search for truth as it rejects, with perfect solar integrity, the notion of truth at the same time? I think he decided in old age that truth could never be understood, only embodied and acted upon.

He spoke several languages – Sun and Mercury in Gemini. His personal air was nourished by the intellectual spirit of the times, particularly expressed by Malarmé, Baudelaire, and Balzac. He got involved with Indian theology and collaborated with a swami on translations of ten of the Upanishads, and that naturally influenced his poetry as well. However, he did not forsake his own air for foreign spirits. He was a passionate Irish Nationalist. Through him we can see the depth of Mercury's field. Next time you read in a book that Mercury in Gemini is "superficial", think of Yeats. He tasted as many different cultural airs as his life could manage, and then, through his 5th house Sun, he turned them into art which reached – Uranian style – beyond the recognisable constructs of his times. He experimented at the edges of consciousness, excluding nothing. He even had a brief flirtation with fascism as an intellectual construct, in the 1930s, but its practise disgusted him and he lost interest. The only belief he held consistently throughout his life was the belief in reincarnation. That seemed to be bone-deep. Everything else shifted and changed positions within him as he absorbed new ideas and found new symbols to express them.

Beauty passing like a dream

Audience: You mentioned his wife. Wasn't she a spiritualist?

Darby: Let's speak about Maude Gonne first, his great unrequited love and the muse of so much of his poetry. He met her when he was twenty-four. She was over six feet tall, breathtakingly beautiful, a passionate revolutionary, and deeply individualistic. She brought her pet monkey with her, the first time they met. Look at this synastry. Although I have no time for her birth, it still shows the intensity of their connection.

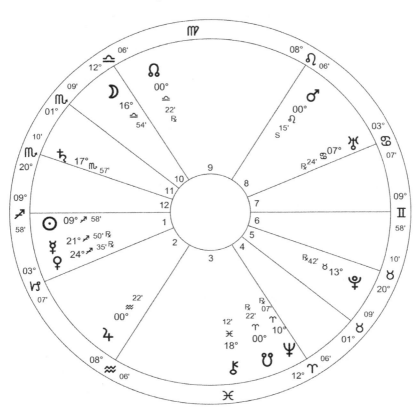

Maude Gonne, 2 December 1866, no birth time (chart set for sunrise in Dublin)

Her Jupiter is on his Ascendant in Aquarius, and opposite his Mars in Leo in his 7th. Her Mercury-Venus is right on his Jupiter in Sagittarius. Pluto has returned to 13° Taurus, on his Venus-Pluto conjunction. Her Moon in Libra opposes her own Neptune and his. How could he not fall in love with her! And, with Venus in Taurus, it was to last for twenty-five years. But there is Pluto-Venus and Venus-ruled Saturn in Libra in the 8th. It was a romantic, idealistic, mostly frustrated, unrequited love. She was the externalisation of his T-square and the outer reason for much of his adult torment. But he never rejected torment, using it to fuel his art, although at times it wearied him. From *A Dialogue of Self and Soul,* written in his sixties, he wrote: "I am content to live it all again / And yet again, if it be life to pitch / Into the frog-spawn of a blind man's ditch, / A blind man battering blind men; / Or into that most fecund ditch of all, / The folly that man does / Or must suffer, if he woos / A proud woman not kindred of his soul."

Audience: He *was* escaping into his head! All that poetry was his escape from a real relationship.

Darby: That is often an accusation leveled at people with lots of air planets. But I am suspicious of it. He has Sun-Uranus trine Saturn trine Moon, all in air signs. How is he supposed to think and behave? He is a true idealist, born to the element of air. Is he really escaping because he does not think and act like an earth or water sign? Can we not accuse very earthy people of escaping from the true realms of imagination, thought and spirit? Again and again he turned his personal, political and spiritual frustrations into, yes, social and political action, but beyond that, always, into poetry. He found one or another side of his oppositions outside himself, certainly, but he also stayed close to the inner tension which held them in place inside himself. And when Saturn finally had got its every drop of blood, through his constant inner and outer work, he married a real and proper woman.

Audience: You don't think that he opposed his own soul by marrying, with his Moon opposite his 7ᵗʰ house Mars?

Darby: It does not seem so. Perhaps he had served his ideal so deeply and so long that he embodied it himself, and this left him free to marry an "other" in the end. The 7ᵗʰ house is all about what is truly "other", and that is why it is such a difficult area. Maude was his creative inspiration – 5ᵗʰ house. Georgie was his true wife – 7ᵗʰ house.

The true wife

It was 1917. His women friends were worried about him, as was he himself. He was middle-aged, fussy, lonely. From his early twenties he had periodically proposed marriage to Maude Gonne. He asked her one last time. She refused again. He had loved her "in the old high way of love", and now it was about to give him up. But he was obviously keen to marry that year, and he asked Maude's beautiful daughter, Iseult, but she also refused. How we would judge him today for such a thing!

Transiting Jupiter was in Gemini, and his progressed Moon was in Capricorn in his 12ᵗʰ house. He was restless and felt cut off from life, with fantasies of a dry and lonely old age. He was fifty-two. The third woman he proposed to that year was Georgie Hyde Lees, and she said yes. She was intelligent, humorous and, most fortunately, she was in love with him. They were married on the 17th of October, on her twenty-fifth birthday.[35]

---

35 According to Richard Ellman (*op. cit.,* Note 12), she was born 17 October 1892.

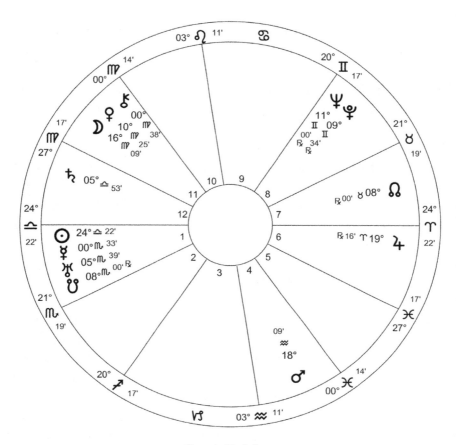

Georgie Hyde Lees
17 October 1892, no birth time (chart set for sunrise in Dublin)

I don't know her birth time, but she had five planets in air. Her Sun at 24° Libra was conjunct his Saturn in the 8th house, while her Mars in Aquarius was conjunct his Moon. The transits are interesting on their wedding day: the Sun was at 24° Libra, conjunct his Saturn (exact to his progressed Saturn), and his progressed north Node was right on his Saturn at 23° Libra – in the 8th house, of course. His progressed Sun was conjunct his Mars in Leo in the 7th, as was transiting Saturn! Uranus was in Aquarius and it was conjunct his Moon – and, of course, her Mars. His progressed Venus was about to conjunct his natal Uranus. Surprising himself, he fell deeply in love with his wife, and their marriage was enduring and deeply happy. What a wise and clever woman she must have been.

They had two children. This is another way his 7th house Mars reflected light back to his 5th house Sun. And another way: on their honeymoon she began to play with automatic writing, which suddenly became serious and went on for several years. He recorded and ordered everything she wrote and said, and turned it into the extraordinary work I mentioned just now, called *A Vision*. This is a translation of the often obscure messages from the spirit world into a mental construction, with an astrological base – a multi-layered map, pure air. It has a grand logic, is geometrical in shape, and explains how souls incarnate and the stages they go through in cycles and spirals of personal and collective history. When asked if he really believed his construction, we hear his Gemini planets again:

> Some will ask whether I believe in the actual existence of my circuits of sun and moon...To such a question I can but answer that if sometimes, overwhelmed by miracle as all men must be when in the midst of it, I have taken such periods literally, my reason has soon recovered; and now that the system stands out clearly in my imagination I regard them as stylistic arrangements of experience comparable to the cubes in the drawings of Wyndham Lewis and to the ovoids in the sculpture of Brancusi. They have helped me to hold in a single thought reality and justice.[36]

He was dramatic by nature, and eventually grew out of his timidity. He concretised his love of the theatrical and brought together his high ideals and his need for self expression by helping to create The Irish National Theatre Company with the help

_____

36   *Op. cit.* (Note 11).

of several friends, notably one of his close women friends, Lady Augusta Gregory. Later they bought the Abbey Theatre in Dublin. He had very strong-minded close women friends all his life, as befits Moon in Aquarius in the 1st house. He was deeply involved with the theatre for a long time, both as a playwright and in every small imaginable way. The mundane side of it eventually exhausted him. If you think about all that fire and air with just the Taurus conjunction, you can see why any involvement on the material plane would be exhausting in the end. When involved he would be obsessed, and so he would have to return to his air space – the place where he worked to fashion life into words that enhanced life. These impulses came from within, as desires and urges, and they had to be brought up into daylight through symbols into poetry. And they came from without, from the upper reaches of thoughts that reached beyond thought to be brought into the time-bound world of everyday life. His poetry is full of symbols, but also of characters in history and in his own life.

Saturn the wordsmith

In 1928 he wrote *The Tower,* and in 1929, *The Winding Stair.* Both use as dominant subjects and symbols the Irish Rising and the Civil War. They also use the image of his own tower which he bought in Ireland and which he lived in, on and off. He drew images and thoughts from the Byzantine Empire, Plato, Plotinus, Porphyry, and his contemporary psychical research. His inner library of images was extraordinarily rich. He picked them up everywhere, with his Mars in fire in the 7th trine Neptune. And then he wove them into the stories in his poems. He used the Sun and Moon, the hawk, the unicorn, the phoenix, horse, hound, and boar. Leda and the Swan, Helen of Troy, and many Irish men and women appear in his plays and poems. And then there are figures such as the Blind Man, the Lame Man, and the Beggar.

His work became richer after his marriage and all through his later years. Some of his greatest works were written between ages fifty and seventy-five. He railed against old age, and yet we experience its richness through his poetry: "An aged man is but a paltry thing, / A tattered coat upon a stick, unless / Soul clap its hands and sing, and louder sing / For every tatter in its mortal dress / Nor is there singing school but studying / Monuments of its own magnificence; / And therefore I have sailed the seas and come / To the holy city of Byzantium." This is from *Sailing to Byzantium,* written in his sixties.

With Saturn in air, it is the mind that is the place of mastery; we work towards developing mental mastery, if we work at all. Freud had Saturn in Gemini. Jung had Saturn in Aquarius. Yeats had Saturn in Libra. Saturn in air demands constant practise in articulating feelings, experiences and vision so that they might be useful to others in understanding their own experiences. Saturn in air demands that one work to give shape to ideas – to incarnate ideas, bring them into local time. Saturn in air demands that one practises communicating; otherwise the machinery grinds to a halt. And that is disastrous.

Some of his most productive work was done through a period which he says was pure drudgery and boredom. He hated being bored, of course – the great Gemini cry. Passion, intensity, and joy were the most important qualities for him, and he managed, against inner and outer obstacles, to retain them, but not at the expense of suffering. All passion is grounded in suffering which endures the unendurable, and he endured personal suffering through his idealism in many different ways, most notably through his twenty-five years of unrequited love. But also, he was both Anglo-Irish and an idealistic Irish nationalist, which had become, by the 1930's, an almost unbearable contradiction. And he was constantly criticised by the public and his friends for his weird occult inclinations and his personal eccentricities. However, he fashioned bitter disillusionment into poetry as another might pour it into painting, writing, or loving service to a person or a garden or with prayer.

The man and the masks

Audience: He was fascinated with masks, and with the *Noe* theatre. It makes me wonder if air Ascendants form their personae out of mental concepts. Are they more constructed than other elements?

Darby: I thought of that, too, when reading him again. Saturn and Uranus co-rule his Aquarius Ascendant. Uranus in Gemini conjunct his Sun in the 5th accounts for the impulse to play with masks, but whatever he began to play with become worthy of serious work, with the trine to Saturn in Libra. And that set off Libra's ruler Venus, which set off the T-square! There were many complex layers of his love of masks, and the masks he wore and the theatre in which he worked grew and developed hand in hand. I mean the Abbey theatre, but I also mean the theatre of his life. I wish I had another hour for this, but I don't, so let me quote him here and there.

He said the mask was "the image of what we wish to become", and it changes with each phase of development. There was a true mask and a false mask, and the Will might choose the wrong one. He also said that "style, personality – deliberately adopted and therefore a mask – is the only escape from the hot-faced bargainers and the money-changers." We hear the sensitivity of the 1st house Moon here. One more thing about masks, this from his early *Autobiographies:* "If we cannot imagine ourselves as different from what we are and assume that second self, we cannot impose a discipline upon ourselves, though we may accept one from others. Active virtue as distinguished from the passive acceptance of a current code is therefore theatrical, consciously dramatic, the wearing of a mask. It is the condition of an arduous full life." That is not to be taken lightly. It is not something to agree with or disagree with quickly. It deserves thought. And is an interesting way to approach the Ascendant.

Audience: Didn't he have some sort of operation to renew his sexual potency in his seventies? It apparently worked, too. His Saturn in the 8th, so well aspected, I imagine. He got a new view of himself through it.

Darby: He did, and it apparently both disturbed and delighted him. This, at the time, eccentric solution to a problem was only one of his many eccentricities. Do you know, in his late years, he signed his cheques, "Yours sincerely, W. B. Yeats"? And once, when he found a cat sleeping on his fairly new fur coat at the Abbey Theatre, he cut the coat around it because he said he knew the cat was having a "magical dream". Then he put on his ruined coat and left – Aquarius rising at its most humanely dramatic, in this case.

I must stop now. I wish we could spend the whole evening reading his poetry to each other. I hope you will go back to it if you have not read him in some time. If you want a wonderful biography, I would recommend Richard Ellmann's *Yeats: The Man and the Masks*. But perhaps even going out into the street and looking at people as they walk along, with their own inner worlds full of thoughts which are trying to make sense of their feelings, of their lives, will be a good enough way to leave this day on air. Keep awake to the air you breathe, the thoughts you entertain in your inner world. Earlier today I read you a stanza from *A Dialogue of Self and Soul*. Let me read you the last stanza before we go:

> I am content to follow to its source
> Every event in action or in thought;
> Measure the lot; forgive myself the lot!

When such as I cast out remorse
So great a sweetness flows into the breast
We must laugh and we must sing,
We are blest by everything,
Everything we look upon is blest.

Thank you for taking to the air with me today. Invisible, all-pervading and life-sustaining, it is perhaps the most difficult element to discuss. In one sense this is because it is the element of discussion, and so we can only speak about it by using mirrors and metaphors.

We walk on air, dance on air, are off the air or on the air. We take the air, we need a change of air. We build castles in the air. We love airing our views but we don't like people who give themselves airs. We open the windows to air the room, we close the windows and air-condition the room. We are breathless with excitement or fear and sometimes moments are so beautiful they are breathtaking.

I guess the most important thing I have to say about air is this: keep it circulating; make sure your flight-paths change periodically. If you don't have any of your own planets in air, breath good air from others, and beware of believing your ideas so much that they block off your communication. If you have many planets in air, let them be the space where you abstract your experience in the pursuit of understanding and wisdom, but beware of hiding in theories and concepts which keep you from feeling the pain and beauty of life. OK, let's go out and enjoy London's air this fair evening.

BIBLIOGRAPHY

Arroyo, Stephen, *Astrology, Psychology, and the Four Elements,* CRCS Publications, 1975

Baring, Anne and Cashford, Jules, *The Myth of the Goddess,* Viking Arkana, Penguin, London, 1991

Costello, Darby, *Water and Fire,* CPA Press, London, 1998

Donoghue, Denis, *Yeats,* Fontana Paperbacks, London, 1971

Ellmann, Richard, *Yeats: The Man and the Masks,* Penguin, 1979

Foster, R. F., *W. B. Yeats: A Life,* Oxford University Press, Oxford, 1997

Hesiod, *Theogony,* trans. Martin Litchfield West, Oxford University Press, Oxford, 1988

Jackson, Eve, *Jupiter,* The Aquarian Press, Wellingborough, 1986

Jung, C. G., *Memories, Dreams and Reflections,* Vintage Books, New York, 1989

Raine, Kathleen, *Yeats the Initiate,* The Dolmen Press, Ireland, 1986

Watson, Lyall, *Heaven's Breath,* Hodder & Stoughton, London, 1984

Yeats, W. B., *A Vision,* Collier Books, New York, 1972

Yeats, W. B., *Autobiographies,* Macmillan Publishers, London, 1955

Yeats, W. B., *Mythologies,* Collier Books, New York, 1959.

ABOUT THE AUTHOR

A consulting astrologer and teacher for over 40 years, Darby Costello has inspired clients and students for decades. She began her teaching career at the Centre for Psychological Astrology in the late 1980s and since has presented for the Faculty of Astrological Studies, the Mercury Internet School of Psychological Astrology, Astrology University, and The London School of Astrology. In 2013 she received the Charles Harvey Award for Exceptional Service to Astrology.

Darby's work demonstrates her fascination with the personal dynamics revealed in the birth chart as well as her commitment to allow an active unfolding of archetypal patterns in every moment, so that her work remains engaging and fresh, both for herself and her students.

Visit Darby online at www.darbycostello.co.uk